Transformational LEADERSHIP

A NEW MODEL FOR TOTAL CHURCH INVOLVEMENT

Phillip V. Lewis

BROADMAN & HOLMAN PUBLISHERS

Nashville, Tennessee

4212-39
0-8054-1239-5

Dewey Decimal Classification: 303.3
Subject Heading: LEADERSHIP
Library of Congress Card Catalog Number: 96-15343

Acquisitions and Development Editor: John Landers
Interior designer: Leslie Joslin

Library of Congress Cataloging-in-Publication Data
Lewis, Phillip V.
    Transformational leadership: a new model for total congrega-
tional involvement / Phillip V. Lewis.
        p. cm.
    Includes bibliographical references.
    ISBN 0-8054-1239-5
    1. Christian literature. 2. Pastoral theology.
I. Title.
BV652.1.L485   1996
253—dc20   96-15343
                                                        CIP

02 03 04 05 06 01 00 99 98 97

Contents

PREFACE:
NEW EYES FOR LEADERSHIP

Jesus Christ challenged his listeners to stay young in their thinking, to accept and entertain new truth, to have an adventurous mind (Mark 2:21–22). Isaiah called on his people to use reason rather than emotion in their thinking (Isa. 1:18). Yet, Albert Einstein may have been correct: "Everything has changed but our ways of thinking, and if these do not change we drift toward unparalleled catastrophe."

A new wind is blowing across the face of the church. One must be aware of the direction and force of that wind; recognize the dangers; attempt balance among groups within a congregation; and discover how to transform church members into kingdom players. Leaders of the twenty-first-century church must shepherd their members with integrity and lead them with skillful hands (Ps. 78:72). New ways of thinking and new models are needed. Churches designed during more placid settings and times will not withstand the pressure of chaotic times. In the business world of the past, the inflexible, rule-driven mass producers were staffed by persons who knew their place. No more! Today, organizations are flexible, porous, adaptive, and fleet of foot; every person is "paid" to chart new courses, to hustle, and to be engaged fully with engendering swift actions, constantly improving everything.[1]

At a time when church members, or potential church members, are questioning many religious practices, the twenty-first-century church must respond to its challenges, just like business must respond to its

v

competitive world. Revolutionary changes are occurring in the world today that will forever alter the way churches meet the needs of a lost world. These changes are so profound they sometimes seem overwhelming. Christian leaders who are out of touch with these changes will fast become obsolete.

This book challenges the status quo (i.e., doing things the same old way) and asks for a paradigm shift in thinking about leadership. It calls leaders to become transformational leaders, to realize that Jesus expects today's leaders of his church to transform themselves and others (Rom. 12:2; 2 Cor. 3:18). Answering this challenge is necessary to avoid catastrophic, misguided, ill-informed, or incapable leadership of the twenty-first-century church.

Therefore, allow the mind to be flexible, to not become fixed and settled in its way; be willing to entertain new ideas and contemplate new ways. And change the way of thinking about Christian leadership. This shift in thinking is requested because of the following assumptions:

1. *Many Christians are afraid to apply business principles to the church.* They are more comfortable about applying Christian principles to business. Yet, most CEOs consider the church misinformed about business, and vice versa. CEOs sometimes feel that the average pastor has little or no understanding of what business people do. They accuse ministers of living in ivory towers, isolated from the everyday realities of business and misunderstanding "the real world." Many pastors (and others) believe business is unethical and only interested in maximizing profit. Both professions probably have too little understanding of each other.

2. *Social science research and its conclusions are applicable to church planning.* Sources are not available that critically blend a theory of business research and applications to church planning.[2] However, that is the fault of researchers in forming a basis for a critical assessment of modes of research. It is not the intent of God to isolate either business or religion. One influences the other. Business is what Christians do to make a living and care for their families. Their Christianity supports their value system while "doing business," whether they are in the business of sales, education, law, government, or whatever. Jesus is the head of all things; he has supremacy over all things (Col. 1:18). Thus he is the head of business (and every other organization or concept) as well as head of the church.

3. *This book applies to small churches as well as large ones.* The bigness mania has had ill effects on American industry, while a passion for the small has been a great advantage to Japanese business. In the same way, the church can achieve great success by valuing the small. A rural church in Alabama has an outstanding record of evangelizing the people in its community. A few years ago debate raged over whether to shut its doors

due to its size. Instead, the leadership changed its thinking and direction and began using small home Bible studies known as *cells;* within three years, the church was averaging ten to twenty visitors each Sunday. Smallness is an attitude, not necessarily a number.

4. *Most churches choose to be the way they are.* Leaders of those churches may argue against this idea, but their actions indicate otherwise. They can talk it, but they cannot walk it. A church will seldom, if ever, be any larger than the vision of its leaders.

Marcel Proust stated: "The real voyage of discovery consists not in seeking new landscapes but in having new eyes." This book will help Christian leaders see with new eyes how to transform themselves, others, and the church.

Acknowledgments

Many ideas in this book have been presented in one form or another to classes, seminars, and workshops in the continental United States and in the Caribbean. Those who have heard some of these messages and have contributed to their refinements deserve a heartfelt thanks.

Two colleagues have made a major contribution to this book and deserve praise: Maureen Riegert, Azusa Pacific University, with her excellent editorial skills; and Dr. Jim Mankin, Abilene Christian University, with his experiential knowledge of what is happening within the kingdom in the United States.

Others also have contributed with critical reviews and suggestions: Steve Cate, Barbara and Kent Houck, Marilyn Lewis, Deloris Mankin, William Mitchell, W. C. "Dub" Orr, Mary Alice Reid, and Paul Vertz. Becky Nelson, Carole Mahaney, and Onita Hill deserve acknowledgment for faithfully "computerizing" early versions of this manuscript. And thank you Debi Cade for arranging all the phone calls, faxes, and appointments relative to finalizing this project.

A thank-you is also deserved by the editorial staff at Broadman & Holman: First, to Forrest Jackson, for his early interest in a manuscript on transformational leadership; then to John Landers, for taking on the responsibility of seeing this project through editorial and marketing review. Thank you, Steve Bond and Kim Overcash. Thank you everyone.

Part One:
TRANSFORMING
CHRISTIAN LEADERSHIP:
Recognizing the Need for Revitalization

"The meeting of two personalities is like the contact of two chemical substances: if there is any reaction, both are transformed."—Carl Jung

"The strongest is never strong enough to be always the master, unless he transforms his strength into right, and obedience into duty."—Jean Rousseau

"Even a thought, even a possibility, can shatter us and transform us."—Friedrich Nietzsche

"Be transformed by the renewing of your mind."—Apostle Paul

The future is now! And Christian leaders must be about the work of transforming themselves, others, and the church. God is calling people to step into a new role: transformational leadership. His call goes beyond the point-of-mind, spiritual, or organizational renewal. His call is for a total revitalization and transformation of thinking and acting, for men and women to be leaders of change in his kingdom.

Who and where are these new leaders? This question is more relevant today than ever before. A *U.S. News & World Report* poll of April 4, 1994, indicates that Americans are as religious as ever, but they are uncertain how to "walk the walk." Highlights of that poll suggest:

1

- Nearly 60 percent say they hold their current religious beliefs because of their parents' example.

- Forty-six percent describe themselves as born again, and 13 percent say their conversion was sudden.

- One-third say God is always with them during a crisis, but another third say they have never had divine guidance.

- Sixty percent say they attend a church or synagogue regularly. Of those, half participate in religious services every week.

- Sixty-five percent believe religion is losing its influence on American life, yet 62 percent feel the influence of religion has increased in their personal lives.

- Seventy-six percent believe that God is a heavenly Father who can be reached by prayer, and 77 percent testify that God has guided them personally in making a decision in their lives.

- Seventy percent think every individual must determine what is right or wrong, and 48 percent hold that there is no one set of values that is right.

- Eighty-four percent feel the government would be better if politics were more directed by moral values.

- Sixty-five percent would approve of a moment of silent prayer in schools.

- More than 80 percent believe that it is possible to be a good Christian or Jew even without attending a church or synagogue.

- Thirty percent believe the United States as a whole is hostile to their moral or spiritual values. Television is considered hostile by 62 percent and newspapers by 46 percent. The president is considered hostile by 34 percent, Congress by 47 percent, and the Supreme Court by 27 percent.

As evidenced above, today's world is challenging. Therefore, today's leaders must face challenges that yesterday's leaders did not have. They must assume that the future will never again be like the past. They must be people of vision, and they must be equipped and inspired to lead. They must be willing to be transformed by God and to transform others and the church.

Eric Hoffer said, "The only way to predict the future is to have the power to shape it." Chapter 1 provides a foundation for how to shape the future, to revitalize and transform the church. It sets the stage for becoming a transformational leader.

The Challenge of Transformational Leadership

1

TRANSFORMATIONAL LEADERSHIP

"They don't make (or do) things like they used to!" Ever made that statement? With knowledge doubling every year or two, the only constant is change. The question is not, "Will change occur?" but rather, "When and how will change occur?"

Change comes to every avenue of life and to all organizations—including the church. There are global changes that may forever alter the ministry of the church. World events such as the end of Communism in Russia, the disintegration of the Eastern bloc, and other socio-economic and political trends demand attention. The last thing a fish notices about itself is that it lives in water. Christian leaders cannot afford to be this oblivious to their environment. They cannot ignore these shifts.

Christian leaders must address many questions to meet the challenges of a changing world:

- What responses do the changes demand?
- How can problems be identified and transformed for the good of all peoples?
- How can one modify personal thinking from the antiquated to the twenty-first century?
- How will people adapt?

The list of questions seems endless. But the answers lie in one's openness to being transformed by God and his Word, and a willingness to respond to the needs of his world.

How to accomplish these goals is a controversial matter. Transformational leaders employ the style that best suits the situation they face. They do not approach every situation in the same way. When something does not work the first time, they do not get a bigger hammer and hit it again. Transformational leaders restudy the situation and look for a better approach. They realize that style is not as important as results.

Transformational vs. Transactional Leadership

Transformational leadership is of considerable importance and will become even more significant in the future. Unfortunately, many leaders operate with a transactional style. To illustrate: In terms of style and practice, transformational leaders inspire others to excel, give others individual consideration, and stimulate people to think in new ways. They transform the people and organizations with which they work. Examples of such organizations include Chick-Fil-A, Interstate Batteries, Mary Kay Cosmetics, ServiceMaster, Tom's of Maine, and TDIndustries.

Transformational Leadership Style

Consider the following characteristics of the transformational style of leadership:

1. Transformational leaders build on the strengths of others, strengths that may have lain dormant.

2. Transformational leaders raise levels of awareness about the issues of consequence and ways of reaching organizational goals for their colleagues, subordinates, followers, clients, or constituents.

3. Transformational leaders enable people to transcend their own self-interest for the sake of others.[1]

Transformational leaders change reality by building on the human need for meaning. They focus on values, morals, and ethics. They are proactive and encourage human potential. Their goal is to transform people and organizations—change minds and hearts; enlarge vision, insight, and understanding; clarify purposes; make behavior congruent with beliefs, principles, or values; and bring about changes that are permanent, self-perpetuating, and momentum building.[2]

Transactional Leadership Style

Transactional leaders promise rewards to followers in exchange for performance. They are reactive, not proactive. Consider the following characteristics of transactional leadership:

1. Transactional leaders recognize what employees want from their work and try to get that for them if their performance warrants it.

2. Transactional leaders exchange rewards and promises of reward for employees' efforts.

3. Transactional leaders respond to employees' immediate self-interests if these can be met by getting the work done.[3]

4. Transactional leaders attempt to build on their followers' need to make a living. They concentrate on power and politics. They are reactive and focus on tactics.

Some writers on leadership have demonstrated the differences between transactional and transformational leadership by comparing managers and leaders. (See box 1.1.) Although the differences between transformational leaders and managers and leaders is broader than depicted, this is a convenient illustration. This book emphasizes the transformational attributes of leadership. Such attributes should be emulated for the good of the church.

Transforming the Church

Jesus had a way of creating vision, shaping values, and empowering change. Can today's Christian leaders do any less? It is time for a revolution in the church. In some ways, that is what has transpired in evangelical Christian churches for at least a decade. Such a revolution will require the transformation of present-day leaders and congregations. It certainly will require a paradigm shift in the way some approach leading.

A paradigm shift is a fundamental change in the way one views the world—the way one perceives, understands, or interprets. The Greek word that describes this shift is *metanoia.* "The word has a rich history. For the Greeks, it meant a fundamental shift or change, or more literally transcendence ('meta'—above or beyond, as in *'metaphysics'*) of mind (*'noia,'* from the root *'nous,'* of mind). In the early (Gnostic) Christian tradition, it took on a special meaning of awakening shared intuition and direct knowing of the highest, of God. *'Metanoia'* was probably the key term of . . . John the Baptist. In the Catholic corpus, the word *metanoia* was eventually translated as 'repent.'"[4]

Box 1.1
MANAGER OR LEADER?

1. Managers make sure that things work well. Leaders create that which works better.

2. Managers solve today's problems by fixing the difficulties caused by changing events. Leaders create a better future by seizing opportunities stimulated by changing events.

3. Managers focus on the process. Leaders focus on the product.

4. Managers make sure the details are taken care of. Leaders set broad purposes and directions.

5. Managers make sure that people put in an honest day's work for their pay. Leaders inspire people to do more than expected.

6. Managers organize and plan to meet this year's objectives. Leaders create a vision of the years down the road.

7. Managers create efficient policies and standard operating procedures. Leaders go beyond the need for standard procedures and create a more efficient system.

8. Managers focus on efficiency. Leaders focus on effectiveness.

9. Managers focus on problem behavior and try to improve it through counseling, coaching, and nurturing. Leaders focus on what is going right and praise it.

10. Managers worry about the present. Leaders look forward to the future.

Adapted from R. Lynch, "Are you a manager or a leader?" *The Nonprofit Board Report, 3* (4), (February 1, 1995): 14.

Transformational leaders motivate people to do more than they envision, by raising awareness of different values and transcending self-interests. These leaders give individual consideration to others and stimulate people to think in new ways. They change markedly (and for the better) the people and organizations with which they work.

In corporate America, since the mid-1980s, such a revolution has been in effect. This revolution is similar to a staged drama. It has protagonists, antagonists, dramatic themes, and a gripping plot played out over three acts:

1. *The awakening*—when the need for change and revitalization is realized.

2. *The envisioning*—when a vision is created and workers are mobilized.

3. *The re-architecting*—when the design and construction of a wholly new organization are detailed.[5]

The final act is exhilarating because it leads to an organization's rebirth. It can do the same for a church. It can transform one's thinking, acting, being, and becoming.

Recognizing the Need for Revitalization

Act 1, the awakening, is a recognition that something needs to be changed, revitalized, or awakened. Not unlike the Dallas Cowboys in Super Bowl XXVIII, when they found themselves trailing the Buffalo Bills 13–6 at halftime. Their awakening resulted in a 30–13 win. Salespeople use the AIDA formula to awaken in customers a need to buy their product—Attention, Interest, Desire, and Action. In a church, such an awakening can be an emotionally wrenching process.

A small church in Arizona was losing members. Some quit because they only attended out of habit, obligation, or to be an example to their children. Others left because they were tired of going home from services depressed by the sermon. The leaders could not admit that there were developments that warranted change or that the status quo was being challenged.

It is human nature to feel safe with the familiar. That is why some people grieve over the disappearance of the old, comfortable ways of doing things. Their feelings are similar to those that people experience when leaving the security of an old job for the challenge of a new position, or parting with a favorite sweater because of moth holes.

A congregation in Texas was formed because a group was disturbed with a renewal taking place in their church. They advertised in the religion section of the local paper, giving the times of Bible study and worship, and called on all those interested in the "ancient paths" (see Jer. 6:16) to join them. These self-appointed guardians of a church (as it was in the 1950s) are missing out on the thrill of renewal in the kingdom.

Two steps are necessary for an organization to begin a revolution, be transformed, or become revitalized:

1. *Kick-start the revolution.* Articulate why the change is necessary; make certain all leaders are in agreement.

2. *Deal with resistance.* Provide people with the facts and the rationales for change; more often than not, they will reach the same conclusions as the leaders.[6]

ex.
forming
storming
norming

Those confronting the need to revolutionize their churches often fear chaos and unforeseen outcomes. Such fear breeds timidity and stifles proactive leadership. Consequently, this first stage of the revolution can be marked by conflict, denial, and resistance. Veteran members may have conflict with the "babes in faith" because of different need agendas. Denial of needed changes may result in a refusal to even think about, let alone talk about, the issues. Resistance to change is common and may take many forms, but it will be strongest when the change is personal. Thus any negative thinking or acting must be dealt with. Unless a majority buys into the needed change, it will be difficult, if not impossible, to implement a transformation.

Creating a New Vision

Act 2, envisioning, focuses on the revolution. It encourages creativity and directs attention toward the future. It seizes the positive force of emotion, channeling frustrations and fears into positive directions.

A congregation in Oklahoma developed a worship committee for special Sundays and events such as New Year's Day, Easter, Mother's Day, Father's Day, Thanksgiving, Christmas, the first day of school in the fall semester, special contribution/budget days, and mission emphases. The committee was charged with involving as many people in the congregation as possible, being creative in their design of worship services, and trying to have something (via logic and emotion) that would edify all members. Like jumper cables used on a dead battery, these special worship services revitalized this congregation.

Creating a new vision requires addressing the technical, political, and cultural systems.[7] These three fundamental building blocks can be viewed as an analytical matrix. (See box 1.2.) Designing a strategy, an organizational structure, or a human resource management program raises certain questions:

- For technical systems, how does one organize people, money, information, and technology?

- For political systems, how does one allocate power, rewards, and growth opportunities?

- For cultural systems, how does one share norms, beliefs, and values?

Let us think of these technical-political-cultural (TPC) issues as three strands of a rope.

- From a distance, individual strands are indistinguishable. Similarly, a casual observer cannot distinguish the TPC systems in organizations.

- Close examination reveals that each strand is made up of many substrands, just as close examination of organizations reveals many TPC systems.

- The strength of the rope depends not only on the strength of the strands, but also on their connection. Just as a rope can unravel, an organization begins to come apart when its systems work at cross-purposes.[8]

That is why leaders must commit themselves to a shared vision to change or realign a church. Transformational leaders bind people together around a common identity—goals, values, and missions. They have a technique for writing their own "movie script" and producing their own future.

Box 1.2

	Strategy	Organizational Structure	Human Resource Management
Technical Systems			
Political Systems			
Cultural Systems			

Building a New Organization

Act 3, re-architecting, is the art of redesigning and rebuilding an organization that evolves to meet the challenges it faces. The concern is often how to ensure the continuity of the organization and its leadership in the future. Transformational leaders build for tomorrow what will be needed in the kingdom at that time.

Several years ago a small congregation in Tennessee was struggling with the need to change the way the worship service was conducted. Young couples and teenagers were leaving to unite with other churches that provided a more exciting, spirit-filled worship experience. Church leaders were unable to reach any consensus among the members as to what kinds of changes would be comfortable and how to bring these about. They shared their frustrations with the congregation, and then announced their resignations. A committee was formed to search among the church for new leaders. During this time a concerted effort was made by the committee to sell church members on the need for a new vision, a new day. Focus groups were formed and members were invited in to share their ideas and feelings. A new leadership was selected. They introduced a new worship and fellowship format. Today this church is renewed and growing. Visitors familiar with this congregation comment that they cannot believe how much this church has changed—and for the better. It is now a dynamic force in its community.

To achieve re-architecting, renewal, or to build a new organization, at least three boundaries (or limiting factors) must be discovered and then taken down. This process is similar to a creative destruction or disintegration of the "old" organization.

- *Vertical boundaries*—the ceilings of hierarchy (the power brokers). To take down these barriers: "de-layer" the hierarchy, reduce perks for leaders, and broaden incentives.

- *Horizontal boundaries*—internal walls (barriers between groups within an organization, such as functional, geographic, or product groups). To take down these barriers: use cross-functional committees or teams and build partnerships.

- *External boundaries*—boundaries between the organization and its external stakeholders. To take down these barriers: create alliances, measure member satisfaction, and build teams with customers and suppliers.[9]

A revolution requires such fundamental redesigns. How people work together to get things done, who relates to whom for what, and how decisions are made are always key areas to explore. The key components in re-architecting are people, time, and space.

This is a continuing process. Once the three-act process is completed, it must be started again. Church leaders must create an environment where members understand that change is not an event, but a process.

Ten Strengths of
Transformational Christian Leaders

As the church changes, so must its Christian leaders. Every congregation is headed somewhere; the question is, Where? Transformational leaders use their initiative to lead people to a closer and more intimate relationship with God. They are open to his transformation so they may in turn transform others. This transformational style of leadership has been referred to as principle-centered power.[10] Ten basic processes and principles characterize leaders' behavior.

1. *Persuasion*—sharing reasons and rationale; making a strong case for personal desires while maintaining genuine respect for followers' ideas and perspective; addressing the whys as well as the whats; committing to stay in the communication process until mutually beneficial and satisfying outcomes are reached. (See 1 Cor. 2:1–5.)

2. *Patience*—maintaining a long-term perspective and staying committed to goals in the face of short-term obstacles and resistance. (See Col. 1:10–12.)

3. *Gentleness*—dealing with vulnerabilities, disclosures, and feelings followers might express without harshness, hardness, or forcefulness. (See 1 Pet. 3:15–16.)

4. *Teachableness*—operating with the assumption that one does not have all the answers, all the insights; valuing the different viewpoints, judgments, and experiences followers may have. (See 1 Cor. 12:28–30.)

5. *Acceptance*—withholding judgment; giving the benefit of the doubt; requiring no evidence or specific performance as a condition for sustaining others' high self-worth. (See Acts 10:34–35.)

6. *Kindness*—remembering the little things (which are the big things) in relationships; being sensitive, caring, and thoughtful. (See 1 Cor. 13:4.)

7. *Openness*—assimilating accurate information and perspectives about followers' potential while affirming who they are now, regardless of what they own, control, or do; giving full consideration to their intentions, desires, values, and goals rather than focusing exclusively on their behavior. (See Matt. 18:15–20.)

8. *Compassionate confrontation*—acknowledging errors, mistakes, and the need for followers to make "course corrections" in a context of genuine care, concern, and warmth; making it safe for followers to risk. (See 1 Pet. 3:8.)

9. *Consistency*—congruity among successive acts, ideas, or events so that one's leadership style becomes a set of values, a personal code, a manifestation of one's character, a reflection of who one is and who one is becoming; not a manipulative technique brought

into play when someone does not get his or her way, is faced with crisis or challenge, or is feeling trapped. (See Eph. 5:8–10.)

10. *Integrity*—matching words and feelings honestly with thoughts and actions, with no desire other than for the good of others, and without malice or desire to deceive, take advantage, manipulate, or control; constantly reviewing the intent as one strives for congruence.[11] (See Titus 2:6–8.)

These ten characteristics are common attributes of notable leaders of distinction—Mother Teresa, Billy Graham, Charles Swindoll, or Pope John Paul II—but they also should be common of all Christian leaders. Certainly it would be difficult to be a transformational leader without these attributes.

Transforming the Self

Transformation leaders know that to change lives, they must first be transformed. Plato said that the unexamined life is not worth living. Until one is willing to examine oneself and see if personal transformation is needed, the church cannot and will not change. After all, Christians are the "built" ones, not the builders, except as "workers together with God" through proclaiming the gospel that the redeemed might be added as living stones to the building (1 Pet. 2:4–10). The human race is God's building, his temple (1 Cor. 3:16).

Unfortunately, many promote and exalt the church building so much that these buildings become monuments to human success. As a result, we have many enormous and elaborate church buildings but little evidence of God's presence in the populace (1 Cor. 6:19).

God's leaders must be dedicated to allowing him and the Holy Spirit to bring about internal transformation while endeavoring to help in the transformation of his church, his people. The philosopher William James said, "The greatest discovery of my generation is that men can change their circumstances by changing their attitude of mind."

Leaders of the twenty-first-century church must examine themselves for four competencies:

1. Can they identify, organize, plan, and allocate the resources of time, money, materials, facilities, and human resources?

2. How are their interpersonal skills, especially regarding team member participation, teaching and coaching, servant leadership, and ethnic diversity?

3. What is their ability to acquire, evaluate, organize, maintain, interpret, and communicate information?

4. Can they understand and design complex interrelationships (or organizational systems)?[12]

In short, can future leaders transform the self, others, and their churches to meet the challenges of the new millennium?

Followers depend on leaders for self-transformation. They are empowered when they view the leader as an ideal model. In fact, the primary objective of bringing about follower self-transformation is to enable them to achieve an inner strength or a set of beliefs about their capacity to pursue and realize a vision.[13]

This book can help people change the circumstances in their church and put into place a continuous revolution. In order to do so, it will be necessary to make people agents of that change. After all, that is what the Lord did with his disciples, and they redefined religion as the world then knew it. Today's Christian leaders are called to do no less—redefine religious dogma for the twenty-first century. They must meet the challenges of a changing environment, and work toward completing the work the Lord has given them.

The next eight chapters will attempt to show, first, how leadership theory and practice have evolved (chaps. 2, 4, 6, 8); and, second, how leadership theory and practice can be transformed into Christlike qualities for effectiveness in the church (chaps. 3, 5, 7, 9). This discussion will then be followed by eight chapters that will deal with strategic issues and leadership practices in the church (chaps. 10–17). Finally, the last three chapters highlight spiritual results of transformational leadership (chaps. 18–20). The goal? To provide the necessary ingredients to start a revolution in the church (or at least a revitalization)!

Until Jesus comes again, thousands of leaders must be trained to carry on his work. Change is never finished.

Pause to Reflect

1. The world is in the midst of a revolutionary change. Standards are constantly being challenged and shifted. What changes have you noticed in the church during the last ten years? What changes do you predict in the next ten years?

2. A revolution in the church will require the transformation of present-day Christian leaders. Do you agree or disagree? Why? What should the transformed church and transformed leaders look like?

3. The goal of the transformational leader is to transform people and organizations. Have you seen this type of leadership in action? Discuss

how people and organizations with which you are familiar have been transformed by a leader.

4. The key to re-architecting is people, time, and space. Is one of this trio more important than the others? Why and how?

5. Christian leaders must be transformed so they may transform. What is the transformational formula for leaders? How can they be transformed so they may transform the church and its members?

Part Two
TRANSFORMING
LEADERSHIP THEORY:
Understanding What Christian
Leadership Is Really About

Bob Dylan captured a generation in the 1960s with his poetic verse, "And the times, they are a changin'." Some fifty years earlier, William Butler Yeats wrote, "Things fall apart; the center cannot hold." Few song phrases or poetic lines have so accurately portrayed the present or predicted the future. The times, indeed, are ever-changing!

A child's riddle inquires: On day one, a large lake contains only a single, small lily pad. Each day the number of lily pads doubles, until on day thirty, the lake is totally full of lily pads. On what day was the lake half full?

Answer: It takes twenty-nine days for the lake to be one-half full and only one more day to be completely full. Remember, the lily pads doubled each day.

Change like this faces Christian leaders and the twenty-first-century church. Lily pads and innovations keep on multiplying. If today is day twenty-nine in the cycle of changes facing the church, how will leaders face this world of discontinuous and escalating change? Not with traditional notions of leadership and organizational behavior! Yesterday's ways of doing things no longer guarantee the results they once did. The church is not like it was in the 1940s, 1960s, 1980s, or any other decade. Each generation brings a new way of thinking, a broader understanding of scholarship, and a different approach to worship.

Such events contribute to unconscious assumptions about the leadership of change. Here are some popular myths:

- It is impossible to understand why people accept or resist change.

- Organizations cannot really be changed.

- What leaders say about change should never be confused with reality.

- Change will always be mismanaged.

- Organizational efficiency and effectiveness inevitably decrease when changes are attempted.

- Those who help implement change are heroes; those who resist, villains.

- Leaders are inherently insensitive to problems caused during the implementation of change.

- People are prone to resist any change that is good for the organization.[1]

How can leadership overcome such widespread misconceptions? The focus of chapters 2–9 is on understanding what Christian leadership is really about. If one is to be a transformational leader, one must deal with the new realities of religious leadership, organizational development, and the knowledge society.

Chapters 2, 4, 6, and 8 represent the traditional approach to studying leadership: *power and influence, traits, behaviors, and situations.* Chapters 3, 5, 7, and 9 represent a transformational leadership challenge to change the above approaches to: *strategy, initiative, possibility, and vision.* I selected this approach because there is a change imperative in the church. Older models or frameworks of how things should be done are no longer appropriate. Thus the former ways of studying leadership, while interesting, must give way to a transformational style of leadership.

If one cannot stop the lily pads of change from multiplying inside the kingdom, then one must learn to expand the capacity to absorb change. The church must learn to flourish in constant transition. This can only be accomplished via transformational leaders who have first been transformed into the likeness of Jesus Christ with ever-increasing glory (2 Cor. 3:18).

Welcome to day twenty-nine!

The Challenge of Transformational Leadership

I. Transforming Christian Leadership: Recognizing the Need for Revitalization
1. Transformational Leadership

II. Transforming Leadership Theory: Understanding What Christian Leadership Is Really About
2. Power and Influence
3. Strategic Leadership
4. Traits of Leadership
5. Initiatory Leadership
6. Leadership Behavior
7. Possibility Leadership
8. Situational Leadership
9. Visionary Leadership

III. Transforming Leadership Strategies and Practices: Responding to the Challenge
10. Strategic Analysis
11. Transformational Change
12. Strategic Formulation
13. Transformational Conflict
14. Strategic Implementation
15. Transformational Communication
16. Strategic Evaluation
17. Transformational Motivation

IV. Transforming the Christian Leader: Guaranteeing the Future
18. Trust
19. Commitment
20. Affirmation

2

POWER AND INFLUENCE

Power is central to the study of leadership. If a group exists, there is a power structure. High-status people in a group influence behavior. Nietzsche observed, "Wherever I found the living, there I found the will to power." But power is usually thought of as one of the less attractive human characteristics. It connotes self-serving, manipulative behavior. "Power corrupts, and absolute power corrupts absolutely" and "He who has the gold makes the rules" are sayings often heard in discussions of power.

Power is the capacity to influence others to do something they would not have done without having been influenced.[1] It is intangible, multifaceted, elusive, and invisible. Yet, it can be felt in a person, a group, an organization, or a country. *Influence* is the ability to change one's behavior through words or actions; power is the ability to exert that influence, which in turn enhances one's status. *Status* is the ability to exercise power to influence decisions and outcomes.[2]

Some people know how to acquire power. They know where power exists, use their abilities to obtain it, and avoid actions that will decrease it. (See box 2.1.) How they use power depends on their status, influence, situation, or need to exercise that power (for good or evil). Transformational leaders use their power to empower church members. They do not tie others' hands. Instead, they give them the knowledge, skills, information, resources, and support to accomplish goals. They give others credit for being able to think, reason, plan, and implement those plans. As a result, members have a vested interest in the work of the church and its impact on the community.

Box 2.1

How People Acquire Power

1. Having something that others want or need grants power. Acquiring money or other resources, having some excess or slack resources, and controlling others' access to what they need, increasing their dependency, enhances power.

2. Having information that reduces uncertainties or otherwise helps others cope strengthens personal and departmental power in relation to those others.

3. Becoming valuable and nearly irreplaceable increases power over the organization.

4. Being able to affect some part of the decision process—problem definition, generation and weighing of alternatives, and selection among them—increases power to affect the decision.

5. Achieving a consensus with others helps a group articulate and press for its preferred result in the political struggle over matters in the organization. Coalitions based on consensus gain advantages over unorganized opposition.

6. Being central in communication networks and being skillful in persuasive communication strengthens power.

Adapted from J. Pfeffer, *Power in Organizations* (Marshfield, Mass.: Pitman, 1981), 67–96.

Most people (especially churchgoers) do not like to admit they want power. Those who have power often go to endless lengths to mask the fact. Some politicians, like Lyndon Johnson or Bill Clinton, openly relish the trappings of power. But the American style of power is to pretend to be powerless. To confess that one has power is to make oneself responsible for using it. Safety lies in an artfully contrived pose of impotence, behind which one can do exactly as one pleases.[3] Although most organizational members do not admit to seeking power, few willingly give it up once they have it. The possession of power is the surest road to promotion and success.

Power is inherent in all organizations. It can be exercised vertically, horizontally, or circularly. *Vertical power is* represented by hierarchy—up and down the organization, top management to the lowest employee, or vice versa. In the church, hierarchical power is perhaps best represented in the Catholic church with its system of members, priests, monsignors, bishops, archbishops, cardinals, and the pope. In the minds of many, however, such hierarchy or levels of status reflect a schism between leadership and spirituality. The focus is on position and dominance, its outcome, control, and submission to authority.[4]

Horizontal power pertains to relationships across the organization—vice president to vice president, manager to manager, department to department. In a church, horizontal power structures are similar: pastor to pastor, elder to elder, and deacon to deacon. The focus is on joint problem solving and coordination of work flow. It typically relates to task coordination, information sharing, decision making, and conflict resolution. Church leaders sometimes de-emphasize horizontal power because they feel it weakens their authority.

Circular power revolves around the leader as a resource member, or an enabler, of a team.

> In the circular organizational structure, the leader does not operate "on top" of others, but is seen as the enabling center of a team. Formal and informal relationships between people are recognized and appreciated, and differences are valued and respected. There is continuous striving for balance between achievement of organizational goals and the care and development of those who serve the organization. The leader is not expected to be the sole originator of the organization's vision but to listen to emerging ideas and from them to discern and articulate the vision. The leader is expected to be knowledgeable and competent; others are viewed as having skills and important abilities also. Successes in the system are communal, and failure is viewed as an opportunity for learning.[5]

Circular organization focuses on people, purpose, renewal, and growth; the outcome is transformation, being, learning, and diversity; the leadership style relies on partnership and collaboration.[6] Such a structure depends on a trusting relationship between leaders and followers.

Interpersonal Sources of Power

Library shelves are filled with books about the use and abuse of power and how it has motivated the great and the greedy throughout history. Henry Kissinger called power the ultimate aphrodisiac. Consider the twenty-five-year president of a Christian college in Mississippi who was considered a quiet, humble, rock-solid moral authority. Yet he was also said to have full, complete, and absolute power over the college and its board of trustees. Labeled by the media as a modern-day "Bible Belt Jekyll and Hyde," he apparently believed he was the college and could do whatever he wanted. His alleged secret life revealed offshore bank accounts, far-flung liaisons with prostitutes, pornographic literature, and a vial of strychnine.[7] Power offers such subtle temptations, especially when one is able to wield virtually unchallenged authority.

How much does one really know about power and power people? (See box 2.2.) The classic model for understanding interpersonal power is referent, legitimate, expert, reward, and coercive power.[8]

Box 2.2

What Do You Know about Power People?

What drives people who seem to be addicted to power? How much do you know about what motivates them and what makes them succeed or fail? Here's a chance to test your views and compare them with those of some experts. <u>True or false?</u>

___ 1. Women are just as likely to be driven by a need for power as are men.

___ 2. Power people share few common characteristics.

___ 3. Power people tend to be attracted to certain occupations more than they are to others.

___ 4. Power people make super traveling companions because they're so cool and well-organized.

___ 5. Spouses of power people always have a rough time, and their marriages are always extremely rocky.

___ 6. Creativity is a common trait in power people and is responsible for their success.

___ 7. Power and sex are unrelated and have nothing to do with each other.

___ 8. Power people don't usually care about the cars they drive because they're preoccupied with other matters.

Answers: F, F, T, F, F, F, F, F. If one answers six to eight questions correctly, she or he is above average in knowledge of this topic.

Adapted from J. Brothers, "What Do You Know about Power People?," *Los Angeles Times* (September 28, 1994).

Referent Power

Referent power is that granted to a leader because the group accepts that person's influence. Followers identify with and admire the leader. They respond voluntarily to her or his requests. They place power in this person to make the right decisions about behavior standards, attitudes, or values.

Imagine a group of leaders composed of laborers, retail store clerks, school teachers, and the president of a local bank. Because of the banker's high profile in the community, his outspokenness, and his "power dressing," the other leaders fall silent when he speaks and apologize when he interrupts their remarks with his own. They reach a unanimous verdict by rubber-stamping the president's judgment and agreeing with his opinion on every congregational decision.

Transformational leaders increase their referent power in several ways: being fair, cultivating a winning personality, developing credibility with the group, building a high *esprit de corps*, and communicating their liking for the members.[9]

Legitimate Power

Legitimate power is granted to leaders who have the right to make certain decisions because of their position. These leaders are authorized (that is, delegated the authority) to make judgments by law, a higher status level, or the group. Recipients of their influence view such sanctions as right. The president of the United States, the chancellor of a university, or the pastor of a church each holds legitimate power.

Supervisors receive legitimate power through their job descriptions and formal places in the organizational hierarchy. However, their formal or official power may be broadened considerably if they earn referent power from employees as well as expert power. Pastors who have received seminary training and passed through formal ordination ceremonies have more legitimate power than lay ministers.

Legitimate power is increased through a climate of trust, respect, and honor. Transformational leaders strengthen their legitimate power base: acceptance of others, compassionate confrontations, consistency, gentleness, integrity, kindness, openness, patience, persuasion, and willingness to learn.[10]

Expert Power

As work groups mature, someone usually becomes competent in a given area. They possess special knowledge to solve a problem, perform a task, or decide on a future course of action. The leader emerges because others see him or her as someone with superior ability. *Because of specialized knowledge, information, or skills, others look to this person as an expert.*

Although a football quarterback may gain legitimate power when the coach says, "You're it!" he must demonstrate ability on the job to have expert power. Teammates must see that he reads defenses and calls plays accurately. He then becomes a leader in fact as well as in name. Such was the case with Steve Young, who led the San Francisco 49ers to a 1995 Superbowl victory, and Troy Aikman, who led the Dallas Cowboys to back-to-back Superbowl wins in 1993, 1994, and then again in 1996.

The best-qualified member of the pastoral staff who is promoted to senior pastor upon the former senior pastor's resignation holds legitimate and referent power. He can call on previous experiences to lead and motivate staff and church members, who view the pastor's accomplishment as a standard to be pursued.

Reward Power

A person's ability to obtain desired responses by offering payoffs is reward power. The rewards may be formal: pay raises, promotions, special recognitions, or gold stars. Rewards may also be informal: pats on the back, the granting of a favor, or dinner for a job well done. "Payments" are usually determined by position. But this type of power is useful only if others value the rewards offered. For example, the power to determine a course grade has aspects of both reward and coercion if students see an A as reward and F as penalty. The same is seen in pastors who emphasize works over faith. Heaven is the reward; hell, eternal punishment. However, the guilt associated with a lack of work to "earn" heaven may increase one's wondering if living eternally with a vengeful God is worth it. Does one want the carrot or the stick? Certainly such emphasis neglects the doctrine of grace and a loving, forgiving Father.

Coercive Power

Coercive power results from the belief that failure to follow directions will result in punishment. Thus while some employees increase productivity to gain a higher salary (i.e., respond to reward power), some may also increase productivity to escape being fired (i.e., respond to coercion). Coercive power produces fear and often provides no way to escape what the leader desires. David wrote: "I have seen the wicked in great power, and spreading himself like a green bay tree" (Ps. 37:35, KJV). Uncontrolled, coercive power was not a pleasant sight then, and it has not been refined with age.

A leader's coercive power is contingent on the follower's perceptions of how probable it is that the leader will exact punishment for noncompliance, and the degree of negative consequences such punishment will entail, minus the probability of punishment from other sources (i.e., the followers) if one does not comply.[11] It should be noted, however: Coercive power will gain compliance, but it will not create motivation. Christian leaders who insist on enforcing their authority and neglecting things like congregational mission, goal achievement, empowerment, and open communication can expect to see their members leave for other, more user-friendly churches.

Of these five power sources, referent and expert power are thought to best support a positive work climate. However, any of the five can get the job done. Note:

1. Referent power is of intermediate importance as a reason for complying with leader directives, but it is positively correlated with organizational effectiveness.

2. Legitimate power, along with expert power, is rated as the most important basis for complying with leadership wishes, but it is an inconsistent factor in determining organizational effectiveness.

3. Expert power is more strongly and consistently related to satisfaction and performance than is any other type of power.

4. Reward power is of intermediate importance for complying with leader directives and has an inconsistent correlation with performance.

5. Coercive power is the least valuable in bringing about compliance to leader directives and is negatively related to organizational effectiveness.[12]

William Hazlitt wrote that the love of power is the love of ourselves, but the love of liberty is the love of others. Power-hungry leaders seldom recognize the needs of others. People are necessary only for increasing personal power. The president of a Christian college in Texas was notorious for running over people, using their talents as long as it met his needs, and then getting rid of them when they were no longer useful to his purposes. Is it any doubt that people felt powerless in the face of such a leader? They were without the informal power that their formal roles demanded. (See box 2.3.)

The ability to gain and use power is essential to a leader's success. Remember, however, that the typical interpersonal sources of power as discussed above have little place in the church. Jesus came into the world so his followers might have an abundant life, not have power over fellow humans (John 10:10; Matt. 5:43–48). The power source he did provide (i.e., the Holy Spirit) was to overcome Satan and the spiritual forces of evil (Eph. 6:12; 2 Tim. 1:7). The New Testament never uses the word *authority* in conjunction with leaders (pastors, bishops, shepherds, overseers, elders, or deacons). It is only used for Jesus (Matt. 28:18). The charge to God's leaders in the twenty-first-century church is to nurture and care for member needs, not to wield a do-it-because-I-said-so power.

Box 2.3

Why People Feel Powerless

1. They lack informal political influence as well as powerful mentors or sponsors. They are not on an upwardly mobile career path.

2. They are unable to get adequate resources: budget money, staff services, supplies, and additional workers.

3. They have little input to, or influence in, the planning and decision making that directly affect them and their subordinates. Their area of independent decision making is too limited.

4. Their situations do not permit them to take risks. Their bosses solve problems for them rather than serve as resource persons.

5. Their authority is undercut by their bosses.

6. They convey a sense of insecurity as leaders and anticipate resistance from their subordinates rather than cooperation.

Adapted from N. Carr-Ruffino, *The Promotable Woman* (Belmont, Calif.: Wadsworth, 1982), 32.

Structural and Situational Sources of Power

Most discussions of power center on its interpersonal nature. However, power may also be determined by the situation and the design of an organization's structure (division of labor or departmentalization). That is, decisions are made as to who does what. Not everyone involved in a job can or should do the same thing. "We have different gifts, according to the grace given us"—prophesying, serving, teaching, encouraging, contributing to the needs of others, leadership, and showing mercy (Rom. 12:6–8). Employees behave more productively as their tasks become specialized. Christian workers increase their effectiveness when moving toward a single, planned, and directed activity (i.e., a unity of direction).

Structural and situational power sources include information, knowledge, resources, and decision making.[13]

Information

The person who possesses information also possesses power. Individuals and groups who control information about current operations, develop information about alternatives, or acquire knowledge about future

28

events and plans have enormous power to influence others.[14] The leader who has information that may be of use to a follower and decides to withhold that information exerts a controlling power over the follower.

A deacon in an Arkansas church was an attorney in the community. He asked to review the financial records. When his request was refused, he sued. This event became gossip fodder for both church members and the community. The church was organized with elders and deacons, and the elders' defense was that, as overseers of the congregation, they had the authority to withhold financial information. The deacon won the case. The elders appealed to the Arkansas Supreme Court, however, who ruled in the elders' favor, saying that as trustees of the congregation they had the authority to refuse access to records. Who really won this case? Certainly not the cause of Christ in that community.

Knowledge

If information is power, it follows that knowledge is power. Knowledge has grown phenomenally over the last century. However, the knowledge explosion places pressures on today's leaders that their predecessors by only fifty years did not have. Organizations that depend on highly sophisticated databases can easily become obsolete unless planned change efforts are continuous. Thus, knowledge is important, but wisdom is crucial. "If any of you lacks wisdom, he should ask God, who gives generously to all without finding fault, and it will be given to him" (James 1:5). God has granted some the ability to speak with wisdom (1 Cor. 12:8), but wisdom is too important to be limited to those few. All Christians should seek it through prayer.

Herodotus said that the bitterest pain is to have much knowledge but no power. Yet to have knowledge without wisdom is equally, if not more, bitter indeed. A leader's power is the product of legitimate power multiplied by his or her ability to use knowledge competently.[15] The competent use of knowledge, however, implies wisdom. As Alfred Lord Tennyson wrote, "Knowledge comes, but wisdom lingers."

Resources

A number of resources affect power in an organization. Which resources are most important depend on the leader, followers, and situation. Typically, the most effective and best-liked leaders are those who command more of an organization's resources, who bring something valuable from outside into the group, and who have access to information affecting the group.[16] Certainly the church needs information, money, facilities, and a host of other resources. But real power exists in spirit-filled people (Eph. 3:14–19).

The history of the church is filled with great leaders such as Martin Luther, John Knox, John Calvin, Ulrich Zwingli, Charles and Susanna Wesley, and Thomas and Alexander Campbell. The twenty-first-century church needs more men and women as resources—people who will pray for and practice God's wisdom. Without such resources, Christians are doomed to share the destinies of worthless leaders.[17]

Decision Making

Decision making is choosing between alternatives. The way problems are solved affects what happens not only to the decision maker but also to those whom he or she leads. Individuals or groups acquire power to the extent they can affect some part of the decision process.[18] That is why some people want the right to make a decision, and others shy from the risk and responsibility.

Most models of decision making include defining the problem, analyzing the problem, establishing criteria for a solution, proposing possible solutions, evaluating the alternatives, selecting a solution, and plotting a course of action. Because decisions involve risk, it should be noted that mistakes are seldom final and devastating. Often they are effective teachers. Thomas Edison tried at least 6,000 vegetable fibers, 1,600 minerals, monkey's hair, and even the hair from a mustache until he hit upon the answer for the electric light bulb filament—a carbon-impregnated cotton thread that had been baked in a furnace.

In May, the leaders of a Texas church announced that the time of the evening service would be changed from 5 P.M. to 6 P.M. beginning the first Sunday in June. All the other churches in their community met at 6 P.M. However, the members were so disgruntled about this decision (which did not have congregational input) that two weeks after the announcement another decision was made that this time change was only for the summer months and would be reevaluated at the end of the summer. After three months of complaints, the September evening services began at 5 P.M. and continue to be held "sacred." Although the leaders were determined to change the time and convince the members that this was a better meeting time, the members wanted no such change. Fortunately, the leaders were willing to listen to the members' wishes before greater problems developed. If a decision is wrong or if it will not work, admit failure and cut losses. Transformational leaders do not compound a bad decision with blind determination to make it work.

The Effective Use of Power

Without power, the Christian leader will find it difficult to influence people. With it, there is always the temptation for abuse.

30

A worker in a Christian service center was promoted to manager, a position of legitimate power from which she supervised the other workers, her former peers. Shortly afterward, the board of directors decided to extend the center's open hours from 5 P.M. until 9 P.M. to better meet the needs of the poor in their community. The new manager asked for volunteers to work evenings, but the employees, led by one vocal individual, refused. Although it caused her personal anguish, the manager invoked her legitimate power and fired the informal leader of the insurrection, warning him that she would do the same with the others if necessary. "It was his career or my career," she remarked. Fortunately for all concerned, the other workers agreed to work an evening schedule as did the remorseful leader, who requested and received back his old job.

Leaders who use their power for the good of the organization exhibit certain characteristics. (See box 2.4.)

Christian leaders must decide among a variety of strategies. Whatever the action, Paul reminds his readers that "whatever you do, whether in word or deed, do it all in the name of the Lord Jesus, giving thanks to God the Father through him" (Col. 3:17).

The true measure of the transformational leader is not the power she or he wields but the power released in others—the power to decide, accomplish goals, and grow. Membership satisfaction increases when Christian leaders empower their followers rather than subjugate them. Power is a two-edged sword. Used properly, it motivates; used improperly, it creates problems. Transformational leaders use a servant-leader model to get others to accept ownership and accountability for the well-being of the church.[19] Such a model requires an understanding of strategic leadership (chap. 3).

— — —

Pause to Reflect

1. Discuss the power structure of your church and how it fits with the pattern described in the following biblical passages: Acts 20:17–35; 1 Timothy 3:1–13; Titus 1:5–9; Hebrews 13:17; and 1 Peter 5:1–4.

2. Describe a time when you felt powerless in the church. Use the journalistic formula to analyze your story—who, where, what, when, and why.

3. Of the five interpersonal power bases, which are most often used in your church to influence others? Is each power base used effectively? If not, why? Could its use be improved?

4. Of the three structural and interpersonal sources of power, which are most often used in your church to influence others? Is each source used effectively? If not, why? Could its use be improved?

5. Review box 2.4. Do you agree with the characteristics listed for effective power use? Why or why not? What would you add to this list?

Box 2.4
Leadership Characteristics for Effective Power Use

1. Effective leaders understand what is and is not legitimate behavior in acquiring and using power. Different power sources demand certain obligations in terms of how they may be used. The misuse or lack of understanding of a power source can destroy its effectiveness.

2. Effective leaders understand the interpersonal as well as the situational and structural sources of power, and the most effective methods of influencing people using these different sources. They often recognize the structural and situational problems that exist in a power relationship and modify their own behavior to fit the actual situation. Unsuccessful leaders rely too much on one or a few power bases.

3. Effective leaders tend to seek leadership positions that allow the development and use of power. These jobs provide opportunities for and, indeed, demand influencing the behavior of others. Successful performance in these positions, in turn, allows them to acquire power.

4. Effective leaders temper their power-oriented behavior with maturity and self-control. They recognize that their actions influence the behaviors and lives of others. While they are not necessarily reluctant or afraid to use their power, they apply power carefully, in principled and fair ways that are consistent with organizational needs and goals.

Adapted from J. P. Kotter, "Power, Dependence, and Effective Management, " *Harvard Business Review,* (April 1977): 125–36; and D. A. Gioia and H. P. Sims, "Perceptions of Managerial Power as a Consequence of Managerial Behavior and Reputation," *Journal of Management,* (1983): 9, 7–26.

3

STRATEGIC LEADERSHIP

The key to transforming power-based leadership (chap. 2) to servant/steward leadership is strategic planning. Abraham Lincoln said, "The dogmas of the quiet past will not work in the turbulent future. As our cause is new, so must we think and act anew." For Christian leaders to rely on historical leadership principles like power and influence is to turn toward disaster. A new, different strategy must be sought.

Two decisions are critical to the survival of all churches: *what* a congregation wants to be, and *how* it should get there. Both are integral to long-range thinking. What a church wants to be sets its direction. How it gets there requires forming a strategy before starting long-range planning and day-to-day decision making. Strategy must be related to the nature and direction of the congregation. (See box 3.1.)

Consider the following dilemma of a start-up church in the Los Angeles area. The congregation began meeting three years ago in a public school building. During this time, the church moved locations four times, each time to a different suburb. With each move a few members were lost and a few gained. The climate was constantly unsettled. Some of the members jokingly compared themselves to the wandering tribes of Israel. Each move necessitated ten to thirty minutes more driving time for some members. To compound the problem, the name initially chosen for the church included the name of a nearby geographical area. The third and fourth moves were out of that designated area, but the church kept the same name. In one sense, this church was going somewhere! But their frequent moves left them little time to decide what they wanted to be. Although this congregation still exists, it has had little influence in the three previous neighborhoods.

Box 3.1

STRATEGIC RELATIONS BETWEEN WHAT A CHURCH WANTS TO BE AND HOW IT SHOULD GET THERE

Strategy: long-range planning, daily decision making, goal accomplishment

---

Every congregation has a momentum—it is headed somewhere. Christian leaders who do not consciously set a strategy risk having their direction (i.e., drive and energy) controlled by others (inside or outside their congregation). Football coach Lou Holtz said, "It's not my job to motivate players. They bring extraordinary motivation to our program. It's my job not to demotivate them." Transformational leaders proactively plan for the future to keep momentum (i.e., to keep from demotivating the members). They "direct the affairs of the church," which is "the body of Christ" (see Eph. 5:23; Col. 1:18, 24; 1 Tim. 5:17).

What Is Strategic Leadership?

A transformational leader is like a physician who prescribes exercise for the patient's internal strength and medication (external influence) in light of the patient's overall health. A competent doctor will certainly not take these steps and fail to ask to see the patient for a year. He or she closely manages the patient's condition, modifying aspects of the treatment to maximize results or recommending radical change if the condition worsens. Transformational leaders continually monitor key internal and external events and trends. They pursue strategies that capitalize on internal strengths, take advantage of external opportunities, mitigate internal weaknesses, and avoid or mollify the impact of external threats.

Strategic leadership is the formulation, implementation, and evaluation of actions that enable an organization to achieve its objectives. This process is an unbiased, systematic approach to making major decisions under uncertain conditions. Strategic leadership is flexible and dynamic rather than dogmatic. It deals with a changing world and evaluates the structure and processes of the church accordingly.

The Need for Leadership

Every leader has a distinctive leadership style. Some are autocratic; others, democratic; some, task oriented; others, relationship oriented; some, transactional; others, transformational. Style is of particular interest to those who follow. People want to follow leaders who establish a warm, supportive, friendly, and accepting climate. They want leaders who encourage innovative and creative approaches to managing, who collaborate in decision making, and who support all results. Style is also an important variable in determining levels of commitment to an organization's mission and purpose. Followers reward leaders with these behaviors with their self-confidence and enthusiasm for work that exceeds minimum standards. These followers are loyal to their leaders, to the cause, and to the organization and its purpose.

Style of leadership determines results. *What is effective is whatever works in a given situation.* Effective leaders find and use the style that is best for the situation they face. Similarly, a transformational leadership style is of considerable importance and probably will become even more significant in the future. May God provide leaders who recognize the stewardship of decisions, power, authority, responsibility, and accountability!

The style of transformational leaders contrasts markedly with that of leaders who want the final decision-making authority but none of the accountability, who want the power but not the responsibility. Some people seem willing to copy behavior in movies such as *Wall Street, The Godfather,* or *Clear and Present Danger.* They use force or coercion and manipulation to seize control. They remind us of Peter's admonition that leaders are not to lord their leadership over the flock (1 Pet. 5:2–3).

The Need for Strategy

Only in the late 1980s and early 1990s did many church leaders first begin using strategic leadership principles. Businesses began using strategic management during the 1950s and 1960s when new markets were emerging and expanding. When the early 1970s brought growth stagnation and the mid-1980s and early 1990s a reduction in production, strategy became a survival technique for managing the organization's resources to achieve long-term objectives.

Churches and businesses share the same strategic needs: *the need for focus* (many statements of strategy are just too abstract to provide guidance to key decision makers); *the need for congruence* (a common point or way to tie direction together is lacking); and *the need to respond strategically to change.*[1] Transformational leaders engage in strategic planning.

First, transformational leaders focus their strategies. Numerous congregational strategies are vague, lack specificity, or are too massive and complicated to serve as a framework to guide key decision makers. Like a camera, they need to focus. For example: In what business is Hallmark engaged? To respond, "The greeting card business," restricts their product line considerably. Using a wide-angle lens, Hallmark executives would say they are in the "social expression" business. This gives them a range of products.

A mission statement and definition of what business an organization is in allows one range of activities and prohibits another. Each person must ask what "business" their church is in—teaching, equipping, missions, edification, benevolence, university work, rebuking, correcting, training, salvation? Whatever that definition, its purpose must be clear to pastors and parishioners alike.

Transformational leaders ask at least two questions:

- What is it that we do uncommonly well?

- If this church were not here, what difference would it make in the community?

Fred Craddock suggests that the church's greatest temptation is to survive. Instead, the purpose of a congregation should be to increase service. Thus the niche of a small church might be full/quality service (i.e., caring/loving service) to the community.

Someone has said that small churches count people, while large churches count furniture. Concentrating on Christian service, not growth, will in all likelihood result in growth.

Second, transformational leaders provide congruence (i.e., agreement, fit) between the strategy they set and the strategies set by others in the church. "Congruence" does not mean that pastors, elders, deacons, or others are pre-empted from having their own strategies. The large modern congre-gation is too complex and too diversified to be a monolith. Various programs of a church require separate strategies. But they must complement one another and support the primary strategy.

Third, transformational leaders are prepared for the future. That is, they respond strategically to change. By observing and assessing current trends and anticipating future challenges, transformational leaders formulate appropriate strategic plans. How will the twenty-first-century church respond to the future without a strategic plan?

Congregational Life Cycles

Most churches go through the same life cycles of many organizations: emergence, growth, maturity, and decline. (See box 3.2.) Their survival keys are the same set of keys congregations must use. Leaders in volunteer organizations (like the church) depend on followers. Baby boomers are reluctant followers; they exert a lot of power and expect adherence to the doctrine of equality. Such groups powerfully affect the church's life cycle.

Box 3.2

Life Cycles

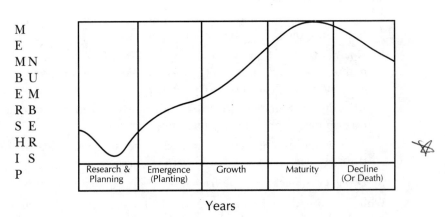

Years

According to organizational life-cycle models, churches pass through various stages. The introductory or *emergence* phase is the start-up stage for a new congregation. During this period, there will be an effort to create widespread awareness and find acceptance in the neighborhood or community. The *growth* phase involves concentration on recognition of the church and emphasis on finding the best service niche. Programs and personnel will be added; leadership will become more centralized. The need to finance rapid expansion will be of paramount importance. Evangelism will become more focused.

In the *maturity* phase, a defensive stance is taken toward changing that which has been successful to date. Although some changes are implemented for improvement, the emphasis often shifts to cash-flow management and related concerns. A declining membership may result; perhaps because the "things" of the church are given more attention than its people. Then in the *decline* phase, programs are pruned and/or phased out, personnel dismissed, and mergers considered. In some cases, divisions (i.e., splits) occur because of disagreements among members. In the worst case scenario, the *death* phase, liquidation is discussed. (At times this may be the wisest decision.)

Cycles of growth and decline can be blamed on generational differences, worldliness, secularization, legalism, narrow dogmatism, lack of conviction, and a failure in responsible study of Scripture.[2] Three things may be necessary to break the cycle of decline and division: individual revival, corporate revival, and prayer for change to end the decline cycle.

Identifying life-cycle stages helps develop market or investment strategies. Here are examples of various industries in their current position in the business trend cycles:

1. *Birth (or emergence):* Pay-per-view, two-way video communications, home shopping, the information superhighway

2. *Growth:* Coffee houses, environmentalism, fish farms, health maintenance organizations (HMOs), home health care, New Age awareness, self-protection, solar energy

3. *Maturity:* Carbonated soft drinks, fast foods, frozen foods, home furnishings, warehouse retailing, hospitals, oil

4. *Decline:* Bartending, chemical lawn care services, department stores, movie theaters, tobacco, variety stores

5. *Dying:* Furs, neckties, typewriters, video stores, nuclear energy[3]

While enjoying the vitality of the top of the life-cycle curve (i.e., before maturity leads to decline or death), transformational leaders establish an environment that consistently encourages building and exploring. It is imperative, however, that this happens *before* the decline ensues. Regeneration requires constant analysis of the how and on continued new vision and energy. (See box 3.3.)

The congregation that scores one big success should not rest on its laurels, but start thinking right away about the next success or project. Transformational leaders focus on the next chapter in this book of never-ending church development. This sequential process must be equal to or surpass the caliber of the last effort. It cannot be like *Karate Kid II* and *III*, *Rocky III* and *IV*, *Star Trek V*, or *City Slickers II*. They were not blockbuster hits like their predecessors, even though critics held them in higher acclaim than the first movie. The atmosphere for growth must always support creative efforts.

A church in a small town in the East has grown consistently over the past twenty-five years. Today they have grown to nine hundred members. This is no fluke. Their growth has resulted from careful strategic planning—a new building, a youth camp, a facility for the elderly, the largest Vacation Bible School in the county, and meeting continuous attendance and contribution goals. Every successful program sets the stage for the next project. Spiritual life is on fire because church members are constantly looking forward to something better.

Box 3.3

Life Cycles in Renewal

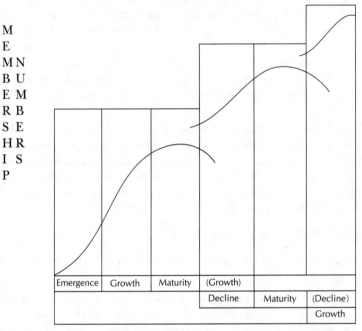

Years

In contrast, a church in a large city in the Southeast with seemingly endless resources went through a five-year growth cycle with successful leadership. Many people, inspired by the church leaders' vision, began attending. Then, the leaders began to ignore the need for visions and dreams. They set no new goals, and the congregation ebbed away. The neighborhood began to change, and there was little incentive to go to the church. Rapid decline forced the congregation to close its doors, ending a sixty-plus-year history.

Most corporations go out of business by the time they are forty years of age.[4] Could it be that the normal life cycle of a church is forty years?

If so, organizational death is not necessarily failure. It is a natural part of the life cycle. Some church growth experts are predicting that future life cycles may be as short as twenty years.

Terminal Illness

Even an unhealthy church can grow, but "ethnikitis" and old age are terminal illnesses.[5]

Ethnikitis is a disease caused by a changing community, mostly urban. It afflicts neighborhood churches that have thrived by ministering to the needs of the local people. Due to uncontrollable circumstances, the neighborhood has changed. New people have moved in, and others out. In advanced stages of this illness, a large number of church members will continue to commute to the worship service from outlying communities. But because the church typically builds no ministry bridge to the new people in the community, they cannot minister to newcomers. So they die.

Old age is caused by a disintegrating, mostly rural, community. As rural communities become smaller, businesses close and family farms are taken over by large agricultural corporations. These churches are like plants denied the nurturing rays of the sun. Churches in these communities are denied access to the essential element of growth—people. Families are forced to relocate, and these churches often die.

Growth-Inhibiting Diseases

Any church can grow so long as it is not infected with a growth-inhibiting disease such as these:

1. *People-blindness* occurs when church leaders do not recognize the important cultural differences that glue large social groups together or become barriers to the communication of the Good News.

2. *Hyper-cooperativism* sets in when church leaders think a growth problem will be solved by joining a cooperative evangelistic program with other churches.

3. *Koinonitis* occurs when Christians develop fellowship to such an exaggerated extent that all their attention and energies are absorbed by other Christians. Evangelistic myopia is likely to settle in.

4. *Sociological strangulation* afflicts only growing churches and occurs when the physical facilities of the church can no longer accommodate the people flow.

5. *Arrested spiritual development* occurs in churches that are not well-fed with the Word of God. True church growth is ultimately God's work.

6. *Saint John's syndrome* refers to lukewarm, second-generation churches that have not added new members regularly. They no longer grow or receive the vital blessing of God (see Rev. 2 and 3).[6]

Like churches struck by terminal illnesses, churches with growth-inhibiting diseases eventually die off. There is little hope for the situation and the leadership responsible for this decline phase of operation.

Barriers to Constant Improvement

The most common barriers to constant improvement are insecurity, arrogance, self-centeredness, apathy, laziness, short-term focus, and distrust.[7] They are barriers because they block an individual's motivation to change, even for the sake of improvement.

A group of elders (all male) in a congregation out West have set themselves up as "guardians of the flock." Their vision is short-sighted at best, nonexistent by most standards. They have told their members that all decisions in their congregation's personal lives are to be made by them—yes, even their finances, frequency of sex, number of children, job changes, etc. Any "mavericks" in the congregation who challenge the elders' decisions are reprimanded severely. There are no church meetings to discuss future plans or programs. This men's-only group is arrogant and self-centered. They seem unable to trust anyone. They are interested primarily in building dependence of their members on their leadership (reaching cult status by most definitions). Consequently, there is little opportunity for change, development, or improvement. And, the pity of it is, all their actions are done in the name of God and Christ. (Interestingly, many highly educated young people looking for security and direction are drawn into the fold.)

Improvement can mean the difference between success and failure and is an extremely complex process. It requires a systematic approach for identifying and analyzing external factors and matching them with a church's internal capabilities. Transformational leaders recognize the telltale signs of decline. They regroup, replan, restructure, or rethink as needed. This proactive response shifts a church's life cycle upward, enabling growth and empowering leaders to focus on the next encore.

Constant improvement is more likely to occur in an environment that reinforces self-respect, loyalty, motivation, and commitment. However, this attitude must be a strategic imperative. It is the result of constant, fervent prayer for transformational leadership. Strategies that are successful in one stage can be disastrous in another. A wise minister once said, "If this program is no longer effective, then we should let it die and embalm it in all its glory."

European mountain climbers tell a story of passing a certain grave along the trail to a famous peak. On the marker is a man's name and the inscription: "He died climbing." Such a statement is a picture of a life of faith—moving toward the goal to which God calls (Phil. 3:12–14). "Therefore, since we are surrounded by such a great cloud of witnesses, let us throw off everything that hinders and the sin that so easily entangles, and let us run with perseverance the race marked out for us" (Heb. 12:1).

To better understand this "great cloud of witnesses," we will see in chapter 4 that certain leadership traits enhance the skills of transformational leaders.

— — —

Pause to Reflect

1. Consider what your church has accomplished in its history. What does your church want to be in the future? How is it planning to get there?

2. Discuss the concept of transformational leadership in action in your church. What would it take to change the philosophy of a leadership group to adopt a transformational frame of reference, if they are not yet at that point?

3. Discuss the concept of strategic planning in your church. Does the strategic plan respond to the need for focus, for congruence, and to change?

4. Describe where your church is on the organizational life cycle in box 3.2. What are the key components for regeneration of a congregation stuck in the maturity stage?

5. Discuss the barriers that block your church leaders' motivation to change in order to stay in a growth frame of mind. What can your leadership do to avoid terminal illness and/or growth-inhibiting diseases?

4

TRAITS OF LEADERSHIP

Are leaders born or are they made by circumstances? Early leadership researchers summarized leaders' qualities and assumed certain traits were inborn. Effectiveness was measured in terms of potential ability and personality characteristics of a leader and group members. Studies of leadership traits between 1904 and 1947 concluded that patterns of leadership traits differ with the situation, and that leadership is not a matter of heredity. (See box 4.1.) How many famous leaders had children who were famous leaders? From Eli and David's sons on down, innate traits do not seem to hold as a true predictor of leadership success.

Management is planning, organizing, budgeting, and controlling; *leadership* is setting a vision, building relationships, creating strategies, and motivating.

Whether in business, education, scouting, or the church, people prefer to be led rather than managed. Leading is not necessarily managing, even though the two terms are often used interchangeably. Have you ever heard of a world manager, educational manager, political manager, religious manager, or community manager? World leader, educational leader, political leader, religious leader, and community leader—yes![1]

Yet, there is no reason to believe a person with the appropriate background, skills, and motivation could not both manage and lead well in some situations.[2]

Box 4.1
Traits of Leadership: 1904–47

age	height and weight	physique, energy, health
appearance	fluency of speech	intelligence
scholarship	knowledge	judgment and decision
insight	originality	adaptability
introversion-extroversion	dominance	initiative, persistence, ambition
responsibility	integrity and conviction	self-confidence
social activity and mobility	emotional control	social and economic status
popularity and prestige	biosocial activity	social skills
cooperation		control of moods and optimism

Adapted from B. M. Bass, *Bass and Stogdill's Handbook of Leadership: Theory, Research, and Managerial Applications,* 3rd ed. (New York: The Free Press, 1990), 61–73.

Follow-up studies of leadership traits since 1948 (see box 4.2) have concluded that "individuals with higher activity and energy levels, with relevant task and intellectual competencies, with relevant interaction skills, and with participative values and orientations tend to emerge as leaders more often than not. As a consequence of these attributes, they tend to be valued as individuals and placed in valued positions."[3]

Yet not all successful leaders possess all the traits typically provided in such lists. In fact, certain recognized leaders possess different traits from other leaders. Analysis of trait research reveals that:

1. Attempts to select leaders by traits has little success.

2. Numerous traits indicate leaders are different than followers.

3. The traits demanded of a leader vary from one situation to another.

4. The trait approach ignores the interaction between the leader and the group.[4]

Are there any traits that are of value to the Christian leader, traits that will facilitate a healthy working relationship with followers? Yes, but as the exhibits have already illustrated, there is not total agreement on which characteristics are most important. For example, which of these lists seem more comfortable?

Box 4.2
Traits of Leadership: A Follow-up (1947–Present)

technical skills	social nearness, friendliness
task motivation and application	supportive of the group task
social and interpersonal skills	emotional balance and control
leadership effectiveness and achievement	administrative skills
general impression (halo)	intellectual skills
ascendance, dominance, decisiveness	willingness to assume responsibility
ethical conduct, personal integrity	maintaining a cohesive work group
maintaining coordination and teamwork	ability to communicate; articulativeness
physical energy	maintaining standards of performance
creative, independent	conforming
courageous, daring	experience and activity
nurturing behavior	maintaining informal control of the group
mature, cultural	aloof, distant

Adapted from B. M. Bass, *Bass and Stogdill's Handbook of Leadership: Theory, Research, and Managerial Applications,* 3rd ed. (New York: The Free Press, 1990), 85.

- Trait List #1: Leaders lead people, gather people around a vision, motivate people, encourage people, are role models, expect excellence, work hard, take risks, love people, and value administration.[5]

- Trait List #2: Leaders exhibit commitment, goal-setting and decision-making ability, motivation, enthusiasm, honesty, courage, responsibility and accountability, and can prioritize.[6]

Each list is valuable, and it is hard to tell which list would have an advantage over the other.

Spiritual Traits of the Transformational Leader

Transformational leaders create a vigorous relationship between leaders and followers. This energetic give-and-take affects a church's activities related to goal setting and achievement. It is not a title granting someone a license to wield authority recklessly over others (see Matt. 20:25–28; 1 Pet. 5:2–3). Leadership is a calling, a vocation, not a position. It is a skill one performs; it is a service one renders. True leadership is a working relationship among group members.

The apostle Paul certainly had expectations of spiritual leaders in mind when he wrote to Timothy:

> Now the overseer must be above reproach, the husband of but one wife, temperate, self-controlled, respectable, hospitable, able to teach, not given to drunkenness, not violent but gentle, not quarrelsome, not a lover of money. He must manage his own family well and see that his children obey him with proper respect. (If anyone does not know how to manage his own family, how can he take care of God's church?) He must not be a recent convert or he may become conceited and fall under the same judgment as the devil. He must also have a good reputation with outsiders, so that he will not fall into disgrace and into the devil's trap (1 Tim. 3:2–7).

Name a church leader who was especially effective or influential. His or her characteristics are probably listed in this passage of Scripture.

These spiritual traits may be classified into five relational characteristics: social, moral, mental, personality, and maturity.[7] Such spiritual standards do not change. They are the same today as they were when the church was established. None of these qualities are optional; they are indispensable requirements.[8]

Social Traits

Transformational leaders recognize and appreciate the work and dignity of each person. They strive to understand human relations and respect others. They understand their own feelings and frustrations and accept others' feelings and frustrations. They are open, friendly, and hospitable. Manipulation is never an option. C. W. Perry said, "Leadership accepts people where they are and then takes them somewhere else." Transformational leaders exhibit expertise or competency in three areas that significantly improve their social skills.

1. *Transformational leaders realize that people need to be needed.* They believe people have unlimited potential and value. They communicate this understanding to those individuals via warmth and openness.

2. *Transformational leaders develop trusting relationships.* Trust begins with leadership. Before followers can be trustworthy, leaders must demonstrate trust, and attitudes such as confidence, reliance, expectation, and hope. Two points are especially important in demonstrating trust:

- There are degrees of confidence bestowed on a trusted person, and trust levels increase with time and demonstrations of trustworthiness.

- Minimal amounts of risk are involved in trusting another person; sometimes it appears dangerous to reach out to others, but the effort usually results in growth.

3. *Transformational leaders provide proper recognition.* People deserve credit and recognition for what they accomplish. Such recognition demonstrates an appreciation of people's contributions. Besides that, it is a biblical principle: "Give everyone what you owe him . . . if respect, then respect; if honor, then honor" (Rom. 13:7). Congregations that have recognized the contributions of their members have flourished.

One church hosts a banquet for its Bible study teachers annually. Another has a ham dinner for those who usher, serve communion, count the contributions, and perform other tasks. Still another congregation gives a Bible to couples who have been married fifty years, recognizes them in church, and acknowledges the tremendous example of their strong marriages. At a Christian campground, the directors regularly recognize those who bring happiness to others with a "Bluebird of Happiness Award"—a plaque for distinguished Christian service. Sometimes a simple gift of a T-shirt, a book, an umbrella, or a pat on the back affirms people and motivates them to continue their good work.

Moral Traits

Someone once penned, "Some of the best fiction of our day can be found on the expense reports of Christian organizations." If there is one trait that should distinguish the Christian leader, it is the moral trait of *integrity.* The present ethical and moral crisis in society screams out for such leadership.

The church is the logical supply house for leaders who inspire followers with a righteous fervor, leaders like Martin Luther King Jr., Billy Graham, Charles Swindoll, and Lloyd Ogilvie. Men and women like this can take charge because God is on their side. Unless Christians show they are redeemed, how will others believe in the Redeemer? (See Ps. 107:1–3; Matt. 5:16.) The church needs leaders. It needs to give leaders to the world who cannot be bought, who put character above wealth, who do not lose their individuality in a group, who make no compromises with wrong, and who are not afraid to stand for truth. The church should not have to deal with those who will follow those so-called leaders who failed to honor God.

Henry Van Dyke said, "You have to live in a crowd, but you do not have to live like it, nor subsist on its food." Consider Rotary International's Four-Way Test of Ethical Behavior:

1. Is it the truth?

2. Is it fair to all concerned?

3. Will it build goodwill and better friendships?

4. Will it be beneficial to all concerned?

Paul said it this way: "Do not conform any longer to the pattern of this world, but be transformed by the renewing of your mind" (Rom. 12:2). Transformational leaders exhibit the highest standards of moral and intellectual honesty. Every action is a testimony. Consider a group of oil executives who hired five young men. Four of those new employees drank heavily with the executives on the weekend. One did not. The one who demonstrated restraint was the one who received the promotions. One's life is a witness to unbelievers every day, even when one thinks no one is watching.

Mental Traits

Some leadership research indicates that leaders have a somewhat higher intelligence than their followers. Transformational leaders typically have greater analytical ability and can see broad problems and complicated relationships. They also excel at communicating ideas, motivating others, and understanding what others are communicating—all activities that are highly dependent on mental capability. They have a greater capacity for differentiation, a rare talent for integration, and distinctive flexibility.[9]

What distinguishes leaders from followers might simply be called "thinking." On a number of instances Jesus addressed his listeners with the question, "What do you think?" (see Matt. 17:25; 18:12; 21:28; 22:42; 26:66; Mark 14:64; John 11: 56). He called on them to analyze a situation, to put it together, or to synthesize a meaning. God's leaders must be great thinkers. They must have the vision to think ten to twenty years into the future. Such thinking enables executives and church leaders to accomplish great things.

Personality Traits

Leaders are often described as "driven." They are motivated to keep accomplishing. They enjoy responsibility, striving for intrinsic rather than extrinsic rewards. Seeing their congregations move smoothly and productively toward a goal also motivates them to do more for the membership. Leaders work for success and set an example of hard work. As they reach one goal, they aspire to a new one. One success becomes a challenge to achieve greater success.

Transformational leaders not only have faith in God but also in themselves. Christian psychologists as well as modern behavioral scientists confirm that a person's self-image is the real key to personality and behavior. The way leaders view themselves is the way they will view their followers. "The person who feels that people are not very important cannot have very much deep-down self-respect and self-regard—for he himself is 'people,' and with what judgment he considers others, he himself is unwittingly judged in his own mind."[10]

Leaders and members alike must analyze their self-image. Many are prisoners of their negative or distorted self-perception. They underestimate their potential. As a result they are unhappy, unproductive, and dissatisfied. In such cases, it is important to realize that God is the Creator and Sustainer of all life. "God don't make junk!"

Maturity Traits

Transformational leaders are emotionally stable and mature. They have a broad range of interests and abilities. They also have healthy self-concepts, are self-assured, and have respect for others. They can understand incoming data, convey ideas, and inspire others. They are neither defeated by failure nor overjoyed with victory. Transformational leaders continue to strive "until we all reach unity in the faith and in the knowledge of the Son of God and become mature, attaining to the whole measure of the fullness of Christ" (Eph. 4:13).

Emotional stability is indicated in the way one deals with people. This stability is expressed in understanding, trust, confidence, tolerance, loyalty, and sympathy. The following are characteristics of mature leaders:

1. They have tact and get along with people.

2. They avoid interfering in others' affairs.

3. They constantly accept change because of their underlying security.

4. They do not blame others when things go wrong.

5. They are able to develop a solid *esprit de corps* because they work well as part of a team.

6. They can handle criticism and differences in others.

49

7. They are not overly critical of others and their methods of doing things.

8. They can cut through trivia and help a group reach its goals and objectives.[11]

Leaders who evidence such immaturity (or perhaps a lack of control) usually fail. God's leaders must exhibit maturity in their dealings with others (1 Tim. 3:16).

These five traits (social, moral, mental, personality, and maturity) have the power to transform both leader and follower. The transformational leader is the epitome of these traits. These prerequisites are the basis of a working relationship with a congregation. However, they need to be coupled with initiative (chap. 5).

— — —

Pause to Reflect

1. Leadership has been defined as a function, not a position. It is a skill one performs and a service one renders. Do you agree or disagree? Why? How is leadership a helping relationship?

2. Two different periods of trait studies are cataloged in this chapter. What attributes have been consistently identified for the past seventy years? In your opinion, are they still relevant for the 1990s? Are they fitting for the twenty-first century? Discuss.

3. Six spiritual traits are discussed in this chapter. Based on your experience in the church, do leaders exhibit those characteristics? Are there other qualifications you would add to this list? If so, what are those?

4. The six spiritual traits discussed are not considered optional; they are indispensable requirements. Do you agree or disagree? Discuss. In your opinion, are any of these traits more critical than others to today's church? Why?

5. Read Titus 1:5–9 and 1 Peter 5:1–4. Contrast the qualifications listed in these two passages with the list in 1 Timothy 3:2–7 discussed in this chapter. Are there any traits in these other passages that should be added to a transformational leader's qualifications? Discuss.

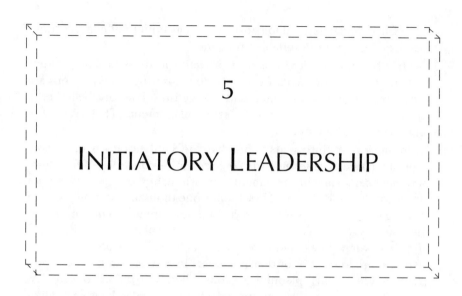

5

INITIATORY LEADERSHIP

Adolphe Monod said, "Between the great things we cannot do and the small things we will not do, the danger is that we shall do nothing." To transform leadership traits into action requires initiative. *Initiative is the willingness to begin and follow through.* Knowing and identifying leadership traits (chap. 4) is important, but far greater is the need to move forward, sometimes through chaos, to tackle the weightier issues, to do something (see Matt. 23:23).

Every religious leader grapples with the question: Where should my church be headed? This is a simple and straightforward question. Yet some Christian leaders seem puzzled, perplexed, and deeply troubled by such queries, perhaps with good reason. These questions cut to the nature and purpose of a church and to the leaders' vision of what that church should become. To ask is to question congregational development and strategy. There is an implied assumption that no matter how strong a church's present position, the status quo is on trial. A church is subject to comparison of both leaders' and followers' expectations about what they want their congregation to be.

Business owners, chief executive officers, presidents, and top managers agree that strategy is vital to success. An increasing number of profit and nonprofit corporations and institutions use strategic management concepts and techniques to make effective decisions. Unfortunately, some Christian leaders fail to consider strategy until their congregations face seemingly insurmountable problems.

They become *reactive* instead of proactive leaders. Reactive leaders blur the real goal of the church—salvation. Growing congregations are very provocative, goal-oriented, and evangelistic. They are believers in the motto, *carpe diem;* their leaders "seize the moment." They take a strategic initiative and move forward to the glory of God.

For more than thirty years a church in the Southeast has planned strategically. Three decades ago, the congregation—consisting of four hundred members—met in a basement auditorium, but the leaders were not afraid to plan and dream. They built a one-thousand–seat auditorium and began to plan for greater growth and development. They promoted their Sunday school, Vacation Bible School, and child care, and dreamed of a time when they could care for the elderly. The leaders began to involve more and more of their members in service and outreach programs and held yearly planning sessions called "Operation Forward." At one of these sessions, they announced a ten-year goal to have a membership of three thousand and an auditorium that would accommodate those in attendance. They reached this goal in seven years and attendance often exceeded four thousand! Throughout this incredible growth, they continued to emphasize benevolence, teaching at home, and mission work abroad. Consequently, the church became one of the largest congregations within its denomination. Why? Because that church's leaders were willing to seize their strategic initiative.

Strategic Initiative and the Church

The word "strategy" is derived from the Greek *strategos* and refers to warfare and a military general.[1] Originally, this term was defined as planning and directing large military movements and the operations of war. Strategy may seem a strange word to link with the church, but it captures the essence of the church's struggle. On an earthly plane, some churches resemble battlefields. Members argue, fight, and sue one another. One congregation defames another. On a heavenly plane, Christians are at war against "the rulers, against the authorities, against the powers of this dark world, and against the spiritual forces of evil" (Eph. 6:12).

These wars raise an interesting question: Who is the church fighting against? Is it Satan? The "world?" One another? Other churches? Corporate America? Hugh and Christie Hefner? The Zionists? United Nations? Congress? Other denominations? Satan does not distinguish between the heavenly and earthly planes; he moves freely between the physical world and the spiritual world. Churches must use strategy in such an uncertain world and when dealing with such a mobile enemy.

Initiative, however, is not a strange word to link with either the church or strategy. Initiative is the determination to take the first step toward a goal (the basic purpose of the church) and then to keep moving toward it. *The American Heritage Dictionary* (Second College Edition) defines initiative as "the power, ability, or instinct to begin or follow through energetically with a plan or task." The apostle Paul wrote, "I press on" (Phil. 3:12) and "encourage others to live up to what we have already attained"(v. 16). In his work, this dual objective is reiterated: never be satisfied with where one is spiritually, and press on using one's God-given initiative. Similarly, a church cannot be content with the status quo. Transformational leaders rise up and begin anew the work the Lord has delegated.

Initiative is a highly prized trait in managers and employees. To avoid stagnation, decline, and death, transformational leaders employ a rational approach toward anticipating, responding to, and altering the future.

> It is the future that dictates the present. . . . People act in the present according to their *judgment* about what the future will hold. They differ only in the span of future time that elicits a judgment and in the nature and scope of present activity that will permit them to live in a period of future time. Thus, in this sense, it can be stated that it is . . . vision of the future which dictates present action.[2]

There will continue to be changes in the social, economic, and political environment. These changes will have profound future effects on the church in issues such as war, diversity, immigration, and gender equality. Every leader needs to identify those changes before they happen and plan accordingly. Christian leaders must continually ask: What does the future hold? Many assume it holds life or death, heaven or hell. But not everyone may agree. Although church leaders may be unable to know or examine in great detail every factor that will affect their church, they can identify and address specific elements. They can specify the depth and nature of their examination. And they can know who holds the future!

God has always used individuals with initiative to accomplish his will, individuals like Joseph, Gideon, Deborah, David, Nehemiah, and Paul. Today is no different. Men and women with vision must act strategically if their congregations are to prosper in a materialistic society. Leaders today, like Queen Esther thousands of years ago, have come into the kingdom to do God's work, knowing that spiritual leadership can be exercised only by Spirit-filled people.

The Search for Initiative

The story is told of a promising Greek artist named Timanthes who painted an exquisite portrait. He was so thrilled with what he had painted that he sat for days gazing at his work. One morning he discovered that his teacher had deliberately ruined his painting. With tears and anger he asked why. His teacher replied, "I did it for your own good. Your painting is excellent, but it is not perfect. Start again and see if you can do even better." Timanthes began anew and created a masterpiece of antiquity, *Sacrifice of Iphigenia.*

Strategic initiative and leadership presents a similar dilemma. Who should be selected as leaders or strategists, either to keep the church headed in the right direction, or to turn it around if it is struggling or failing? Who can be depended on to never be content with accomplishments, but rather to continue to try and reach even higher plateaus of service?

Studying the types of people Jesus called to his ministry provides a partial answer. He selected individuals who were ready to work, obedient to his commands, honest in assessing themselves, and willing to make sacrifices.[3] In essence, his followers were willing to exercise their initiative.

Ready to Work

Jesus picked people who worked with their hands. Peter, Andrew, James, and John were the principal actors in this drama. These men did not fish for fun. This was not a weekend fishing/camping expedition. This was a job that gave them only the afternoons to themselves. Night was the best fishing time; morning, the worst. So they fished all night and then spent a good part of the morning cleaning their nets. That is what they were doing when Jesus arrived on the scene and offered them a provocative solution to their fishing problems. They were willing, despite a frustrating night and morning filled with hard labor, to go fishing again simply because Jesus asked.

A lack of work was what got the Thessalonian church into trouble. Many had quit their jobs because they thought the Lord would come soon. They had fallen prey to "busybodiness." Sometimes those who work the least talk the most. Paul exhorted them to work in quietness; to earn a living; not to be a burden on others; and to not grow tired of working (2 Thess. 3:6–13).

Jesus picked people who were accustomed to work and who were not afraid of it.

Obedient

Peter and the others obeyed seemingly without reservation. They may not have completely understood why the Lord was commanding certain things, but they obeyed anyway. Sometimes believers do not understand either. Remember when Abraham was told to sacrifice his son; Ananias to baptize Saul; or Peter to eat of the animals that God showed to him in the dream? Abraham, Ananias, Peter, and many others did not understand, but they obeyed.

Obedience is particularly hard in the United States where individuality and independence are emphasized. It is an acknowledgment that someone else knows what is best. Families are testimony to the struggle between individuality and obedience, between freedom and anarchy. Parents hold on to their teenagers, hoping obedience will keep their children from the evils of the world. Teenagers struggle to break free of the parental grip to live their own lives. At some point, parents let go, taking comfort in the promise that as God provided for Abraham, he will also provide for their families. But obedience is hard. Giving up self-control is hard, even to the one who taught his children what love is.

Honest in Assessing Themselves

Peter realized that he was a sinner. In fact, he was so painfully aware of his depravity that he fell to his knees. The incredible thing about Peter throughout the New Testament (and David in the Old Testament) was his self-assessing powers. He stumbled often and realized his limitations. Consider the denial, the walk on water, and the time Paul rebuked him for his hypocrisy among the Gentiles.

Christians also live with certain limitations, and this incident raises a question: *How often is personal assessment conducted?* Judging others is so much easier than looking inside oneself. In fact, one may judge others to avoid judging oneself. Does it say something about one's self-concept? Yet, the followers of Jesus constantly evaluate themselves: "Be careful that you don't fall!" (1 Cor. 10:12). Although this command is negative, the plight within the evangelical and Catholic churches illustrates the point that leaders who sin ask for forgiveness. When one realizes that he or she is a sinner in need of the Savior, the first step toward growth is taken: *honest self-assessment.*

Willing to Make Sacrifices

There was no free ride for these early followers. They left their catch, their boats, their jobs, and their homes to follow Jesus. Their lives took on a new focus. The discipline once devoted to fishing now was devoted to spiritual ends. There is a remarkable trust here. It is based on this assumption: *Jesus can supply any need just as he supplied the fish.*

Remember the story of the would-be followers on a Samaritan road who were asked to count the cost and follow Jesus, but could not? The sacrifice involved in following Christ has not changed. "No one who puts his hand to the plow and looks back is fit for service in the kingdom of God" (Luke 9:57–62).

The cost of following is high. It involves giving up the self, recognizing one's reliance on cheap grace, and a willingness to let Christ lead.[4] Think of the early saints who were martyred because of their faith. Or today's missionaries who are jailed or killed abroad because of their stand for God. There are many who leave comfortable lives to follow him. Listen to these words of one of God's greatest followers:

"For to me, to live is Christ and to die is gain" (Phil. 1:21). "Each of you should look not only to your own interests, but also to the interests of others" (2:4). "Continue to work out your salvation with fear and trembling; for it is God who works in you to will and to act according to his good purpose" (vv. 12–13). "I know what it is to be in need, and I know what it is to have plenty. I have learned the secret of being content in any and every situation, whether well fed or hungry, whether living in plenty or in want. I can do everything through him who gives me strength" (4:12–13).

All these statements were written by Paul while in prison for following Jesus. What is a modern Christian's willing-to-make-sacrifices quotient? How honest is his or her self-assessment?

Initiators

When one inquires as to why Jesus selected the followers he did, the answer partially lies in the fact that he recognized in them a willingness to exercise *initiative.* When he sent out the Twelve on a trial-run missionary campaign, he told them: "I am sending you out like sheep among wolves. Therefore be as shrewd as snakes and as innocent as doves. Be on your guard against men; they will hand you over to the local councils and flog you in their synagogues. On my account you will be brought before governors and kings as witnesses to them and to the Gentiles" (Matt. 10:16–18).

Jesus knew his apostles were capable of using their own initiative to perform his work. But he also knew that before they could develop their initiative, he must empower them to do his work. Thus he allowed them to act on their own and then to report back to him what happened. His empowerment was what caused them to do his work in ways that turned the world upside down (see Acts 17:6). "They went out and preached that people should repent. They drove out many demons and anointed many sick people with oil and healed them" (Mark 6:12–13). On another occasion, Jesus sent seventy-two people two by two to proclaim the good tidings of the kingdom. He equipped them (i.e., he transferred initiative to them), and they returned from their missionary campaign with joy, proclaiming, "Lord, even the demons submit to us in your name." Jesus replied, "I saw Satan fall like lightning from heaven. . . . Rejoice that your names are written in heaven" (Luke 10:17–20).

Notice how Jesus used positive reinforcement by enjoying and rejoicing in their fruits. He showed them that their risk paid off. The leader's job, so ably demonstrated by the Lord, is to give followers no choice but to choose to master their own initiative.

A classic article on time management and delegation says there are five degrees of initiative a leader can exercise:

- Wait until told (lowest initiative);
- Ask what to do;
- Recommend, then take resulting action;
- Act, but advise at once;
- Act on own, then routinely report (highest initiative).[5]

Two of the gravest problems in the church today center around people who do not use their God-given initiative and leaders who stifle people from using their initiative. Unfortunately, it puts the church in a double bind.

Response to a Changing Membership

Whether perceived as a world of somewhat ordered chaos and purposeful confusion or one violently turned upside down, the world requires flexibility, adaptation, and action for operational success. The church cannot afford to be inflexible when the world demands flexibility and adaptability. The church cannot sit and wait for others to do something when the world is screaming for someone with the initiative to reach its hurting masses. The church must undergo constant fine tuning to make these timely adjustments.

It may be a cliché to say that change is the only constant in the world, but change is changing the face of the modern church. These changes are created by leaders who are responsive to the external environment. With a wide range of educational and cultural backgrounds, as well as levels of biblical knowledge and understanding, the church is being pulled in one direction or the other. Transformational leaders use their initiative not only to incorporate change within scriptural boundaries in order to meet the realities of the marketplace, but also to meet the changing needs of Christians and non-Christians alike. The members should not be the proverbial "tail wagging the dog," causing leaders to make panic decisions.

A young mother with children at home decided to have a Bible study in her home for other young mothers. Her church leaders questioned the validity of this practice because they would not be meeting in the church building. Their apparent lack of flexibility, spontaneity, and respect for initiative blinded them to the way the first church began—meeting in homes—and it denied the potential for future growth within the Lord's kingdom.

Transformational leaders use new models of vision, communication, and motivation. They actively compete for leaders, souls, members, funds, and a new strategic initiative. Such changes must be made before churches lose this generation and the next one. Congregational leaders must stop being so worried about doing wrong that they cannot do what is right. They must be proactive and exercise their initiative.

A new vision for the Lord's work is necessary because without a vision God's people perish (see Luke 9:57–62). A new emphasis on strategy is important because our struggle is not against flesh and blood (Eph. 6:12). A new emphasis on communication is demanded because dreams must be put into words (see Joel 2:28–29; Rom. 10:13–18). New styles of motivation are welcomed because there are still people to be saved and churches to be grown (see Matt. 28:19–20; Acts 2:14–47).

A number of writers have suggested using strengths to take advantage of opportunities, turning stumbling blocks into stepping stones. However, they typically ignore other important relationships, such as the challenge of overcoming weaknesses in order to free up the opportunities. Strategic factors like strengths, weaknesses, opportunities, threats, vision, communication, and motivation may not be new, but matching them with initiative in a systematic fashion is.

Communication and motivational techniques used to be directed toward winning the world and saving lost souls. The result was growing churches. Has the church forgotten this goal of saving the world, or lost it in the hustle of everyday life? Have churches lost their primary strategy for channeling resources into supporting the church at large?

Christian leaders must use their congregations' strengths to compensate for any weaknesses, ward off possible threats, and take advantage of emerging opportunities. Leaders must be open to change, encourage change, and control the dynamics of change. They must take the strategic initiative and respond to a changing membership.

In other words, *do something!*

— — —

Pause to Reflect

1. Describe the tendencies of leaders in your church regarding *reaction* versus *proaction*. How willing are they to seize their "strategic initiative"? Describe the same tendency and willingness in yourself.

2. Define the terms *strategy* and *initiative*. Do you believe there is a need for strategic initiative in the church today? Why?

3. Discuss the recruitment of the apostles relative to their personal characteristics. What made them worthy of being called by Jesus?

4. Do you think what congregations need today is a change in the way they think about and do things? Why? What are some of the things that could be changed without endangering the commands of God at your church?

5. What do you personally need to do to take the strategic initiative? How can you and the present leaders of your congregation serve together?

6

LEADERSHIP BEHAVIOR

Instead of traits, attributes, or characteristics of leaders (chap. 4), many researchers look to behaviors or styles to understand leadership. Those interested in a stylistic approach have been concerned primarily with autocratic or leader-centered behaviors of leaders like Hitler, Stalin, Mao, Hussein, or Castro as contrasted with democratic or group-centered behaviors of leaders like Thatcher, Aristide, and Clinton; and they are interested in the various components of each.

Leadership is a social influence exerted on individuals and/or groups to achieve goals. Four components are involved: the leader, the followers, the context, and the results. The style of the leader determines the results (or accomplishment of goals).

Autocratic leaders have also been labeled authoritarian, directive, Theory X, coercive, and persuasive; they are production-minded, lone decision makers, initiators of structure, goal emphasizers and work facilitators, task oriented, and concerned about performance.[1] The authoritarian approach contributes to order, consistency, and the resolution of conflict.

Democratic leaders also have been classified several ways: considerate, consultative, participative, consensual, supportive, employee-centered, relationship-centered, interaction-facilitating, concerned with people and the maintenance of good working relationships, endorsers of joint and group decision making, and Theory Y ideologists.[2] The democratic style contributes to commitment, loyalty, involvement, and satisfaction of followers.

Box 6.1 contrasts a task-centered autocrat with a people-centered leader. This continuum contrasts boss-centered leadership with participative leadership. The autocrat shows concern for getting work accomplished. His or her communication and behavior indicate that concern. The participative, or democratic, leader displays concern for relationships. His or her behavior and communication do the same. This distinction asks how power is distributed, whose needs are met, and how decisions are made.[3]

In a business context, the range from left to right would include seven stages:

1. The leader makes the decision and announces it.
2. The leader "sells" the decision.
3. The leader presents ideas and invites questions.
4. The leader presents tentative decision, subject to change.
5. The leader presents the problem, gets suggestions, and makes a decision.
6. The leader defines limits, then asks the group to make a decision.
7. The leader permits the group to function within limits defined by him or her.[4]

At the center of the continuum is a leader whose consultative decision-making style encourages both leaders and followers to play active roles in making decisions and assuming joint responsibility for those decisions. This "happy medium" is a common style for many successful church leaders. Participation and collaboration are welcomed and encouraged.

In addition to autocratic and democratic leadership, there is the behavior known as situational leadership (see chap. 8). This third type of leadership matches the style of the leader to the incident. That is, it reveals who would be best to lead in a given situation. Which style seems to make better sense for a church?

Autocratic Leadership

Autocratic leadership emphasizes authority. Autocratic leaders in a church often give orders, limit church membership participation, and emphasize the work of the church. Autocrats decide all goals, set all policy, structure all tasks, and try to force all people to accept their decisions. They tend to be personal in their criticism and remain aloof from group participation. Biblical examples of autocratic leaders include Saul, Ahab, Nebuchadnezzar, Herod, and Diotrephes, among others.

Box 6.1
Church Leadership Continuum:
When Your Walk Does Not Match Your Talk

TASK <————————————————————————> PEOPLE

Task-Oriented Behavior:	Relationship-Oriented Rhetoric:
1. I supervise my group closely so that the members work harder and do better work.	1. My door is always open.
2. I decide on appropriate goals and objectives for my group and convince the members of the value of my plans.	2. Let's hear your ideas.
3. I establish controls to make my group accomplish its tasks.	3. I believe in strong incentive plan.
4. I plan my groups' work load for them.	4. Let's keep the lines of communication open.
5. I meet with my group to find out if they are following my plan.	5. Our employee-development program is there for you.
6. I require my group members to make frequent progress reports.	6. I value diversity.
7. I set up new controls immediately if the quality of my groups' work drops.	7. Let me know how I can help.
8. I push my group to meet deadlines and production schedules that I set up for them.	8. My group is a team.
9. I restrict my group from establishing their own goals.	9. I like a person who shows initiative.
10. I prohibit my group from making decisions without consulting me.	10. This will be great for morale.

Adapted from M. Vanterpool, "Rhetoric and Behavior: Theory X and Theory Y," *The 1991 Annual for Group Facilitators* (San Diego: University Associates, Inc., 1991): 51–64.

Consider the dictatorial/autocratic leadership style of King Neb-uchadnezzar. After dreaming, he commanded his magicians, enchant-ers, and sorcerers to interpret his dream for him even though he had forgotten what the dream was about and could not explain it to them. On three separate occasions the king's wise men suggested that this was an impossible task, but he replied, "'If you do not tell me what my dream was and interpret it, I will have you cut into pieces and your houses turned into piles of rubble.' . . . 'If you do not tell me the dream, there is just one penalty for you. You have conspired to tell me misleading and wicked things, hoping the situation will change.'. . . This made the king so angry and furious that he ordered the execution of all the wise men of Baby-lon" (Dan. 2:5, 9, 12).

Autocratic leadership has many defects, especially in a church setting, but some autocratic behavior may be preferable to democratic leader-ship in certain situations. A *benevolent autocrat* is a leader who, with love or concern and respect, uses autocratic behaviors in situations where they are needed. Nehemiah is an example. However, the benevolent autocrat does this in an effective way, knowing what must be accom-plished, but without creating resentment.

> The benevolent autocratic manager is usually perceived as one who places implicit trust in himself and in his way of doing things. He is concerned with, and effective in, obtaining his production in both the short and long run. His main skill is in getting other people to do what he wants them to do without creating undue resentment. He is seen as having much of the orientation of the autocrat but as a bit smoother. . . .

> The benevolent autocrat in top management has little sympathy with participation or bottom-up management. He will sometimes use a par-ticipative approach before reaching his decision but not after it. He knows allowing subordinates to comment beforehand may produce a good idea, will alert him to problems he must deal with, and almost always will reduce resistance to change.[5]

In the church, the benevolent autocrats probably have special knowl-edge and expertise. They must be listened to, if only because they will insist upon it. They have a love for the people with whom they work and a burning desire to achieve the mission of their organization. Leaders such as James Dobson and Bill Hybels are sometimes described as full-speed-ahead leaders. There is some evidence to suggest that most orga-nizations with proven growth records and successful programs have benevolent autocrats for leaders.

Democratic Leadership

Democratic leadership is group-centered and participative. Leaders' authority proceeds from the membership. The leader facilitates communication, acts as a resource, and helps in membership development. This approach allows participative leaders and followers to interact and attain common goals in problem solving. Biblical examples of democratic leaders include Solomon and Josiah, although Josiah was apparently better able to stand against the majority when necessary than was Solomon.

Participative leaders display four traits:

1. Members of the team are considered equal with the leader in terms of input and ideas. Everyone's ideas are considered equally.

2. The leader assumes the role of a player/coach and becomes the team's facilitator.

3. The leader often accepts the team's ideas, even when they disagree with his own.

4. The leader focuses on stimulating creativity and innovation within the team.[6]

Looking at the downside, the democratic leader may be more interested in harmony than effectiveness, "a kindly soul who puts happy relationships above all other considerations. He is ineffective because his desire to see himself and be seen as a 'good person' prevents him from risking even mild disagreement in order to improve production." Such a leader spends "much of his time trying to find ways to make things easier for his people. . . . He avoids those who argue and prefers that difficult human problems be solved by transfer, promotion, or pay raises." The democratic leader "rationally discusses all issues with the staff. He is willing to change his mind to keep the peace. What is worse, he thinks this is always the best thing to do." In doing this he "gives up his role as manager."[7]

The effective democratic leader must remain the leader while emphasizing group needs much more than personal needs.

Free-Rein Leadership

Some researchers suggest a third style of leadership: free-rein, a permissive, hands-off style that avoids power and responsibility. This style implies that a leader can lead without leading. This *laissez-faire* leader is primarily a contact person or consultant who provides members with information or resources they need to accomplish their goals. Otherwise, the leader leaves the group alone to assume operating authority, define goals and procedures, and resolve problems as they occur.

Slightly different is loose-hands leadership, a style in which the leader empowers the group with stewardship but holds them accountable for their actions.

For most issues of governing, Ronald Reagan as president was much more *laissez-faire* than Lyndon Johnson.[8] The ethical scandals during and after Reagan's administration testify to his hands-off style of leadership.

Ezekiel 34:2–4 denounces free-rein leadership at its worst: "Woe to the shepherds of Israel who only take care of themselves! Should not shepherds take care of the flock? You eat the curds, clothe yourselves with the wool and slaughter the choice animals, but you do not take care of the flock. You have not strengthened the weak or healed the sick or bound up the injured. You have not brought back the strays or searched for the lost."

Because these leaders neglected their responsibility, the Lord declared that he would hold them accountable for his flock, remove them from tending the flock, rescue the flock from them, search for his sheep, and look after them himself. For similar reasons, most leadership experts reject hands-off style.

Styles of the Transformational Leader

Transformational leaders focus on using the skills and ideas of others to formulate, implement, and evaluate strategy. They rely on strategic visions, communication, decisions, and motivation to accomplish their work. Any time leaders are making decisions that will affect others, they should seek input from those people. Seeking others' ideas before making decisions, allowing them to help make the decision, or turning decision-making power over to them is an expression of trust and provides a great opportunity for involvement. It also results in greater commitment.

The most effective Christian leaders are those who combine a task orientation with a people orientation. The least effective are those who make no attempt to do either, let alone combine them. "Ministers, like shepherds, lead. They do not drive. The Bible teaches that God's leaders set an example (1 Pet. 5:3). They lead by kindness, gentleness, and patience (2 Tim. 2:24–26). They also see leadership as a means to serve (Luke 22:24–27). . . . The skilled leader sets up situations in which others are willing to follow and are happy to work with her. The church's leaders demonstrate this skill by interpreting and applying biblical principles through thoughtfulness, enthusiasm, and sharing responsibility with others."[9]

Box 6.2

A Combination of Consideration and Initiating Structure

High		
	High Initiating Structure Low Consideration **PEOPLE LEADERSHIP**	High Initiating Structure High Consideration **TEAM LEADERSHIP**
Initiating **Structure**	**MINIMUM LEADERSHIP** Low Consideration Low Initiating Structure	**TASK LEADERSHIP** High Consideration Low Initiating Structure
Low		**High**

A people orientation is sometimes called *consideration.* A task orientation is referred to as *initiation of structure.* (See box 6.2.) Both are critical for the church and the transformational leader.

People Orientation

Consideration is the concern a leader exhibits for the welfare of the group. This relationship-oriented behavior creates and maintains good will.

A large congregation learned of the indiscreet behavior of its college minister with the youth minister's wife. Realizing the impact such news would have on the sizable student population at this church, as well as the general membership, leaders of the congregation called a meeting of everyone in the church. Without discussing the particular problems involved, they explained about the resignations of both ministers, acknowledged that the transition would be rough, expressed their concern, detailed what they were doing for the spiritual and marital health of both couples, answered questions about the future, and encouraged people to come to several designated future meetings to discuss their concerns. The considerate behavior of these leaders defused a potentially explosive situation that might have occurred if they had not involved the congregation in the decision process.

Consideration includes being supportive and friendly; representing others' interests; providing open communication, recognition, and respect; and sharing concern. Thus the considerate leader:

1. Expresses appreciation for good work.

2. Stresses the importance of being satisfied with the job or position held.

3. Maintains and strengthens the self-esteem of others by treating them as equals.

4. Makes special efforts to help others feel at ease.

5. Puts worthwhile suggestions into operation.

6. Obtains others' approval on important matters before going ahead.[10]

Acts 6:1–7 gives a scriptural example of the positive outcome of consideration in the early church. The number of Christians was growing, but there was a problem because the widows of the Grecian Jews were being neglected in the daily distribution of food.

> So the Twelve gathered all the disciples together and said, 'It would not be right for us to neglect the ministry of the word of God in order to wait on tables. Brothers, choose seven men from among you who are known to be full of the Spirit and wisdom. We will turn this responsibility over to them and will give our attention to prayer and the ministry of the word.'
>
> This proposal pleased the whole group. . . . They presented these men to the apostles, who prayed and laid their hands on them.
>
> So the word of God spread (Acts 6:2–7).

Task Orientation

The second factor that best describes transformational leadership behavior involves task-related behaviors. *Initiation of structure describes the extent to which a leader initiates activity in a group, organizes it, and defines the way work is to be done.*

One church decided to change the objective of its morning worship service from "edifying the members" to "preaching to unchurched visitors" because of a large number of visitors on Sunday mornings. They provided the initiating structure to the members by describing the change in worship service format, the use of more guest speakers, a Saturday evening seeker's service, a more active involvement in evangelism, and new ministry themes. As a result, total attendance, including those who attended on Saturday, doubled within a year.

Initiating structure behaviors typically involves scheduling, deciding what needs to be done and how and when, directing followers, planning and coordinating, problem solving, and maintaining standards. Thus initiating structure includes:

1. Insisting on maintaining standards and meeting deadlines.

2. Deciding in detail what will be done and how to accomplish it.

3. Establishing clear channels of communication and patterns of work organization.

4. Concentrating on the task.

5. Acting directively without consulting the group.

6. Defining and structuring the leaders own role and those of the followers toward attaining goals.[11]

Nehemiah is a good Old Testament example of how to initiate structure. He surveyed the work to be done, suggested to the people what was needed, obtained their commitment, then proceeded to outline who should do what and how. In the New Testament, look at how Jesus worked with the apostles—from calling them, to teaching and training them, and finally leaving them with a mission (Matt. 28:18–20). At each stage, Jesus was indeed the master teacher, exhibiting concern for the welfare of his disciples and for the kingdom.

Leadership takes many forms—autocratic, democratic, and free-rein. However, "it is only when leadership takes on a more truly transformational form that the spiritual dimension comes to the fore."[12] A complementary style to the behavior theory of leadership that highlights the transformational style of leadership is possibility leadership (chap. 7).

— — —

Pause to Reflect

1. One typical distinction between autocratic and democratic leadership involves the distribution of power. Do you agree or disagree? Discuss. What church experiences have helped mold what you believe about autocratic and democratic leadership?

2. In your opinion, is the following an accurate statement? "Most congregations with proven growth records and successful programs have benevolent autocrats for leaders." Discuss.

3. The downside to democratic leadership may be that it emphasizes participation when such behavior is appropriate or that it is overly interested in harmony. Do you agree or disagree? Why?

4. Free-rein leadership is described as a permissive, hands-off style that implies that the leader can lead without leading. How is this possible? Have you seen it in operation in your church? Describe.

5. The two factors that best describe transformational leadership behavior are consideration and initiation of structure. Do you agree or disagree? Why? Read 1 Samuel 13:1–15. How does this passage of Scripture pertain to consideration and initiation of structure?

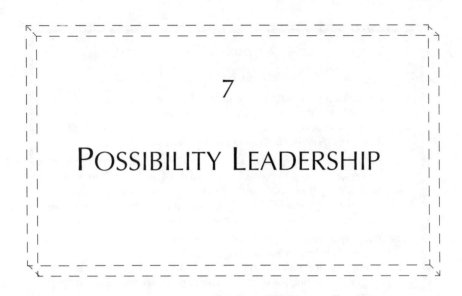

7

POSSIBILITY LEADERSHIP

"Occasions are rare; and those who know how to seize upon them are rarer" (Josh Billings).

"I feel that the greatest reward for doing is the opportunity to do more" (Jonas Salk).

"Ability is of little account without opportunity" (Napoleon Bonaparte).

"A task without vision is drudgery. A vision without a task is a dream. A task with a vision is hope" (author unknown).

To transform behavior or style leadership (chap. 6), one must understand *possibility leadership*. The traditional emphasis on leadership style centers on how to handle obstacles. Possibility leadership focuses on opportunities.

The implications are clear. If the church is to be ready to enter the twenty-first century, it must have a transforming dream. It must envision possibilities. (See box 7.1.)

A congregation with a transforming dream will reap rich rewards. Its leaders will not fear change. They will listen to members and look forward to the future. Such leaders will be heard to say, "The future is always more interesting than the past." The church contains the seed of life. Christian leaders must promote congregational health and longevity.

Box 7.1
The Need to Keep Dreaming

1. *Churches must constantly be revitalized.* They must dream again! Stagnation is the death of any organization, especially a church. Weekly worship and study offer a regular opportunity for individual and corporate refreshment and to refocus on the dream.

2. *Pastors help congregations keep their vision clear.* They empower their organizations to refine "here is who we are" and "here is how we work together best" norms. They enable their congregations to turn dreams into reality. They help build morale by focusing on the energy and hope generated by a new vision of the dream.

3. *Structure grows out of the dream, beliefs, and goals of a church and exists to implement and extend the vision.* A warning may be appropriate for new ministers: The honeymoon period is a time when restructuring is easier than later. But do not restructure before understanding the church's dream.

4. *A church needs to be committed first to its vision, and second, to its program structure.* Programs too weak to develop the dream should be allowed to die; innovative programs energized by the dream must be created.

5. *A dream is a necessary foundation for a healthy organization.* Nothing less than a kingdom dream will turn a church toward aggressive ministry.

6. *A planning cycle rooted firmly in the dream is an indispensable aid to organizational health.* Each cycle renews and stretches the organization. Kingdom ministry thrives on dream planning.

7. *Organizations contain the seeds of their own lives and deaths.* Even congregations founded on healthy dreams can drift into destructive patterns. When organizations become aware of their decline, they can decide to dream again. This decision is a life-or-death choice.

Adapted from R. D. Dale, *To Dream Again* (Nashville: Broadman, 1981), 16, 18.

The Dreamer Leader

Transformational leaders are dreamers—visionaries. They have learned how to lead and manage by vision.

Despite partisan affiliation, most Americans agree that Ronald Reagan was a visionary leader. He is credited with restoring the image and vitality of the role of president, of rallying the American people, of restoring pride. Think of all the voters—Republicans, Democrats, and Independents—who endorsed his bid for the presidency. He may not have shared all of his fellow Americans' beliefs, but Reagan had the foresight and the ingenuity to gain broad support that transcended party lines.

When Peter preached the first Christian sermon on Pentecost in Jerusalem, he quoted the prophet Joel: "Your young men will see visions, your old men will dream dreams" (Acts 2:17). Today's churches still need young people who see visions and older adults who dream dreams.

To understand the possibility leader, we must understand dreams and visions. We must explore four areas: brain styles, reflection/meditation, positive thinking, and imaging. (We will expand this discussion in chapter 9.)

Brain Styles

People sometimes remark about others they have just met: "We just do not think alike. I cannot understand that person." They are right! At first glance, people sometimes seem weird or at least different. They look at a new church building and see the architectural beauty of the structure. Someone else looks at the same building and sees only inadequacies in seating and parking. People are wired differently. That is why these situations sometimes remind us of John Godfrey Saxe's parable about six blind men and an elephant. (See box 7.2.)

Scientists have known for decades that the brain is divided into two equal-sized hemispheres. The *left-brain* hemisphere stores rules, systems, schedules, and order. It is dominant for verbal memory and analytical and mathematical skills. The ability to work with words and numbers and to process sequential information are left-brain activities. The focus is on deductive, analytical, and linear reasoning. The *right brain* amasses emotions, fantasies, and ideas dealing with colors, textures, shapes, and smells. It comprises spatial thinking and the ability to envision patterns. Processing different information simultaneously is also a right-brain activity, as are artistic and intuitive abilities. The focus is on inductive, relational, and nonlinear skills.

Integrative thinking uses both hemispheres and is necessary for most tasks. Most people, however, seem to have a dominant side. Leaders with a dominant left brain have the ability to solve problems in an organized, logical, step-by-step way. Those leaders with a dominant right brain tend to think about problems in a global, all-at-once fashion. They tend to be more creative, but appear disorganized to left-brain dominants. Christian

Box 7.2

The Parable of the Blind Men and the Elephant

It was six men of Indostan
　　To learning much inclined,
Who went to see the elephant
　　(Though all of them were blind),
That each by observation
　　Might satisfy his mind.

The First approached the Elephant,
　　And happening to fall
Against his broad and sturdy side,
　　At once began to bawl:
"God bless me! but the Elephant
　　Is very like a wall!"

The Second, feeling of the tusk,
　　Cried, "Ho! what have we here
So very round and smooth and sharp?
　　To me 'tis very clear
This wonder of an Elephant
　　Is very like a spear!"

The Third approached the animal
　　And, happening to take
The squirming trunk within his hands
　　Thus boldly up he spake:
"I see," quoth he, "the Elephant
　　Is very like a snake!"

The Fourth reached out an eager hand,
　　And felt about the knee:
"What most this wondrous beast is like
　　Is very plain," quoth he;
"'Tis clear enough the Elephant
　　Is very like a tree!"

The Fifth, who chanced to touch the ear,
　　Said: "E'en the blindest man
Can tell what this resembles most;
　　Deny the fact who can
This marvel of an Elephant
　　Is very like a fan!"

The Sixth no sooner had begun
　　About the beast to grope
Than, seizing on the swinging tail
　　That fell within his scope.
"I see," quoth he, "the elephant
　　Is very like a rope!"

And so these men of Indostan
　　Disputed loud and long,
Each in his own opinion
　　Exceeding stiff and strong.
Though each was partly in the right,
　　They all were in the wrong!

John Godfrey Saxe

leaders, whether left-brain dominant or right-brain dominant, must strive to develop an *integrative* brain style.

Women seem to be very adept at using both sides of their brain simultaneously. Men, as a general rule, seem able to use only one side at a time. Research suggests that men are inflexible in dealing with multiple problems concurrently or with multifaceted problems. Women, however, tend to adjust well to dynamic, broad, multi-problems. This situation raises an interesting question: *Why then are so many men in leadership positions,* not only in business but also in the church? Conservative Christians and their congregational leaders must address this question.

A survey of more than nine thousand managers who graded male and female superiors on twenty skills reveals that women are better bosses than men. The gaps between women and men are biggest on planning, making changes, and evaluating employee performance. In fact, women were rated best in every category from communication to decision making. The president of the surveying firm said: "Women are still brought up to be more social. Those skills pay off in the workplace."[1] They also pay off in the church when women are allowed to use their God-given gifts.

Women were far from marginal figures in the first-century church. From the beginning, women were active in nearly every area. Priscilla, Phoebe, Chloe, and Lydia were only a few of the female leaders (see Rom. 16:6, 12). They established congregations, provided homes for Christian assemblies, prophesied, prayed, and instructed converts. In the face of such evidence, church leaders must examine their "scriptural biases" toward females taking active roles in the church.

Consider also the traditional quality of womanhood demonstrated in the character of God (see Isa. 49:15; Hos. 11:3–4); the esteem with which Jesus dealt with women such as Mary, Martha, and the other Marys; the way Paul demonstrated the relational qualities of sensitivity, expressiveness, and care (1 Thess. 2:5–8). Today's church leaders must re-examine their views of women in leadership roles. Just as they may try to place various age groups on a committee, so should they think of the gender makeup.

A churchwide meeting discussed the need to form a committee to recommend new board possibilities. It was announced, however, that this would be a male-only committee. After a number of nominations were made of men to serve on this committee, one of the female members recommended another male. This male member thanked her for the nomination but refused to serve on the committee, stating aloud that he refused to serve on a church committee that did not recognize the importance of women to this task. Unless more Christian leaders are willing to take such a stand, they may find their female membership declining. (And the married females may be taking their husbands with them to another church.) Five years after the above event, several married couples still thank this individual for his stand, affirming that now there are no committees formed without female representation.

For efficient, effective leadership, visionaries must be whole-brained. They must allow both hemispheres to work together cooperatively and interactively. One way some transformational leaders bridge the hemispheres is to ask themselves questions such as these:

- How can I be more logical about this?
- Have I gathered all the facts?
- Do I have all the numbers I need?
- How do others feel about this, and why?
- How will this look when we are done, and how will we feel?

This technique is important because leaders work with many different dominant-brain types and function best in dynamic environments. The excellent leader can move from left to right brain and vice versa to modify behavior or exact program changes. Christian leaders who develop an integrative brain style will use both a deductive and an inductive leadership style interchangeably and as appropriate.

Reflection/Meditation

The golden rule of time management says: *Make time for reflective planning.* Every hour spent in planning saves three to four hours in execution.

God told Joshua to meditate day and night on the book of law (Josh. 1:8). The psalmist also spoke of the value of meditation on the law, (Ps. 119:97) and Paul wrote of the importance of study (2 Tim. 2:15). Improved use of time is important for anyone in a leadership position. It is not the number of hours that a person puts in but what a person puts in the hours that counts. The more time a person spends in reflective/meditative planning, the more he or she will be able to accomplish.

A 1988 survey of executives by Heidrick and Struggles indicates that senior executives spend an average of seventeen hours a week in meetings, six hours preparing, and more hours recovering. A separate survey that same year by the Wharton Center for Applied Research revealed that senior executives spend an average of twenty-three hours a week in meetings, while middle managers reported eleven hours of meetings. Only 58 percent of the senior executives and 54 percent of the middle managers felt the meetings were productive; 22 percent of the senior executives and 29 percent of the middle managers thought the meetings could have been handled over the phone or with a memo. If these figures are indicative of how church leaders spend their time, one can see there is not much time left for quiet moments.

A concept that helps explain the importance of reflection/meditation is *reflective openness,* which is the capacity to continually challenge one's own thinking; an openness to inward examination.[2]

Two New Testament examples of reflective openness are Saul of Tarsus and the Bereans. The blinded Saul spent seventy-two hours in Damascus in reflective silence after his encounter with Jesus (Acts 9:9). The Bereans were more noble minded than the Thessalonians because of reflectiveness and eagerness to examine the Scriptures (18:11). Reflective openness requires courage, faith, and commitment. The exposure of heart and mind to the light of God's Word is often fearful because some cherished beliefs or behavior may have to be sacrificed at the foot of his altar.

However, reflective openness certainly is not foreign to biblical teaching. What is crucial is that one reflects and meditates on the right things.

"Blessed is the man who does not walk in the counsel of the wicked or stand in the way of sinners or sit in the seat of mockers! But his delight is in the law of the Lord, and on his law he meditates day and night" (Ps. 1:1–2).

"Finally, brothers, whatever is true, whatever is noble, whatever is right, whatever is pure, whatever is lovely, whatever is admirable—if anything is excellent or praiseworthy—think about such things" (Phil. 4:8).

Reflection and meditation allows the mind to contemplate thoughts that can streamline various work activities. Such thinking provides the means for refinement, self-examination, and identification of those areas that need to be addressed.

Positive Thinking

The power of a positive mental attitude (PMA) has received much attention in the last couple of decades from leaders like Norman Vincent Peale, Cavett Robert, Napolean Hill, Zig Ziglar, and Robert Schuller. Society has been inundated with information about optimists and pessimists, positives and negatives, possibility thinkers and impossibility thinkers. One can think and grow rich; one can have anything in life if one will just help enough other people get what they want; and any goal imaginable is achievable.

Many church leaders reject positive thinking as impractical and illusive. It smacks of mysticism, mental tricks, magic, or the religion of Pollyanna. Yet the Bible is replete with individuals who displayed positive attitudes. God wants his people to believe in themselves, in others, and in him. Such faith is an unbeatable combination that leads to success and happiness.

Joshua and Caleb were possibility thinkers. Moses sent twelve spies into the promised land to look things over. When they returned, they all agreed that it was a land "flowing with milk and honey" (Num. 13:27). However, ten of the twelve spies concluded there were insurmountable obstacles they would be unable to fight against. These ten negative thinkers saw the size of the enemy, the height and thickness of the city walls, and concluded they were like grasshoppers in the enemy's sight. But two spies—Joshua and Caleb—were not afflicted with this grasshopper complex. Instead they said, "We should go up and take possession of the land, for we can certainly do it" (Num. 13:30). These two positive thinkers inherited their portion of the new land and enjoyed God's blessings. The ten negative thinkers all died in the wilderness.

The apostle Paul stands out as the greatest possibility thinker because of the power of this statement: "I can do everything through him who gives me strength" (Phil. 4:13). Paul did not see himself as inferior or insignificant; he believed in himself (1 Cor. 10; Eph. 3). He could do as much if not more than any other human being could do. And his "boasts" about his sufferings support that belief!

> Five times I received from the Jews the forty lashes minus one. Three times I was beaten with rods, once I was stoned, three times I was shipwrecked, I spent a night and a day in the open sea, I have been constantly on the move. I have been in danger from rivers, in danger from bandits, in danger from my own countrymen, in danger from Gentiles; in danger in the city, in danger in the country, in danger at sea; and in danger from false brothers. I have labored and toiled and have often gone without sleep; I have known hunger and thirst and have often gone without food; I have been cold and naked (2 Cor. 11:24–27).

Caleb, Joshua, and Paul were possibility thinkers because they believed in God's power. They could do anything that God sanctioned and supported. Biblical commands to think positively suggest some keys to maintaining a positive mental attitude:

1. Focus on God instead of self. No problem is a match for the Creator. Thus the key to positiveness is to focus on God—not on self and/or circumstances.

2. Look to the future, not the past. Refuse to dwell on past failures or achievements. Instead focus on the present and anticipate the future (see Phil. 3:13–14).

Don't get distracted

3. Always have a goal. Goals keep one oriented toward achievement and success; they give meaning to life and work.

4. View problems as opportunities for improvement. Negative attitudes produce negative actions; positive attitudes, positive actions (see James 1:2–3).[3]

A Christian professor recently wrote for a campus publication: "Students and colleagues often ask me, 'How can you always be happy and positive each day?' My response is always the same: I have absolute faith in God, and I know He will lead me to whatever it is that He wants me to do. His will be done, not mine. Jesus is the wind beneath my wings, and He carries me onward and upward each and every day of my life. He has guided me through MBA and Ph.D. programs so that I could be at this wonderful paradise.'"[4]

What would be the state of Christianity if today's leaders believed and practiced positive thinking. First, because it is sound psychology and, second, because it is sound theology.[5] No wonder Doris Day's hit tune encourages listeners to "accentuate the positive, eliminate the negative, hold on to the affirmative."

Imaging

Imaging attempts to take positive thinking one step further. One does not merely think about a desired goal. She or he "sees" it with tremendous energy. Imaging is "a form of mental activity . . . [consisting] of vividly picturing, in your conscious mind, a desired goal or objective, and holding that image until it sinks into your unconscious mind, where it releases great, untapped energies. . . . When the imaging concept is applied steadily and systematically, it solves problems, strengthens personalities, improves health, and greatly increases the chances for success in any kind of endeavor."[6]

Imaging, like positive thinking, works better when combined with strong religious faith and reinforced by prayer. Thus imaging also has biblical roots. Solomon suggested that as people see themselves, so they are (Prov. 23:7). Jesus advocated a form of imaging when he told his followers, "I tell you the truth, if you have faith and do not doubt . . . you can say to this mountain, 'Go throw yourself into the sea,' and it will be done. If you believe, you will receive whatever you ask for in prayer" (Matt. 21:21–27).

Imaging brings desired results. When predicated with fervent prayer, it opens doors, solves problems, and achieves goals. For example, Jesus prayed *before* beginning his ministry (Luke 4:1–15), *before* choosing the Twelve (6:12–16), and *before* Calvary (Mark 14:32). However, imaging is much more than a mental activity. It must also be coupled with action once a door is opened. If it is not, problems will not be solved and dreams will not become reality. Before the miracle at Pentecost, the apostles were praying; afterward came the vision (Acts 1:12–24). If a leader prays and images something for his or her church long enough and hard enough, if a leader commits the resources necessary when the time is right, she or he should achieve what is imaged.

Norman Vincent Peale adds a cautionary word: "Make the Lord the silent partner in all forms of imaging, because He is the touchstone that will keep your desires on the high plane of morality where they belong. Imaging can be applied to unworthy goals as well as worthy ones. Praying about goals is essential, because if there are any selfish aims or sinful motives, they will appear as you pray. Pray to be sure your goal is right, for if it isn't right it is wrong, and nothing that is wrong ever turned out right."[7]

Imaging with God motivates Christian leaders and church members. It provides a challenge for which to strive, a course to pursue. What would the church be like today if its leaders believed in and practiced the kind of imaging Jesus recommended?

A gifted leader often reminded people, "There is more love per square inch on this corner than anywhere on the planet." With that mindset, his congregation constantly practiced being the salt of the earth, demonstrating love, fellowship, and goodwill. The congregation has never had a division or split in its fifty-plus-year history.

Creativity

Creativity is closely related to the ability to dream, and it can be learned. Stanford University teaches a course on creativity in business that has revolutionized the art of success. The designers of that course say:

> One of the main problems in U.S. business today is that there are too many ideas, not too few. Dozens of solutions appear and disappear in chaotic piles of data, crowds of expert opinion, and a jumble of contradictory statistics and reports on every aspect of every issue. The pressure of limited time is increased by indecision and, beneath it all, the nagging suspicion that others will find your efforts insufficient and the results poor.

> As we looked at the problem in the late 1970s, it became clear that its solution lay in cutting through the chaos to reach the underlying answers. And the key to doing that lay in the creativity of the individual business person.[8]

The same is true of the church. *Creativity is the ability and power to develop new ideas and translate them into practical applications.* Creativity can enrich a church, its leaders, and its members. Witness the expanded use of puppets, drama groups, and humor to enliven and enhance worship services.

Although creativity is often the fruit of extensive labor, there are several techniques for nurturing creative thoughts. (See box 7.3.) You can improve your creative ability.

Dreaming with Others

Leaders must dream and be creative, but dreaming alone is not enough. Visions are future-oriented. Transformational leaders discover ways to involve others in creating dreams. They help others dream about how the situation will be different in two, five, or ten years down the road.

Several successful Christian leaders take a yearly retreat with other church leaders to review the past year, plan the next year, and take a look at the future. One congregation in Texas does this quarterly. The objective is to focus on who they are, where they are, and where they should be. They pray for individual church members. Leaders always return with a renewed enthusiasm for the immediate future and greater love and appreciation for one another.

Coaching Others to Create Dreams

The transformational leader helps others work toward their goals. *Coaching is helping others to improve their skills and knowledge.* It involves helping others to overcome a specific problem by giving them advice or encouragement. Thus coaching requires patience. According to a five-step coaching format, leaders should:

1. Observe and analyze performance.

2. Identify the area that needs improvement.

3. Demonstrate how the task should be performed and ask if there are questions about the instructions.

4. Have the person demonstrate the task; then give feedback on that performance.

5. Set up a date to review subsequent performance.[9]

In a church, the obvious coach is the pastor. Although other leaders may be available as role models or mentors, the minister is usually the most visible. The pastor is the "spark plug" for the congregation, the one who fires things up by making things go. Thus it is the pastor's responsibility to provide the dream and jump start others to dream and seek.

Box 7.3
Steps Toward Becoming More Creative

1. *Ask the Creator.* Ask God for wisdom and trust Him for it; He will answer. Knowledge will rise from God's Spirit that works within us.

2. *Arrange a Creative Setting.* Work with these variables: The temperature needs to be comfortable or even a little on the cool side to maximize alertness. "Position yourself" for your own creativity. Control the sounds around you. Control the scene. And protect your privacy.

3. *Sharpen Your Objectives and Become Committed to Them.* God provides extra adrenaline when creativity is stimulated by an enthusiastic desire to accomplish a particular objective.

4. *Be Open.* Our very growth as Christians hinges on our mind's ability to be open to the movement of God.

5. *Harness Your Natural Energy.* Schedule brainstorming and other kinds of creative projects during times of natural high energy and alertness. Schedule more routine activities for your slower times.

6. *Stimulate Your Thoughts.* Brainstorm with people who stimulate your creativity. Read books and articles on the subject on which you need creativity. Consult an expert. Think of other situations that are parallel (or of different unrelated items) to this one, try to relate them, and see what they add to your understanding. Roll up your sleeves, dig in up to your elbows, and get involved.

7. *Push the Boundaries.* Push beyond what now exists, test assumptions, explore boundaries, and seek to exceed them.

8. *Employ Your Subconscious.* Obtain a broad base of exposure to whatever facts are involved and perhaps even to what trial alternatives have been thought of. Then allow a time of simmering. The subconscious mind mulls over and reflects on ideas and generates intuitive thoughts which later surface to the conscious mind.

Adapted from S. B. Douglass and L. Roddy, *Making the Most of Your Mind* (San Bernardino, Calif.: Here's Life, 1983), 151–63.

Dreaming the Impossible Dream

Don Quixote was right! To dream what might seem impossible to some, to reflect and meditate, to think positively, and to image are critical ingredients in the Christian leader's vision. If a revitalization of the church is to occur, as discussed in chapter 1, leaders must think creatively about the future. Transformational leaders fortify their congregations with a positive climate for ministry and mission. One church uses signs at exit points in its parking lot that read "You are entering mission territory" to remind members of their positive calling.

Here are three techniques for building a positive, creative, and imaging climate:

1. Modeling positive behavior in one's life and ministry.

2. Building on success.

3. Developing programs to make people feel valuable.[10]

Never, never fear to dream "the impossible dream." Jesus even gave this matter a sense of urgency by saying, "As long as it is day, we must do the work of him who sent me. Night is coming, when no one can work"(John 9:14). Is the church ready for the twenty-first century?

— — —

Pause to Reflect

1. Discuss the idea that dreaming is critical to organizational leadership. Do you agree that "nothing less than a kingdom dream will turn a church toward healthy and aggressive ministry"?

2. Explain the statement, "If you wish to increase the numbers of those who are involved in your congregation, you must learn how to lead and manage by vision." Do you agree with this sentiment? Why?

3. Discuss the concept of "positive thinking." Do you believe it could play an important role in the future growth and development of your church? Support your views with Scripture.

4. Discuss the role of creativity in the church today. On a scale of one to ten, with ten being the highest, how would you describe the creativity of the leadership in your congregation? What can you do to help them think more creatively, or vice versa?

5. Describe a person you know who leads and/or manages by visions. What are this person's characteristics that set the individual apart? Are there techniques that she or he uses that could be used by leaders who do not understand the need to dream?

8

SITUATIONAL LEADERSHIP

There is no one best leadership style or behavior. Different situations call for different leadership styles. Each situation involves varying personalities, interest levels, motivation, physical setting, or group size.

Each situation is different, and each needs to match specific traits and behaviors. Leadership behaviors in the Book of Acts include the decision-making process for the replacement of Judas (1:12–26), the appointment of special servants in Jerusalem (1:1–7), the establishment of the church in Antioch (11:19–30), the Antioch church sending Paul and Barnabas on their first missionary journey (13:1–3), confrontation in Antioch and Jerusalem (14:21–25), and the appointment of elders in the church (15:1–21). Those Christian leaders were relational oriented, for they knew their people; they were task oriented, for they knew their task; and they were goal oriented, for they knew where they were going. They also knew how to lead by example and how to marshal their followers; and they knew the value of serving. The apostle Paul became what was necessary in a given situation to save some individuals (1 Cor. 9:22).

However, Jesus Christ is the classic case of the situational leader.[1] He was autocratic with those who would turn his "Father's house into a market" (John 2:13–16), but welcomed little children (Mark 10:13–16). He loved and understood the rich young ruler (Mark 10:17–25). He was a servant-leader with his disciples (John 13:1–17), but he judged and condemned the teachers of the Law and the Pharisees (Matt. 23).

85

"Jesus was a determined leader whose very character was like granite. He was at times compassionate and tender and at other times furious with the status quo. The poor and powerless stirred the deepest mercy in him. The rich and the powerful religious could arouse his consternation and anger."[2]

Jesus' leadership style changed to meet each situation, but his purpose remained the same; his goal was to do God's will by bringing in the kingdom (John 6:35–40; Matt. 16:13–19).

Leadership Situations

Situational leadership is a leadership style that matches the style of the leader to the incident. It reveals what type of person would be suited to lead in a given situation. A group with a high need for control and direction should not be saddled with a democratic leader. A mature, well-functioning group should not have an autocratic leader.

A church in Honolulu draws many military officers from a local air base. The congregation is often exasperated that these officers sometimes try to run the church like they run their unit. Despite their earnest and honorable intentions, the results are often disastrous. Decisions and rules are force-fed, and the locals are stuck with them when the officers are relocated. Persons who are successful in one leadership role can be ineffective in another.

Three primary conditions define the situational leader:

- The power of the leader,
- The nature of the task,
- The human relationships within the group.

Power

David sang, "It is God who arms me with strength and makes my way perfect" (2 Sam. 22:33). The years that he spent alone with God as a shepherd and as a fugitive prepared him for leadership. Centuries later Paul wrote, "I can do everything through him who gives me strength" (Phil. 4:13). How different this kind of power is from the type James and John's "stagemother" may have been seeking:

Then the mother of Zebedee's sons came to Jesus with her sons and, kneeling down, asked a favor of him. . . . "Grant that one of these two sons of mine may sit at your right and the other at your left in your kingdom." . . .

When the ten heard about this, they were indignant with the two brothers. Jesus called them together and said, "You know that the rulers of the Gentiles lord it over them, and their high officials exercise authority over them. Not so with you. Instead, whoever wants to become great among you must be your servant, and whoever wants to be first must be your slave—just as the Son of Man did not come to be served, but to serve, and to give his life as a ransom for many" (Matt. 20:20–28).

Jesus' concept of the use of power is quite different from the sought-after power espoused by secular society (see chap. 2). Ambitious executives wrestle for and seize control and stay in power by political tactics and Machiavellian means. Such manipulative methods smack of calculated alliances, compromises, and "deals." These executives little realize how their misuse of power disturbs interpersonal relationships on the job and undermines organizational effectiveness. Conflicts arise because they do not understand the effects of negative power on behavior. These abuses have no place in the church.

Power, in and of itself, is not bad, but it can have bad effects. The power behind the transformational leader is God himself. Transformational leaders find their power in the Word, in prayer, and in obedience (see 2 Tim. 3:16–17; James 5:16; John 14:21).

Tasks

Task roles deal with goals of an individual or group—solving a problem, making a decision, or completing a project. These task roles facilitate and coordinate effort. They help a group select and define its objectives and work toward solutions. Such tasks include forming ideas, thinking critically, giving suggestions, providing information, analyzing problems, evaluating alternatives, making decisions, and establishing work procedures.

Paul tells the Corinthians that he "will stay on at Ephesus until Pentecost, because a great door for effective work has opened to me" (1 Cor. 16:8–9). He recognizes a number of tasks that are before him and his fellow workers in order to accomplish spiritual goals. Transformational leaders are concerned with task roles, delegating tasks to those whose talents and interests will further the kingdom.

Relationships

A Christian leader's emphasis on human relationships is dependent on his or her attitude toward God, others, and self. Two crucial inner characteristics enhance a leader's relationship with those who follow.[3]

1. *The transformational leader has a servant's heart* (Mark 10:45; Luke 22:27). Interestingly, when Christ established the church and formulated

the job descriptions for its membership, the only job openings seemed to be for slaves or servants. "If anyone wants to be first, he must be the very last, and the servant of all" (Mark 9:35).

2. *The transformational leader has a sensitive heart.* Like Jesus, leaders must have compassion for the multitudes (Mark 8:1–3). This benevolence must be not only for "those who belong to the family of believers" (Gal. 6:16) but also for those who are "idle" (i.e., the disorderly and unruly), "timid" (the faint-hearted and feebleminded), and "weak" (those plagued by besetting sins; 1 Thess. 5:14).

Transformational leaders pray with Solomon: "So give your servant a discerning heart to govern your people and to distinguish between right and wrong. For who is able to govern this great people of yours?"(1 Kings 3:9). Note how this prayer shows respect for followers and makes use of emotions and feelings.

Leadership Functions

Having seen what situational leadership entails, one can grapple with *what* an effective church leader does. For example, most group activities relate to task accomplishment. Some groups might stress goals, focus attention on membership growth, or review ministry effectiveness. Or, they may solve problems, make decisions, and complete projects. Such activities facilitate and coordinate effort and are the functions a group undertakes to do a job.

In addition to these task roles, the Christian leader must meet the following expectations of followers: to communicate effectively, respond creatively and innovatively, and to set priorities; and possess a results orientation, an empathetic attitude, and a supportive attitude. The transformational leader consistently practices these functions.

Communication

Everyone wants clear instructions about what they need to do. Transformational leaders clearly explain the goals and procedures designed to accomplish these goals. Good communication is the key to sound organizational practice and successful group relationships. Unfortunately, many communicators either cannot or do not give accurate, clear, brief, but complete information.

Transformational leaders know that people are not mind readers. They recognize that communication is vital in order to make effective decisions. Leaders provide clear, accurate facts and figures so that others can effectively complete spiritual tasks. They seek feedback when there is potential for misunderstanding—which is often!

Results Orientation

Transformational leaders are interested in results. They want to be measured by what they do, not by who they are. Consider Joe Roth, the chairman of Walt Disney Motion Pictures Group, who works closely with Michael Eisner, CEO of Disney. Eisner is a business celebrity, but Roth is respected for his keen decision-making ability and his behind-the-scenes approach.

Think of the DreamWorks SGK, the new production company formed by Steven Spielberg, David Geffen, and Jeffrey Katzenberg. This team will be a force in Hollywood because they are known for their big results. ABC, Silicon Graphics, and Microsoft have already agreed to be strategic partners with them. Samsung Electronics, Bell Atlantic, and others have emerged with up to $900 million to invest in DreamWorks. Bankers Trust and Chemical Bank may assemble up to $1 billion in credit for them. Success breeds success.

Transformational leaders work to ensure that their flock sticks closely to performance expectations, not only to get better results but also to maintain higher levels of morale and production. They couple effectiveness with efficiency by allowing God to arrange the parts in the body, every one of them, just as he wants them to be (1 Cor. 12:18).

Innovation

Christian leaders face many challenges. They explore all possibilities and search for the best answers to questions like these:

- What needs do people in the community have?
- How can the church use its building more effectively?
- What can be done to expand missions ministry?
- What different approaches can be taken in Bible classes?
- In what ways can the media be of assistance?[4]

Possibilities can be limited by previous experiences, worn-out excuses, or another's negative attitude. If so, Christians will live in a world void of accomplishment, growth, and possibilities.[5]

Innovative leaders play several roles. When searching for new information, they are explorers. When turning resources into new ideas, they are artists. When evaluating the merits of an idea, they are judges. When carrying an idea into action, they are warriors.[6]

Priority Setting

Some leaders are unable or unwilling to establish priorities. They soon become the victims of crisis management, better known as firefighting.

Even leaders with a clear objective can fall into the "activity trap," so enmeshed in the activity of getting there that they forget where they were going.[7]

Transformational leaders decide what is to be done and in what sequence. They articulate priorities so everyone knows what needs to be done and when. They do not get caught in the activity trap. They know that they might accomplish more by doing less. Rather than exhorting members to support activities with no hint of a worthwhile payoff, transformational leaders question every program that uses time, energy, and money. They ask pointed questions about church-related activities:

This is very important

- Does this activity have any relationship to helping the leadership or anyone else become more like Christ?

- Will this activity bring glory to God?

- Does this activity contribute to the church's task of leading people to Christ and helping others become like Christ?

- Does this activity alleviate suffering, and thereby give dignity to human beings who are made in the image of God?

- Can this activity be redesigned so that it will serve the purpose for which Jesus established the church?[8]

Unless the answer to at least one of these questions is yes, the activity should be abandoned. It has no spiritual destination.

An Empathetic Attitude

Empathy is placing oneself in someone else's position, seeing the world from another's vantage point. Transformational leaders project themselves into their members' personalities. These leaders are viewed as approachable, interested, and understanding. They exercise their intuition to predict how certain information will affect others and whether it will be understood, accepted, rejected, or ignored.

Empathetic leaders may not always agree with a certain member's views and certainly will not be dominated or brainwashed. Yet these leaders remain accessible while holding onto their own beliefs, standards, and expectations. They are sensitive and sincere.

Supportive Attitude

Church members want their leaders to focus on personal relationships. They want leaders to strengthen, regulate, and perpetuate the group's way of doing things so long as the group's way is effective. They want to interact with leaders in a climate for growth. They want to work with leaders who build a supportive and helpful environment.

William James wrote, "I will act as if what I do makes a difference." Just as a transformer changes energy into electricity to help those in its service area, the transformational leader transforms situations for the good of the kingdom. The most effective way to transform the present situation and to transform situational or contingency leadership is through visionary leadership (chap. 9).

— — —

Pause to Reflect

1. Situational leadership is defined as a leadership style that matches the style of the leader to the incident. What are the primary differences between situational leadership and transformational leadership? Is there a place for situational leadership in the church?

2. This chapter suggests three factors that define the situational leader. In your opinion, which of these factors is most critical to understanding the relationship of the situation to the transformational leader? Discuss.

3. Followers seem to have at least six expectations of leaders. In your opinion, which of these factors are most critical to understanding the power and influence of the transformational leader? Discuss.

4. Are there certain situations where you tend to lead best, or where you will be called upon to lead others? Describe those situations. What does this say about your leadership style?

5. Transformational leaders transform the situation for the good of the kingdom. Have you seen such events unfold? Describe one such incident.

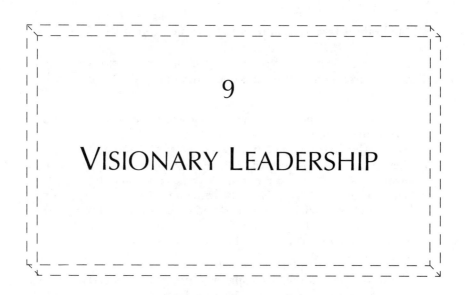

9

VISIONARY LEADERSHIP

To transform situational leadership (chap. 8) into visionary leadership necessitates expanding one's understanding of possibility leadership (chap. 7) and coupling it with spiritual insight. Fred Smith, founder of Federal Express, said, "We will deliver the package by 10:30 the next morning." His vision changed the basis of competition in that industry. Would a similar inspiring vision do the same for your congregation?

Vision is an expression of faith and hope (Heb. 11:1). Those who accomplish great things have a great aim. They fix their gaze on a high goal, sometimes a goal that seems impossible.

Transformational leaders paint a compelling picture of the future. When visionaries stop dreaming or allow others to squelch their dreams, their churches suffer or even die. Success is the distance between one's origin and final achievement. Vision is fundamental to all leadership.

Great leaders envision the future and imagine possibilities. Think of Ghandi, Sadat, Begin, Churchill, Walesa, and Carter. Leaders possess a sense of what could be. They are willing to risk their lives to accomplish their dreams. Moses endured "because he was looking ahead to his reward" and "because he saw him who is invisible" (Heb. 11:26–27). Elisha saw the host of heaven when his servant saw only an encircling army (2 Kings 6:15–17). Similar stories could be told of the foresight, optimism, and hope of Gideon, Barak, Samson, Jephthah, David, Samuel, and others because "none of them received what had been promised" (Heb. 11:32, 39).

To dream or inspire people to perform, leaders must leave the predictable environment of the status quo. They must risk entering uncharted territory.

> When we choose the frontier, we're choosing an unmeasurable and unknowable future. This is a vulnerable choice. If we are forced to explain why we choose that future, how we're going to get there, or whether that future is possible, we have no solid response that we can count on. Moving toward the frontier, creating a vision of greatness, demands an act of faith. Faith, by its nature, is immeasurable and indefensible through the use of data and external evidence. An act of faith moving toward a preferred future is a leap beyond what is now being experienced. This act of faith and act of courage are demanded of each of us.[1]

The world does not always appreciate dreamers. Typically, they are not taken seriously—especially those without connections, financial backers, or big names in their address books. However, God has always supported and commended leaders with vision and assembled those who have firm images of the desired future. Shaping the future is a task shared but a task primarily entrusted to the leader.

The vision—whatever it may be—is the ideal for which to strive. It must be strategically focused on the membership and dedicated to a church's mission. It must capture the imagination and spirit of a congregation. Vision motivates an organization to action. "It provides an overarching framework to guide day-to-day decisions and priorities and provides the parameters for planful opportunism."[2]

The Vision Leader

A number of possibilities exist for understanding visionary leadership.[3] Chapter 7 discussed three approaches: reflection, positive thinking, and imaging. This chapter applies these concepts to holistic, visionary leadership.

David used most of the visionary approaches in his battle with Goliath. Visualizing the end result before facing the Philistine giant helped David plan his attack and determine how to achieve the goal. This understanding motivated him to act.

David said to the Philistine, "You come against me with sword and spear and javelin, but I come against you in the name of the Lord Almighty, the God of the armies of Israel, whom you have defied. This day the Lord will hand you over to me, and I'll strike you down and cut off your head. Today I will give the carcasses of the Philistine army to the birds of the air and the beasts of the earth, and the whole world will know that there is a God in Israel. All those gathered here will know that it is not by sword or spear that the Lord saves; for the battle is the Lord's, and he will give all of you into our hands" (1 Sam. 17:45–47).

David could visualize the result, but he was clearly trusting God for results.

Centuries later Jesus told this parable: "The kingdom of heaven is like a mustard seed, which a man took and planted in his field. Though it is the smallest of all your seeds, yet when it grows, it is the largest of garden plants and becomes a tree, so that the birds of the air come and perch in its branches" (Matt. 13:31–32). When his disciples were unable to heal an epileptic known to fall into fire and water; when they asked why they could not drive out the demon, Jesus replied: "Because you have so little faith. I tell you the truth, if you have faith as small as a mustard seed, you can say to this mountain, 'Move from here to there' and it will move. Nothing will be impossible for you" (Matt. 17:20–21).

Jesus told his followers that even seed-sized faith is atomic power to a believer. Faith, deep inside them, furnishes power to be and become, even faith the size of the mustard seed. When church leaders visualize with God, the results will be similar: victory over giants and power to move mountains.

Vision addresses a congregation's possibilities. The specific ingredients of a Christian vision include:

- Positive appraisal of reality,
- Specific and attainable objectives,
- Worthwhile and possible forward movement, and
- Faithful application of the gospel.[4]

The vision of the leader describes the present and determines the future. For the Christian leader, a vision is a response to God's guiding hand. Transformational leaders grasp the vision's challenge, commit to the mission, and implement the goals that will accomplish the mission and fulfill the vision.

Planning the Vision

The motto of Epcot Center is "If you can dream it, you can do it." One way to plan a vision is to set S-M-A-R-T goals. According to this plan, goals, whether short-range or long-range, are organized according to:

- Specificity,

- Measurability,

- Attainability,

- Realism, and

- Tangibleness.[5]

Think of the future this way: Assume it will be the past repeated; recognize there will be change in the future, but that it is impossible to forecast what the changes might be; deal with the future by developing organizational plans; or recognize that an organization can live and grow in a changing future only if it has a deliberately built-in permanent planning capability.[6]

Transformational leaders have faith in their dream, their ability, and God's power to bring their dream into reality. They have the ability to think and plan, plus a sense of being called by God. They put words to their visions and share them with others, for either the day-to-day accomplishment of good works or the achievement of greatness.

Putting your vision into words has three effects:

- Putting your vision into words implies you are disappointed with what exists now. To articulate a vision is to come out of the closet with your doubts.

- Putting your vision into words exposes the future that you desire and opens you up to potential conflict with the visions of others.

- Putting your vision into words forces you to hold yourself accountable for acting in a way congruent with your vision. Once you create and communicate a vision, the vision becomes a benchmark for evaluating all your actions.[7]

Transformational leaders *create* a vision, *communicate* that vision to others, *coach* others to create visions, and *build support* for achieving the visions. Imagine the possibilities if each church had a broad-based strategic-planning committee—a "dream committee."

One church group in Texas does just that. Members meet every month to plan, dream, and be excited about the future of the church. Their enthusiasm for continued growth drives them to present, challenge, and amend some ideas others might consider off-the-wall. Members of this group must be realistic optimists. Just as Jesus set his eyes on Jerusalem (Luke 18:31–33), just as Paul set his direction to gather enough money to help those in need (1 Cor. 16:1–4), this group set their hearts on the future. Solomon, the temple builder, said, "Where there is no vision the people perish" (Prov. 29:18, KJV). He knew that "a mind is a terrible thing to waste."

Communicating the Vision

Transformational leaders become communications champions. They know that the essence of vision achievement is communication. Vision does not eliminate the need for careful planning; rather it provides a framework for planning that enables a church to direct its plans more effectively.[8] They consistently articulate the vision to make it a recognizable, discernible, driving force in congregational activity. Effective communication of a vision depends on four things:

1. *A clear presentation that captures the attention of the audience.* This takes careful planning and the dedication of a person who champions the vision.

2. *Multiple and periodic communication of the vision.* This improves the chances of the vision being understood.

3. *Evaluation of the communication effort results.* This provides a basis for improving and reinforcing the vision.

4. *Leaders' support of the vision in word and deed.* This ensures that all procedures and structures within the congregation, in turn, support the vision.[9]

There are at least three ways to talk about a vision that help command attention, interest, and understanding. Those are: optimism, emotion, and metaphors.

Optimism

Transformational leaders communicate faith, hope, and optimism. Their statements show commitment and conviction. Their verbal behavior matches their nonverbal behavior. Or in plain language, they talk the talk and walk the walk. These optimistic communications are doubly blessed:

- *The more leaders talk about the vision, the more they believe in it and the more committed they become to it.* Politicians know that the more they appeal to their constituents, the more they garner support to capture a positive vision.

- *The more followers hear leaders talk about a vision, the more they come to believe in that vision and commit themselves to that vision.* The best coaches excel at pep talks that fire up their players to go out on the field and win!

A Tennessee minister tried to excite the members of his church about Vacation Bible School. He challenged his church to bring two hundred or more each day to Vacation Bible School. He said so much about it and was so enthusiastic about the possibilities that the people began to look forward to VBS. They volunteered to help with refreshments, classes, and crafts. The first day they had 186 in attendance. That was the only day the attendance mark was under 200. For the week, the average was 233 people. The results fulfilled the minister's communicated vision, a challenge that could not go unrealized.

On a high school campus, a student saw the need for a special mission project and dreamed how to raise the support for that effort. The Ethiopian famine was at its height. She mobilized a plan to do something to help alleviate that plight. She collected money, sold T-shirts, and sent the money. She rallied the support of others as they bought into her dream to help those starving people.

On a university campus a candidate for president of the student body dreamed about what he could do in that position. He won by getting others to buy into his dream of championing the need for diversity at their college.

Emotion

Leaders use emotionally charged words to get their followers excited about a vision. Many tradition-bound congregations frown upon emotion. Yet, emotionally-charged words give substance to visions. Transformational leaders salt their comments with words like "greatness," "service," "perfection," "integrity," "love," and "compassion." One church leader starts each worship service by saying, "This is a great day for service to the Lord!" A respected university president in California launched every school year by saying, "This is the greatest year in the history of this university."

Metaphors

Transformational leaders captivate others with their vision by using metaphors, parables, and pictures. Images can include the human body, a tree, a sports team, machinery, or an orchestra. Christ used words like "salt," "leaven," and "light." Listeners respond best to an image they care about.

One leader refers to his congregation as "the family of God." Another leader uses the motto: "With one hand we reach out to the very young, and with the other, the very old." A university president says, "Our belief is that education enlightens the mind and inspires the heart so that the hands can serve."

One minister inspires his congregation by saying, "This church is on the march. Great days lie ahead!" Another minister asks members to greet visitors by saying, "We want the love of this church to flow from hand to hand, and from heart to heart."

Building Support for a Vision

Transformational leaders build team support for their vision. Some do this by brainstorming and by challenging traditional assumptions. One Christian leader built this step-by-step sequence for holistic vision development:

1. Call a meeting of five to seven people from the congregation and talk about everything relative to the idea; be very open.

2. Listen to everything said, take notes, and clarify the discussion.

3. Dismiss the formal meeting, then begin to meet one-on-one with other members of the congregation to test the ideas previously generated.

4. Synthesize and interpret the information received; this process requires judgment, intuition, and creativity.

5. Call a second meeting of the original group, summarize what has been learned, and make suggestions related to goals.

6. Let the group react to the proposal and listen for ways to refine it.

7. Develop a set of priorities. This may involve strengthening certain areas, closing any gaps or holes, or managing ministries differently.

8. Select two or three individuals most likely to succeed in bringing the vision into reality.

9. Talk to these people privately about what it means to take responsibility, how to match authority with responsibility, and why teamwork is important.

10. Reach a consensus on the new vision—the right vision, one that should be dreamed.

Notice that the vision involves a team. It does not necessarily originate with the leader, and others have input too. The leader builds immediate support by involving others from the beginning. Soon the whole congregation is pursuing the vision.

Maintaining the Vision

Even if the vision uses the gifts of the church members and leaders, even if it has been entered into with prayer and devotion, and even if it is shared by both the leaders and members, still the vision will need to be nurtured. Transformational leaders take four actions to maintain a vision:

1. *Define the vision specifically.* Defining the vision in writing disciplines thinking and allows one to see its breadth and boundaries; it focuses on what will and will not be done.

2. *Express the vision so clearly that others understand it.* A written statement of purpose or vision statement must be straightforward and to-the-point. It is more than a slogan or an image: it is a purpose that strongly attracts people.

3. *Get both organizational and personal acceptance of the vision.* This must go beyond majority support to personal involvement. People must commit themselves personally to the vision.

4. *Repeat the purpose over and over.* Leaders must repeat the essence of the vision over, and over, and over. This constant repetition keeps people from straying, gives meaning to the congregation, and produces intensity and direction.[10]

Once the church and its leaders have a clear vision, once they view everything in that light, they will view every activity in light of the vision. Soon they will make decisions more easily and allocate their resources in light of the vision. When the members share the church vision, only God can prevent accomplishment. But if God is a part of the vision, nothing can stand in the way of achievement.

Spiritual Insight

Vision is always a fundamental shift away from the norm. Leaders are dealing with an ideal that is not yet realized. They see the gap between what is and what will be (or can be). Breaking with the past requires a change of assumptions, values, and paradigms. A new vision must replace past and present ways of solving problems. As Max DePree has said: "In the end, it is important to remember that we cannot become what we need to be by remaining what we are."

The transformational leader takes a new vision for the church and systematically develops a blueprint that will marshal and motivate the people who will make the dream come true. This may require breaking with a staid, unwilling-to-change congregation. People may have to leave and establish a new, dynamic congregation. Such a change requires hope, courage, wisdom, insight, foresight, optimism, and spiritual vision.

> The man of God must have insight into things spiritual. He must be able to see the mountains filled with the horses and chariots of fire; he must be able to interpret that which is written by the finger of God upon the walls of conscience; he must be able to translate the signs of the times into terms of their spiritual meaning; he must be able to draw aside, now and then, the curtain of things material and let mortals glimpse the spiritual glories which crown the mercy seat of God. The man of God must declare the pattern that was shown · him on the mount; he must utter the vision granted to him upon the isle of revelation. . . . None of these things can he do without spiritual insight.[11]

Few churches go about planning with this quality of insight. Vision requires leaders to project images, dreams, and ideas into the future rather than use a static planning model.

One sixty-year-old congregation had stable leadership and an older membership. They were committed to Christ, but they tended to be staid in their approach to just about everything. Then they called an enthusiastic young minister who challenged them to grow and develop. Soon things started changing. Attendance increased. Young couples with families and children soon filled the building, even the balcony. Activities multiplied: youth camp, area-wide training for service, community outreach and involvement, even long-range plans for a home for the elderly. Soon the church remodeled and redecorated the building. As attendance increased, contributions soared. During a thirteen-year ministry, the congregation changed dramatically. The people had bought into the vision that this congregation was a citadel of righteousness, a pilot light in the city, with wide-reaching influences.

Transformational leaders "dream the impossible dream." They are like the Red Queen in *Alice in Wonderland*. When Alice protested that there was no use in believing impossible things, the queen replied, "I daresay you haven't had much practice. . . . When I was your age I did it for half an hour a day. Why sometimes I've believed as many as six impossible things before breakfast." God is able "to do immeasurably more than all we ask or imagine" (Eph. 3:20).

— — —

Pause to Reflect

1. Consider the statement "All great leaders seem to have an unusual ability to dream and imagine." Describe your own abilities and those of the leaders in your church. Who do you know who is a visionary leader who could teach you and others how to develop a vision?

2. Discuss the importance of involving others in creating a vision. Does your church have a "dream committee"? If not, consider forming one and serving on it.

3. Explain why communicating the vision to the entire congregation is important. Describe your experience when the vision of the leaders was not shared with the church. What happened and what were the results?

4. Illustrate the importance of spiritual vision for the Christian leader. How will spiritual vision affect the church's dream and its accomplishment?

5. Develop a plan for moving your church into a vision-setting mode of operation. What components of your plan require coordination with others? What will be necessary to achieve teamwork? Who is the most likely person to speak to the congregation and lead it into a growth-oriented future? Can you solicit this "communication champion" to do so? How?

Part Three
TRANSFORMING LEADERSHIP
STRATEGIES AND PRACTICES:

Responding to the Challenge

William James once stated that after age thirty, one becomes set like plaster and does not change. Although there are individuals who seem unfixed and immovable, James was wrong. People *can* and *do* change. That is why there is always hope for those who are unchurched, and for the church to be all that it can be.

John D. Rockefeller, at age fifty-three, was a miserable billionaire who could not sleep, was unloved, needed bodyguards, and had a rare disease. He lost too much weight and all his hair. The medical doctors gave him a year to live. As he began to think about eternal issues, he decided to change his ways of thinking about money. He established the Rockefeller Foundation and began to give away his money to help hospitals and health research, schools, and churches. His health improved, and he lived to be ninety-eight.

By grace and power, God can transform anyone. Thus, again, let the call go forth for leaders who are willing to be transformed and transform others and the church. Make no mistake about it, thousands of people in the U.S. alone need the transforming power of God. Note the following statistics:

1. More than two million child abuse cases and 114,000 attempted child kidnappings are reported annually in the U.S.

2. More than one million men are raped in U.S. prisons each year.

3. One in four women and one in five men are sexually abused by the age of eighteen.

4. Eighty-nine percent of school-age children today report being sexually harassed; 39 percent say they are harassed on a daily basis; and 83 percent report the sexual harassment includes pinching, grabbing, or touching.

5. More than 1.6 million abortions take place each year (4,200 each day) and an estimated 27 million since the 1973 Roe v. Wade decision legalized abortion.

6. Twenty percent of the boys and girls attending school carry weapons at least once a month.

7. Sixty percent of school-age children admit to having sex before graduating from high school.

8. One in fifty teenagers who are tested for HIV will be positive, according to the Center for Disease Control.

9. Fourteen percent of the girls attending high school will become pregnant by the age of nineteen.

10. Four out of eight students will try drugs by the time they finish high school.[1]

These staggering statistics are a cry for help from a suffering world. Who has the vision to go and minister to these individuals? Where are the leaders who can help transform these situations? All need salvation. All need the church. But to deal with these thousands, Christians leaders must transform their thinking accordingly.

Joshua had a mission: "Be strong and courageous, because you will lead these people to inherit the land I swore to their forefathers to give them" (Josh. 1:6). Ruth had a vision: "Where you go I will go, and where you stay I will stay. Your people will be my people and your God my God" (Ruth 1:16). Likewise, Paul: "To preach to the Gentiles the unsearchable riches of Christ" (Eph. 3:8). Jesus also had a mission: "The Spirit of the Lord is on me, because he has anointed me to preach the good news to the poor. He has sent me to proclaim freedom for the prisoners and recovery of sight for the blind, to release the oppressed, to proclaim the year of the Lord's favor" (Luke 4:18–19).

What twenty-first-century vision of the church will rally Christian leaders to transform their strategies and practices and respond to the needs of present and potential members? Chapters 10–17 are written with those challenges in mind. The even chapters (10, 12, 14, 16) represent the traditional approach to studying strategic leadership: *analysis, formulation, implementation,* and *evaluation.* The odd chapters (11, 13, 15, 17) represent transformational strategic leadership challenges: *change, conflict, communication,* and *motivation.*

This approach attempts to advance leadership beyond the current framework of strategic planning. Although this material is pertinent, one must move beyond theory to application. Until that happens, Christian leaders will find themselves surrounded by the discouraged and despondent. A new vision and mission for the church requires new ways of dealing with the challenges of leadership.

Like the cowboy who spurs his horse to gain speed, may God's leaders spur themselves toward renewed energy and higher ground. Jesus gave his disciples a vision better than themselves, but he also gave them the means by which to meet the challenge. He is still providing followers the skills and abilities to advance his kingdom. Rise up, and *just do it.*

The Challenge of Transformational Leadership

I. Transforming Christian Leadership: Recognizing the Need for Revitalization
    1. Transformational Leadership

II. Transforming Leadership Theory: Understanding What Christian Leadership Is Really About
    2. Power and Influence
    3. Strategic Leadership
    4. Traits of Leadership
    5. Initiatory Leadership
    6. Leadership Behavior
    7. Possibility Leadership
    8. Situational Leadership
    9. Visionary Leadership

III. Transforming Leadership Strategies and Practices: Responding to the Challenge
    10. Strategic Analysis
    11. Transformational Change
    12. Strategic Formulation
    13. Transformational Conflict
    14. Strategic Implementation
    15. Transformational Communication
    16. Strategic Evaluation
    17. Transformational Motivation

IV. Transforming the Christian Leader: Guaranteeing the Future
    18. Trust
    19. Commitment
    20. Affirmation

10

STRATEGIC ANALYSIS

Eighty-five percent of America's Protestant churches are either stag-
nating or dying.[1] In 1937, the Gallup Poll revealed that 73 percent of
Americans were members of a church or synagogue. In 1988, that number hit an all-time low—65 percent. That year was the first time Catholics
were no more likely than Protestants to be church members.[2]

In light of this situation, Christian leaders must understand the needs
of various age groups in order to meet their felt needs. Baby boomers are
members of the generation born between 1946 and 1964. They charac-
teristically lack institutional loyalty, including denominational loyalty.
Yet they have high expectations for those institutions. Baby Boomers are
not known for building strong relationships. They are typically ill-
equipped to understand and live life. They have a high tolerance for
diversity in individuals and life styles. They are comfortable with change
and seem energized by variety and risk.[3]

The generation born after 1965 is known as the Baby Busters, the
X-generation, or the Thirteenth Generation. They feel entitled to the
best of everything and expect immediate gratification. They typically
live isolated lives that are fast-paced, unfocused, and indecisive. They
are comfortable with contradictions, accept the idea of unisex, and
find the serious humorous.[4]

Many of today's church leaders were born before or during World
War II. How will these older leaders motivate boomers and busters? How

can leaders who are boomers motivate busters? Or vice versa? How do leaders keep those over fifty from retiring their talents and gifts too early? Can leaders identify new gifts that arise from life experiences? (See box 10.1.)

Diagnosis and analysis are necessary to move leadership from a theoretical phase to a transformational style to a strategic planning mode. In other words, environmental scanners and market analysts are critical in the church. Leaders need to keep up with the megatrends the world is encountering. Church leaders must adapt to change to survive the confrontation with the New Age movement and other forms of "spiritual competition." This requires research, analysis, decision making, commitment, and discipline.

Establishing a Scanning Program

Social forces and their impact on the church are hard to measure. Nonetheless, a congregation's changing values, attitudes, and demographic characteristics are important factors in forming strategy. Church leaders who want to establish an environmental scanning program need to ask themselves three questions.

1. *Who should do the scanning?* The obvious answer is one of the congregation's leaders. However, a committee could be charged with this responsibility. One particular congregation has a ministry purpose group that continually reviews church programs and dreams for the future. This group provides quarterly reports and assessments to the church leaders. To execute their task well, they must be aware of what is happening on local, national, and international scales.

2. *What sources of information should be scanned?* A variety of publications provide excellent environmental information, including many church publications. Church growth organizations often provide information with a broad perspective about changing demographics.[5] Religious periodicals such as *Christianity Today, Christian Science Monitor, Theology Today,* and others help. Secular publications such as the *Wall Street Journal, Fortune, Time,* and *U.S. News and World Report* are also helpful. All stay in touch with what is happening nationally and globally.

3. *What system should be used to implement a scanning program?* Here are some guidelines:

- Place someone or some group in charge of scanning.

- Have the responsible person or group review important publications for data that impact the local church's mission.

- Prepare an abstract on the items read.

Exhibit 10.1
Generational Generalities

	Pre-Boomers	Baby Boomers	Baby Busters
Religious Factors	Commitment to Christ = commitment to church	Commitment to Christ = commitment to relationships	Commitment to Christ = commitment to community
	Program-oriented	People-oriented	Community-oriented
	Money to missions	Money to people	Money to causes
	In-depth Bible study and prayer	Practical Bible study, prayer/share	Issue-oriented, Bible study, prayer/share
	Loyalty to denomination	Loyalty to people	Loyalty to causes
	Minister out of duty	Minister for personal satisfaction	Minister to confront issues
Program	Relate to missions	Relate to people	Relate to causes
	Stress in-depth Bible study & prayer	Stress fellowship & support groups	Stress Bible studies on issues
	Maintain stability	Use variety	Use variety
	Focus on marriage & retirement	Focus on marriage & family	Focus on marriage & singles
	Be formal	Be relational	Be spontaneous
	Encourage contact with baby busters	Encourage involvement in small groups	Encourage involvement in community issues
Worship	Quietness	Talking	Talking
	Hymns	Praise songs	Praise songs
	Expository sermons	"How-to" sermons	Issue-oriented sermons
	Pastoral prayer	Various people pray	Various people pray
	Guests recognized	Guests anonymous	Guests anonymous
	Organ/piano	Guitars/drums	Jazz ensemble
	Low audience participation	Higher audience participation	Lower audience participation

Implications for Future	Ability to carry on programs and projects will wane	Support of people-oriented projects will continue	More involvement with issue-oriented projects
	Giving will continue until retirement	Giving will be related to people projects	Giving will be related to issues & causes
	Revivalistic evangelism will continue to decline	Friendship evangelism	12-step evangelism events will grow
	Loyalty to institutions will continue to decline	Loyalty to people will continue strong	Loyalty to issues or causes will grow

Source: G. L. McIntosh, "What's in a Name?" *The McIntosh Church Growth Network, 3* (5), (May 1991): 2.

- Submit the abstract (with applications, if any, in the community) to congregational leaders to determine relevance.
- Recommend actions that can be taken.
- Disseminate the information, encouraging interested parties to discuss concerns with the leaders.

This systematic approach enables leaders to scan outside forces and evaluate how they will affect the church's internal mechanisms. The focus should be on trends with churchwide relevance. The effective church takes advantage of its internal capabilities to satisfy its external demands.

A Chinese proverb says, "Every change brings an opportunity." Change also can bring a threat. All churches confront change. How well they negotiate the hurdles of change is key to survival and success. *External change* occurs "outside" the church and is beyond a congregation's immediate control. *Internal change* occurs "inside" a church and is directly within its sphere of decision-making capability. In spite of these differences, external and internal change have one important similarity: both require that strategic questions be posed before action is taken—who, what, where, when, why, and how.

SWOT Analysis

Because so much research, analysis, and prayer are required to formulate strategy, Christian leaders should know how to adeptly analyze their environment. SWOT analysis, an easy-to-use technique to help any church capitalize on its strengths, overcome its weaknesses, take advantage of its opportunities, and avoid threats, has been designed for business organizations.[6]

SWOT refers to internal strengths and weaknesses and external opportunities and threats. It is a systematic identification of those factors and the strategy best suited to them. Its logic is that an effective strategy makes the most of strengths and opportunities while minimizing weaknesses and threats. This simple assumption, if accurately applied, has powerful implications for successfully choosing, designing, and selecting a winning strategy for a church.

Be patient and stick with the process. Even though the SWOT analysis may sound and look difficult, keep reading. SWOT analysis is very simple.

Three Tasks of SWOT Analysis

SWOT analysis helps Christian leaders find the best match between environmental trends and internal capabilities. The first task a leader faces in developing an effective strategy is to identify distinctive competencies. What can the congregation do very well? What are its unique resources and capabilities? What are the strengths of the members? What is their ability to overcome any weaknesses?

Task #1: Define strengths and weaknesses. In order to identify distinctive capabilities, one should consider the church's strengths and weaknesses. A *strength* is any resource or capacity a church can use effectively to achieve goals and objectives. Examples are a zealous young couples' class, strong benevolence program, state-of-the-art facilities and teaching program, a great choir or singing congregation, friendliness and hospitality, depth of Bible knowledge, maturity of members, or monetary blessings. A *weakness* is any limitation that will keep a church from achieving its goals and objectives. Examples are poorly trained teachers, inadequate facilities, lack of a clear strategic direction, oversupply of weak leaders, or weak financial resources.

Task #2: Define opportunities and threats. After defining the church's strengths and weaknesses, leaders should look for niches their church is well suited to fill. The church interacts in many social and/or economic situations, or niches. Transformational leaders position their congregations to take advantage of their opportunities and avert threats from the environment. An *opportunity* is any favorable situation in the external environment that permits a church to enhance its position. The following examples are opportunities: community need for preschool programs, expansion of evangelistic worldwide efforts and community involvement programs, people experienced at working with surrounding racial and ethnic groups. A *threat* is any unfavorable situation that is potentially dangerous to a church. Threatening situations would include anything that might inflict problems, damages, or injuries. The following examples are threats: government regulations, adverse demographic changes of neighborhood, vulnerability of member contributions due to recession.

Task #3: Match distinctive competence with available niches. Transformational leaders understand their opportunities and threats. They are able to identify where they can be most effective. They understand their strengths and weaknesses. They identify their distinctive competencies. An effective strategy takes advantage of opportunities by employing strengths and wards off threats by minimizing weaknesses. And in some cases, threats can become opportunities, depending on one's outlook and/or resources.

SWOT Analysis of New Testament Churches

Example #1: The seven churches of Revelation. Jesus Christ is depicted as walking among the churches, reminding one of Management by Walking Around (MBWA), a modern-day management technique. As Jesus moves among the churches, he sees strengths, weaknesses, opportunities, and threats. It is a time of Roman persecution against Christians because they will not call the emperor "God." The Christians face arrest, loss of possessions, economic boycott, and death. These fears and threats are very real. No doubt they wondered if they had the ability to overcome the Roman threat. Thus as Christ identifies with each church, judges it, and appeals to it, one becomes aware that victory is the ultimate opportunity. In the final battle, Christ will defeat Satan.

Let us apply a SWOT analysis to the seven churches:

1. Ephesus—the church that left its first love (Rev. 2:1–7)—weakness
2. Smyrna—the rich poor church (2:8–11)—strength
3. Pergamum—where Satan's throne was (2:12–17)— threat
4. Thyatira—the home of Jezebel (2:18–29)—threat
5. Sardis—a dead church (3:1–6)—weakness
6. Philadelphia—the church with an open door (3:7–13)—opportunity
7. Laodicea—the lukewarm church (3:14–22)—weakness[7]

Only two of these congregations (Smyrna and Philadelphia) receive praise. One (Laodicea) receives only censure. The other four hear both good and bad news. "Is it not the same with the local bodies of the Lord's people in any generation? Because this is the case, much is to be learned from a careful study of the epistles to these seven churches. Insights, counsels, warning, and encouragement come to us and challenge us to be more nearly the churches heaven wants us to be at our time in history. We dare not neglect the valuable lessons to be found here."[8]

Example #2: The Ephesian church. Box 10.2 gives a SWOT analysis of the Ephesian church based on the Books of Acts, 1 Corinthians, Ephesians, 1 Timothy, and Revelation.

SWOT Analysis of Your Own Church

Study Box 10.3 and fill in the matrix provided as it relates to the congregation you presently attend. Do not read further until you have completed this exercise.

Forty West Coast church leaders recently participated in a Creating a Vision Workshop. You will find the results of their analyses in Box 10.4. How do their results compare with your results in Box 10.3?

The SWOT Matrix

As a follow-up to a SWOT analysis, the SWOT matrix is an important tool for developing four types of strategies: SO strategies, WO strategies, ST strategies, and WT strategies. Successful business organizations pursue WO, ST, or WT strategies so they can then apply an SO strategy. When a firm has major weaknesses, it will strive to overcome them, making them strengths (e.g., a church building is paid for but it needs modernization or an addition). Note, however, overcoming a weakness does not necessarily mean that a strength will be created or found. When business executives face major threats, they will either confront them or avoid them in order to concentrate on opportunities. Christian leaders can do the same thing.

A Schematic Representation

You will find in box 10.5 a model of the SWOT matrix based on information in Box 10.4. Note that a SWOT matrix is composed of eight cells: four key factor cells and four strategy cells. The four strategy cells (labeled SO, WO, ST, and WT) are developed after the four key factor cells (labeled S, W, O, and T) are completed.

To construct a SWOT matrix, assemble a team of five to nine people of different ages, genders, levels of membership, and personalities; get together; and do the following:

1. List the church's key internal strengths.

2. List the church's key internal weaknesses.

Box 10.2
SWOT Analysis: Ephesian Church

STRENGTHS	**WEAKNESSES**
GENERAL	EPHESIANS
Ephesus most easily accessible city both by land and sea	Once walked dead through trespasses/sins (2:1–2)
Climate exceptionally fine; soil of valley unusually fertile	Lived in passions of the flesh (2:3)
Commercial center	Following desires of body and mind (2:3)
	Children of wrath (2:3)
ACTS	Children tossed to and fro and carried about with every wind of doctrine (4:14)
Paul performs extraordinary miracles (19:11–12)	Live as Gentiles in futility of mind (4:17–19)
EPHESIANS	Falsehoods (4:26)
Apostle Paul (1:1)	Anger (4:26)
Every spiritual blessing (1:3)	Stealing (4:28)
Chosen before foundation of the world (1:4)	Evil talk (4:29)
Destined in love to be God's sons (1:5)	Bitterness and wrath (4:31)
Grace freely bestowed on Ephesians (1:6, 8; 2:5, 8)	Clamor and slander (4:31)
Redemption (1:7)	Malice (4:31)
Forgiveness of sins (1:7; 4:32)	Walking as children of darkness (5:8)
Know mystery of his will (1:9)	Being foolish (5:17)
Sealed with Holy Spirit (1:13)	Drunkenness/debauchery (5:18)
Faith in the Lord Jesus (1:15)	Fathers provoking children to anger (6:4)
Love toward all saints (1:15)	Masters threatening slaves (6:9)
Fellow citizens with saints and members of household of God (2:19)	
Built upon foundation of apostles and prophets (2:20)	1 TIMOTHY
Bold and confident of access through faith (3:12)	Devotees to myths and endless genealogies
Equipped with gifts (4:7–13)	
	REVELATION
REVELATION	Forsaken first love (2:4)
Good deeds (2:2)	Fallen from height (2:5)
Hard workers (2:2)	
Perseverance, endure hardships, do not grow weary (2:2, 3)	
Cannot tolerate wicked men (2:2)	
Test false apostles (2:2)	
Hate practices of Nicolaitans (2:6)	

Exhibit 10.2 (Continued)
SWOT Analysis: Ephesian Church

OPPORTUNITIES

GENERAL

Location favored religious development
and presented an advantageous field
for missionary labors of Paul

ACTS

Correction of teaching on John's
baptism (19:2–7)
Paul establishes church (19:2–9)

1 CORINTHIANS

Great door open for effective work
(16:9)

EPHESIANS

Live for praise of his glory (1:12)
Spirit of wisdom (1:17)
Spirit of revelation in the knowledge
of God (1:17)
Eyes of hearts enlightened (1:18)
Know the hope to which have been
called (1:18)
Know immeasurable greatness of his
power (1:19)
Created for good works (2:10)
Dividing wall of hostility broken
down (2:14)
No longer strangers and sojourners (2:19)
Body a dwelling place of God in Spirit
(2:22)
Power to comprehend love of Christ
(3:18,19)
To be filled with fullness of God
(3:19)
Lead a life worthy of calling (4:1, 2)
Forbearing one another in love (4:2)
Maintain unity of Spirit in bond
of peace (4:3)
Grown up in every way into him (4:15)
Renewed in spirit of mind (4:23)
Put on new nature (4:24)
Be angry but do not sin (4:26)
Labor, doing honest work with hands
(4:28)
Edifying talk (4:29)
Be kind to one another (4:32)
Be tenderhearted, forgiving one
another (4:32)

THREATS

GENERAL

Home of native goddess Diana (or
Artemis)
Temple of Diana a place of worship,
a treasure-house, a museum,
a sanctuary for criminals

ACTS

Sorcery (19:19)
Riot led by Demetrius (19:23–41)

1 CORINTHIANS

"Wild beasts" (15:32)
Opposition to the Way (16:9)

EPHESIANS

At one time had no hope,
without God (2:12)
Suffering and imprisonment
(3:1, 13; 4:1; 6:20)
Opportunities for Satan through
lies and anger (4:25–27)
Grieving the Holy Spirit (4:30)
Immorality, impurity, covetousness
(5:3)
Filthiness, levity, silly talk (2:19)
Deceit with empty words (5:6)
Association with sons of
disobedience (5:6–7)
Taking part in unfruitful works of
darkness (5:11)
Evil days (5:16)
Wiles of the devil (6:11–16)

1 TIMOTHY

Teachers of false doctrines (1:3)
Controversies created by myths
and genealogies (1:4)
Some Christians wandering away
and turning to meaningless talk
(1:6–7)

REVELATION

Removal of lampstand (2:5)

Box 10.2 (Continued)
SWOT Analysis: Ephesian Church

OPPORTUNITIES (Continued)
Imitators of God (5:1)
Walk in love (5:2)
Thanksgiving (5:4)
Learn what is pleasing to Lord
  (5:10)
Walking as wise men (5:16)
Make most of one's time (5:16)
Understand will of Lord (5:17)
Filled with Spirit (5:18)
Address one another in psalms,
  hymns, songs (5:19)
Giving thanks to God (5:20); pray
  at all times (6:18)
Being subject to one another (5:21)
Wives respect and be in subjection
  to husbands (5:22, 24, 33)
Husbands love wives (5:25, 28, 33)
Children obey parents (6:1)
Fathers bring children up in
  discipline and instruction
  of Lord (6:4)
Slaves obedient to masters (6:5)
Rendering service with a good will
  (6:7)
Be strong in Lord (6:10)
Wear armor of God to stand against
  Satan (6:11–16)
Keep alert with all perseverance
  (6:18)

REVELATION
Repent and keep lampstand (2:5)
Hear what Spirit says to the churches (2:7)
Overcome and inherit paradise of God

Box 10.3
SWOT Analysis

STRENGTHS: What makes your church strong?	WEAKNESSES: What weakens your church's mission?
OPPORTUNITIES: What opportunities exist for strengthening your church?	**THREATS:** What are potential threats to your church's mission?

Box 10.4
A Church's SWOT Analysis
Sample

STRENGTHS: What makes your church strong?

Talented, educated people

Restorationist doctrinal position

Commitment to caring for others

Warmth of people; acceptance of others

Metro area wide-open for evangelism

Vision of leadership

Strong sense of members bonding together

Commitment to giving

All voices can be heard

Cultural diversity; accepted and welcomed

Awareness of need for change

Readiness for worldwide awareness

WEAKNESSES: What weakens your church's mission?

Need heightened spirituality

Need active female members

Reluctance to show exuberance in worship

No full-time minister; not growing

Need more open and regular meetings

Not reaching the hurting people

Too much emphasis on youth

Lack of young families and teenagers

Too many differing opinions

Tied to a building/one location

OPPORTUNITIES: What opportunities exist for strengthening your church?

Opportunities (Hispanics)

Help the poor and needy

Building used daily (child care/youth)

Campus ministry (11 colleges nearby)

Children, youth, single ministries

Examine practices; shed traditions

Build relationships; grow closer together

Community service

THREATS: What are potential threats to your church's mission?

Lack of permanent facility

Changing community; seedy environment

Society's negative attitude toward religion

Satan; beaches, mountains, rivers, etc.

Media treatment of Christianity

Anti-church government legislation

Return to past (traditional thinking)

Unwillingness to change

Complacency; stagnation; inferiority

Lack of evangelism

Disunity/loss of unity

Focus on technique; loses sight of principle

Box 10.5
The SWOT Matrix

	STRENGTHS--(S) List strengths.	WEAKNESSES--(W) List weaknesses.
	1.	1.
	2.	2.
	3.	3.
	4.	4.
	5.	5.
	6.	6.
	7.	7.
	8.	8.
	9.	9.
	10.	10.
OPPORTUNITIES--(O) List opportunities.	SO STRATEGIES List ways to use strengths to take advantage of opportunities.	WO STRATEGIES List ways to overcome weaknesses by taking advantage of opportunities.
1.	1.	1.
2.	2.	2.
3.	3.	3.
4.	4.	4.
5.	5.	5.
6.	6.	6.
7.	7.	7.
8.	8.	8.
9.	9.	9.
10.	10.	10.
THREATS--(T) List threats.	ST STRATEGIES List ways to use strengths to avoid threats.	WT STRATEGIES List ways to minimize weaknesses and avoid threats.
1.	1.	1.
2.	2.	2.
3.	3.	3.
4.	4.	4.
5.	5.	5.
6.	6.	6.
7.	7.	7.
8.	8.	8.
9.	9.	9.
10.	10.	10.

3. List the church's key external opportunities.

4. List the church's key external threats.

5. Match internal strengths with external opportunities and record the resultant SO strategies in the appropriate cell.

6. Match internal weaknesses with external opportunities and record the resultant WO strategies.

7. Match internal strengths with external threats and record the resultant ST strategies.

8. Match internal weaknesses with external threats and record the resultant WT strategies.

The preceding SWOT processes can be done successfully with forty or more people in a workshop environment if small groups are used for discovery and reassemble to share results and clarify.

A Personal Representation

If you have completed Box 10.3, fill in the SWOT matrix in Box 10.5 on the congregation you are presently attending. Do not read further before doing this.

Matching Internal and External Factors

The most difficult part of developing a SWOT matrix is matching internal and external factors. The matching process requires good judgment, but no one answer is best.

SO Strategies

SO strategies use internal strengths to take advantage of external opportunities. Any congregation should be able to use its strengths to exploit external opportunities. A congregation with a strong financial base, a dynamic and well-respected pastor, and an interest in media evangelism should be able to reach thousands of listeners in a global preaching effort. Or, a talented single professionals' group (internal strength) coupled with an unsaturated evangelistic market (external opportunity) could suggest that increased advertising and outreach are appropriate SO-type strategies.

WO Strategies

WO strategies aim at improving internal weaknesses by taking advantage of external opportunities. Sometimes key external opportunities exist, but a congregation has internal weaknesses that prevent those opportunities from being seized. A congregation with a dynamic preacher and evangelistic mission is expanding rapidly. New membership growth is the young couples with small children. However, the number of Bible class teachers and classroom space are inadequate. Possible WO strategies are to recruit and train members with the needed teaching expertise, initiate an expansion study, or offer two Sunday school times instead of one.

A church lacking state-approved facilities (internal weakness) coupled with a strong demand by the community for a preschool program (external opportunity) could suggest a WO strategy of renovation and remodeling or building.

ST Strategies

ST strategies use internal strengths to avoid or reduce the impact of external threats. A congregation faced with many threats must muster all its strengths to avoid failure.

A congregation is facing declining membership because some members are transferred by their companies. Church income has declined and the future existence of the congregation is in peril. If, however, the remaining members are financially solvent, the church building is paid for, or funds are readily available because of a strong credit rating, the congregation might be able to continue on its own until it is able to build membership back up.

WT Strategies

WT strategies seek to overcome internal weaknesses and avoid environmental threats. These strategies attempt to minimize both weaknesses and threats. WT strategies are defensive. Poorly trained teachers (internal weakness) coupled with unavailable professional education programs for purchase (external threat) could suggest the need for an educational committee to write one's own curriculum as a feasible WT strategy.

A church faced with many external threats and internal weaknesses is in a precarious position. In fact, such a church must fight for its survival, merge, cut spending, or choose to liquidate. "When a church starts dying, it is almost impossible to turn it around. The elements that started the demise will continue like a fungus to destroy it. . . . Very few, if any declining congregations have ever been revived. They dwindle until they die or else heroically merge themselves out of existence with some other dying church."[9]

The purpose of the SWOT matrix is to generate plausible alternative strategies, not to select or determine which strategies are best. Therefore, not all of the strategies developed in the SWOT matrix will be selected for implementation. Sometimes several internal factors will be matched with

Box 10.6

The SWOT Matrix Applied

	STRENGTHS—(S)	WEAKNESSES—(W)
OPPORTUNITIES—(O)	**SO STRATEGIES**	**WO STRATEGIES**
	1. Flexibility in worship styles should lead to a variety of worship services that would appeal to many different ethnic/age groups.	1. Meeting in small groups separately would eliminate the impression of too much emphasis on one group to the neglect of others.
	2. Availability of talented people could result in several smaller groups or congregations, meeting together only on special occasions.	2. Spirituality could be heightened in small group meetings, if leaders are properly trained.
	3. Commitment to "restoration principle" could mean meeting in homes for weekly Lord's Supper and fellowship.	3. Women in small groups could be as active as the individual groups would allow.
	4. Meeting separately in small groups would allow groups worshiping in many different languages.	4. Small individual groups could be as exuberant or staid as felt best by the group.
	5. Meeting separately in small groups could open the door for evangelism on the eleven campuses in the area.	5. Small groups could make use of the talents of all leaders instead of singling out one.
	6. Meeting separately in small groups would make it easier to evangelize the whole "diocese."	6. In small groups, members of each group would know who of their number was hurting and be able to offer assistance immediately.
THREATS—(T)	**ST STRATEGIES**	**WT STRATEGIES**
	1. Small groups meeting separately could meet where the people are and avoid the "seedy" environment for the building.	1. Continual emphasis from elders on need to make services relevant and remain flexible and open to change will help overcome the threat posed by traditions.
	2. Beaches, mountains, etc., can be turned from a threat into a strength by allowing the small groups to meet wherever they wish (e.g., the lake).	2. Continual insistence from elders on the need to keep the groups small will keep groups growing and resist stagnation and complacency.
	3. The intimacy of the small group can counterbalance the pull of the media and government anti-Christian bias.	
	4. The wealth of talented, educated, strong leaders can work together to counterbalance the threat of disunity or loss of identity.	
	5. Intimacy created by small groups meeting separately will appeal to those feeling isolated and disconnected.	

several external factors to generate an appropriate strategy. One church listed the strategies in Box 10.6 (based on results of Box 10.3) after completing the SWOT matrix.

Strategies should be tailored specifically for a church. They do not necessarily have to be developed for all four strategy cells. Leaders need to implement strategy with caution. When change is involved, it is necessary to move people from step 3 to 4 on a scale of 1 to 10 rather than quantum leaping from step 3 to 9.

Chapter 11 will transform the idea of strategic analysis by highlighting change process. As suggested at the beginning of this chapter, if Christian leaders are to survive in today's competitive religious market, they must identify the need for change and be able to adapt to it.

— — —

Pause to Reflect

1. Discuss the idea that environmental scanners and market analysts (people who keep up with megatrends) are needed within the church. Do you agree? Why or why not?

2. Determine the impact of social forces on your church. What are some of the changing values, attitudes, and demographic characteristics of your city, state, and the nation?

3. Identify the distinctive competencies of your church. What can your congregation do very well? What are its unique resources and capabilities? What are the strengths of the members? What is their ability to overcome any weaknesses?

4. Find the niche for which your church is well suited. What are the social and/or economic situations in which your congregation interacts? Are your leaders positioned in such a way that they can take advantage of the opportunities that present themselves and avert threats from the environment?

5. Match your church's distinctive competence with its available niche. Have you completed the SWOT analysis in Box 10.3? If not, why the delay? You will get a wealth of information quickly and inexpensively.

11

TRANSFORMATIONAL CHANGE

Change is a state of mind. Transforming the church requires a change of attitude or mind-set. In many respects, the members are the most crucial parts of the church and the most critical to the change process (see Rom. 12:1–8; 1 Cor. 12; Eph. 4:11–12). Yet systems are easier to change than the people. Changing either an individual or the system requires altering the human and technical features that hinder the congregation from achieving its full potential.

Asbury Church and Highland Park Church were located at the same street corner. Highland Park Church had an average attendance of more than five thousand, a fleet of buses, a Christian school, a ten-week summer camp for children, and other dynamic programs. Highland Park Church continued to grow and expand yearly, even though it was located in an older, changing neighborhood.

Across the street, Asbury Church was declining from year to year. Membership stood at four hundred, but only about a hundred attended. Only five children attended Sunday school, and two of those were the pastor's. Leaders made no plans for growth or development, opting to "keep house." The pastor explained that the church could not attract new people because the neighborhood was declining.

Why did one church advance while another declined? The answer is simple: the advancing church had effective, knowledgeable team players who knew and promoted the congregational vision, aggressively campaigned for new members, and offered appealing services.

Change

Church analysis that leads to growth or development is planned change. Change is a response to pressure. It substitutes one thing for another. It modifies the behavior patterns of people within an organization. To survive, organizations must periodically change to meet the challenges of a changing world. People within the organization must also change.

Reinhold Niebuhr originally wrote the Serenity Prayer for a service in the Congregational church of Heath, Massachusetts. Millions have used this prayer in Alcoholics Anonymous and other recovery programs:

God, give us grace to accept with serenity the things that cannot be changed,
the courage to change the things which should be changed,
and the wisdom to distinguish the one from the other.

Everyone talks about the necessity of change, but the fact is, very few people want to change. Change is painful. However, it is often a prerequisite to survival.

Present and Predictable Changes

Societal change cannot be isolated from global change. Yet there seem to be distinctive national changes and trends. (See box 11.1.) These present and predictable changes have tremendous potential for helping or harming the church, depending on the response of leaders and members to these changes.

Like it or not, these changes are pervasive. They are altering the face of religion, including church attendance. Churches are becoming more informal. This calls for different styles of worship: skits, live interviews, children on stage, guitars and rock music, and informal dress for worship leaders.

The Church Cannot Be Isolated

As American culture changes, the church changes. Heraclitus said, "All is flux; nothing stays still," and "Nothing endures but change." Christians cannot isolate the church from change, although some may try. The church is not an island. Its task is to make the Bible relevant to today's listeners. Religious leaders must understand people and their culture. God never changes, but human culture changes constantly. Leaders must learn that the Bible is for every culture, language, and generation. God is absolute, and his Word does not change.

Box 11.1

Demographic Highlights of the Twenty-First Century

By the year 2000:

- 33 percent of all Americans in population will be nonwhite.
- Hispanic population will grow by 45 percent.
- African-American population will grow by 22 percent.
- Asian and other people of color will grow by 18 percent.
- 85 percent net new entrants to the workforce will be women, people of color, and immigrants.
- Immigrants will represent the largest share of new workers.
- Women will increase to 47 percent of the workforce.
- Men will decrease to 53 percent of the workforce.
- African-Americans will increase to 12 percent of the workforce.
- Hispanics will rise to 11 percent of the workforce.
- Asians will increase to 5 percent of the workforce.
- 51 percent of the workforce will be between the ages of thirty-five and fifty-four, and 11 to 13 percent will be over age fifty-five.
- There will be more disabled workers in the labor force due to the Americans with Disabilities Act.
- Baby boomers, who were aged thirty-six to forty-four in 1990 and will be aged forty-six to fifty-four in 2000, will pass into their prime income years during the decade.

Adapted from M. F. Winters, *Widening the Circle—Inclusive Practices and Community Foundations* (Washington, D.C.: Council on Foundations, March 1995).

Forces of Change

How does change come about? Organizations change because of a variety of forces. These forces may be analyzed accordingly.

Change begins with the emergence of either external or internal forces. These forces create a need for change in some part of the organization.

External forces are competition, resource availability, technology, values, environmental opportunities, and constraints (economic, political/legal, and social). Internal forces are the knowledge explosion, desire for more leisure time, stress and conflict in congregational activities, interactions, sentiments, performance results, and new technology.

Organizational effectiveness depends on the ability to predict these forces of change to maintain stability. If the environment is constant, organizational structure may remain stable. However, if the environment is chaotic, the structure must be more adaptable and flexible. (The process of analyzing these forces is called "environmental scanning" and was discussed in chap. 10.) Thus churches face an ever-present dilemma: how to be sufficiently organized to operate efficiently, and how to be sufficiently adaptable to new forces demanding change.[1]

One of the techniques to better understand the forces of change is Kurt-Lewin's Force Field Analysis. In essence, this theory says that change occurs when the forces pushing in one direction are greater than the forces pushing in the opposite direction. (See box 11.2.)

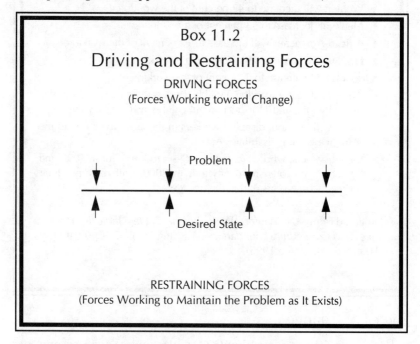

Box 11.2
Driving and Restraining Forces
DRIVING FORCES
(Forces Working toward Change)

Problem

Desired State

RESTRAINING FORCES
(Forces Working to Maintain the Problem as It Exists)

Driving forces encourage change, growth, and development. Restraining forces encourage stability and the status quo. Both driving and restraining forces produce distinct attitudes toward other people and happenings and affect responses to what must be done. Combining external and internal forces with driving and restraining forces gives us four kinds of forces to consider:

- *External driving forces* include shorter life cycles; needs for different channels of evangelism; or changing markets for ministry, status of members, and culture and social values.

- *Internal driving forces* include increased demand for greater spiritual satisfaction, desire by members to have more say in decision making, increased knowledge of how to organize, and higher expectations of members.

- *External restraining forces* include continuing demand of older members for tradition, existence of strong pressure groups to maintain status quo, and inability of groups promoting change to mobilize into effective forces for change.

- *Internal restraining forces* include existing power and social relationships and traditions, vested interests and coalitions, fear of the unknown, and lack of strategies for introducing and implementing change, and confidence to cope with change.[2]

Transformational leaders do everything possible to communicate the need for change and to enable their churches to change. Therefore, it is often helpful to consider five types of change goals.

1. *Strategic change goals* seek to alter the relationship between the organization as a whole and its environment (i.e., revised objectives, expansion, a change in competitive emphasis).

2. *Technological change goals* seek to alter physical parts of the organization such as installing new computer equipment.

3. *Structural change goals* seek to alter internal features of the organization including relationships or processes of communication and decision making.

4. *Behavioral change goals* aim to change beliefs, values, attitudes, interpersonal relationships, group behavior, intergroup behavior, and similar human phenomena.

5. *Program change goals* seek to alter the structure or features of the technical implementation of plans.[3]

Once the type of change goal is identified, then one may choose the target of change and how to implement the change. Those implementing change must be carefully matched to the particular change target and resources available. Also, authority and responsibility of both the *changers* and the *changees* must be explicitly defined to prevent conflict.

Change results will depend on member identification with change needs and goals. Although it is usually initiated to improve efficiency and/or effectiveness, change can be either positive or negative. However, since change is inevitable, the transformational leader might as well accept change and development as positive and deal with it in a positive spirit. As Max DePree said, "In the end it is important to remember that we cannot become what we need to be by remaining what we are."

Resistance to Change

If you have tried to change an organization, you have already met resistance. You know about the difficulty in accurately forecasting major problems. You know something about the enormous amount of time that is needed to iron out problems and get people to accept change. And you have seen that many people hardly commit themselves and show this by refusing to take initiative and help make the plan work.[4]

The classic case of resistance to change was probably Henry Ford. He assumed the black Model T was the only car anyone needed. So when people started asking for different colors, he responded, "You can have any color you want as long as it's black." And that's when his decline started. The door was opened for General Motors and others to take away market share in the automobile industry.

Churches and other religious institutions seem to resist change even more than other groups. Think about these barriers to change:

1. *Focus on the institution rather than the purpose.* The best organizations are purpose-driven. They know why they exist. Those who focus on the institution oppose change because they fear it will threaten their institution.

2. *Socially self-perpetuating.* Most churches and religious organizations attract people who are very much like those who are already members. Common denominators may include race, income, education, a doctrinal idiosyncrasy, loyalty to the founder, commitment to a specific lifestyle, or just about anything else. Such self-perpetuating organizations can be very stable but very slow to change.

3. *Minority rule.* Just because the majority is supposed to rule does not mean things actually work that way. Often, the majority goes along in deference to the minority—a few who do not want change. These fearful few who resist change immobilize many churches.

4. *Yesterday's innovator.* Some organizations are blessed with extraordinarily gifted innovators. They are so good they cannot be matched, and no one wants to try. But even good ideas become

obsolete. This can curtail innovation. All that is left is to perpetuate yesterday's innovations and implement yesterday's dreams—a formula for failure.

5. *Not inclined to risk.* All change involves risk. The greater the change, the greater the risk. And to attempt to relate to modern western culture without losing faith and integrity is high risk indeed. But today's standard answer to change is, "Be conservative."

6. *Unwillingness to suffer pain.* Change is always uncomfortable for some people in the organization. Rather than suffer the pain of dealing with a problem and unintentionally inflicting pain on some individuals, most religious organizations choose to live with the problem.

7. *Complacency.* The congregation is already successful and no one feels self-criticism and change are urgent. "Leave well-enough alone," the people say.

8. *Disruption of interpersonal relationships.* Change sometimes means individuals who have been close associates for years are assigned to different task groups. This may interrupt friendships and common social activities. People may even find themselves among new associates they either really like or intensely dislike.

9. *Threat to status.* Realigning duties and activities often threatens the self-image and status of those directly affected by the change. They feel they will be less highly regarded by their peers.

10. *Fear of increased responsibilities.* Some resist change because they fear they will be unable to handle increased responsibilities. Consequently, some refuse to accept certain ministries. (Of course, some people do welcome such opportunities.)[5]

Some people resist change more than others because they feel more threatened. As George Trusell has written, "People do not basically resist change; they resist 'being changed.'" Thus, those who have the most to lose will resist the most. Cohesive groups are highly resistant to change, but resistant churches are seldom very evangelistic. Can anything be done about this tendency to resist change?

Guiding Change in a Congregation

Resistance to change is a recurring problem. Most leaders know the justification and logic behind their decisions. They expect their members to accept their judgment without question. Fat chance! Transformational leaders follow certain communication rules to gain compliance with their decisions.

Box 11.3

An Agenda for Guiding Change in a Congregation

Strategy 1: Become an Entrepreneurial Leader

The *entrepreneur* is an agent of change who is comfortable working within the system. Entrepreneurial leaders create change by applying a few central principles:

- They get ready for change. They know luck occurs when preparation meets opportunity.
- They decide what they want and go after it.
- They recognize that all ministry ideas do not succeed and that failure can be a growth opportunity, too.
- They find a ministry that is needed and not being attempted; then they do it.

Strategy 2: Sharpen the Congregation's Vision

Jesus preached the kingdom of God. It was his vision, his dream, his passion. What did (and does) the kingdom of God provide for Christ's followers? A positive image of ministry. Motivational pull. Mobilizing energy. A force to launch action. A collage of possibilities. A mission and purpose. A map for the future. A rallying point. A set of ministry priorities. A congregational vision does the same things for a local church. Leaders can define the congregational vision:

- They recognize that shaping the congregation's vision is the most important impact they will have on their church.
- They guide a congregational dream process.
- They emphasize by word and deed the core values represented by the congregation's dream.
- They organize the congregation's ministries around their vision with one central hope: Members will pull together because they share the dream, too.

Strategy 3: Champion the Vision

Leaders in healthy congregations are pacesetters and motivators who champion the congregation's dream. They have one obsession—to publicize the church's vision. They champion this vision through a cluster of behaviors:

- They epitomize the dream and its resulting atmosphere.
- They set the standards of ministry.
- They put the congregation's vision in their hearts and their hearts into the vision.
- They work persistently to actualize the congregation's dream in discernible ministerial deeds.

- They represent the congregation to the outside world.

Strategy 4: Incorporate the Congregation's Dream into the Ceremonies of the Church

Leaders "call the family together." They incorporate the congregation's vision through ceremonies of the group: worship services, homecomings, revivals, fellowship meals, and the ordinances. Ceremonies put the dream on display. Leaders can demonstrate "the way things are done here" accordingly:

- They recognize people's contributions and say thank you in public and private settings.
- They design and host the festivals that embody the congregation's dream.
- They give the congregation permission to relax and play in order to relieve tension and stimulate creativity.
- They orchestrate the symbolic events as well as the daily routine of the church.

Strategy 5: Tell and Retell the Congregation's Story

Leaders are the organization's storytellers. They know that the tales of past congregational heroes and events are motivational parables. They have detailed information and tell imaginative stories. They preserve the congregation's vision by explaining and giving meaning to the church's history in a way that illuminates the future.

Strategy 6: Develop Healthy Alliances

Alliances linking members together provide strength, backing, and protection for the congregation. Alliances can build on and reinforce the shared dream, since humans are naturally social creatures who enjoy each other.

Strategy 7: Improve the Congregation's Atmosphere

There are four primary options for significantly shaping or reshaping the congregation's atmosphere: (1) Plant a congregation. Founders have one huge advantage in climate shaping—they write on blank sheets. Their dreams are fundamental climate creators for new churches. But established or traditional congregations face other options. The climate-changing process, however, can become abrasive and feel like sandpapering. (2) Crisis breaks the continuity of old habits and assumptions. Trauma bounces congregations out of their ruts—at a high cost sometimes. (3) New members introduce new dynamics and vitality to old institutions. (4) New leaders—by force of personality, the clarity of their dreams, or reorganization—launch a new era of congregational life and change the future of the church.

Adapted from R. D. Dale, *Keeping the Dream Alive* (Nashville: Broadman Press, 1988), 148–52.

Rule #1: Provide accurate and detailed information about any change as soon as possible. This advance notice helps curtail disruptive attitudes and forestalls rumors. If members are forewarned about changes or told that the new direction may present short-term difficulties, they adjust more quickly to the change.

Rule #2: Allow people time to accept change. People normally accept change if they have time to become accustomed to the idea. Sudden change usually arouses people's fears, but moving slowly helps to prepare members and make the change less formidable.

Strategies available to transformational leaders for overcoming resistance to change and guiding a congregation through change are detailed in box 11.3. In summary, the transformational leader is "entrepreneurial," sharpens and champions the vision, puts the dream on display, tells the story of the church's history, links members together, and shapes the church's environment. They also find it helpful to remember some sage advice from John Maxwell: "Every new idea goes through three phases: It will not work; it will cost too much; and I thought it was a good idea all along."

Transformational leaders are agents of change. They are the difference between a vitalized and deteriorating organization.

— — —

Pause to Reflect

1. The author states that to change either an individual or a system one must alter the human and technical features that limit the achievement of full potential. Do you agree? Discuss. Why is it often easier to change the system than the people?

2. Ten present and predictable changes are listed in this chapter. In your opinion, which of these are likely to have the most prominent impact on the church as a whole in the twenty-first century? Why?

3. The process of implementing change has been described in three steps—unfreezing, changing, and refreezing. Do you agree or disagree? Explain, and describe a time you have witnessed this process in action.

4. It has been said that the only person who likes change is a baby with a wet diaper. Why do people (including you) resist change? How may resistance be tempered?

5. What kind of changes seem to bother you most? What kind seem to bother you longer than most? Discuss these two types of personal changes.

12

STRATEGIC FORMULATION

Coaches study their opponents' weaknesses. They then formulate a game plan, using those plays best suited for beating the competitors. They plan how to overcome their opponent's strengths and maximize their own. The coach dedicates the week before the game to training, practicing, and attempting to simulate the events in the game. The question both coaches and team members wrestle with during the week is, "When the heat is on, how will we perform?"

Business leaders conduct environmental analyses to learn their strengths and weaknesses. They formulate plans to capitalize on their competition's weaknesses and minimize their own. They attempt to take advantage of opportunities and to avoid and overcome threats. They prepare to meet challenges and changing conditions in order to continue growing and profiting.

Church leaders must take these same actions. They must formulate and implement strategies to effect change. They base their growth strategy on research and analysis to determine internal strengths/weaknesses and external opportunities/threats. Their strategies capitalize on their church's strengths, overcome its weaknesses, take advantage of key external opportunities, and avoid external threats. Transformational leaders *plan* for the future.

Deciding What to Do

Formulating strategy is essentially deciding what to do. To accomplish this, transformational leaders analyze their environment (chap. 11) to provide pertinent information. Specifically, they answer these questions:

1. Where has the congregation been? What has been accomplished?

2. What are the congregation's specific purposes? target market? talents and interests? outreach possibilities/opportunities?

3. Where is the congregation presently heading?

4. What critical environmental factors does the congregation face? This would include economic, political, demographic, and legal/ethical forces.

5. What can be done to achieve objectives more effectively in the future?

Christian leaders must not shy away from these questions. Jesus emphasized the importance of such strategic analysis when he said:

"Suppose one of you wants to build a tower. Will he not first sit down and estimate the cost to see if he has enough money to complete it? For if he lays the foundation and is not able to finish it, everyone who sees it will ridicule him.

"Or suppose a king is about to go to war against another king. Will he not first sit down and consider whether he is able with ten thousand men to oppose the one coming against him with twenty thousand?" (Luke 14:28–31).

Transformational leaders think about implementing strategy even while they are forming their strategy. They think about implementation at each step of strategy development, evaluation, and decision making.

Identifying Values and Aspirations

Our values, aspirations, and ideals influence the future of our churches. Transformational leaders know that what needs to be done is critical to deciding what to do, that is, in formulating strategy. There is no way to divorce a strategic decision from the personal values of those who decide.[1]

Awareness that our own preference for an alternative opposed by another stems from values as much as from rational estimates of economic opportunity may have important consequences. First, it may make us more tolerant and less indignant when we perceive this relationship between recommendations and values in the formulations of others. Second, it will force us to consider how important it really is to us to maintain a particular value in making a particular decision. Third, it may give us insight with which to identify our biases and pave the way for a more objective assessment of all the strategic alternatives that are available.[2]

Transformational leaders know that members sometimes cannot agree on a future direction for their church. They diagnose potential conflict by dealing with the values implicit in how people choose paths. These values ultimately influence motivation and commitment.

One way to deal with individual values and aspirations is to ask the congregation to write a statement of tenets and a statement of mission. *Tenets are the fundamental principles or doctrines held by a person or an organization, the values that underlie all actions.*

After I was elected dean of Azusa Pacific University's School of Business and Management, the school adopted the following tenets:

1. *Christian Witness*—Impacting students' lives for Christ through example and leadership.

2. *Ethics*—Teaching biblical principles in the ethical conduct of business.

3. *Relationships*—Nurturing a caring relationship between student and teacher.

4. *Learning*—Sustaining a learning environment which fosters open inquiry, expression of thought, critical analysis, and creative thinking.

5. *Practicality*—Linking learning to life in practical ways.

6. *Excellence*—Demonstrating excellence in teaching, service, and research.

7. *Academic Freedom*—Creating an environment for faculty characterized by academic freedom and responsible autonomy, professional development, and collegial relationships.

8. *Community Development*—Enhancing the development of organizations and communities served by the university.[3]

Though formulating such a list is time-consuming (it may take a year), it is an exercise that will yield results and bond the members in a way that may have been impossible before. A church went through such a process and concluded that it was committed to these tenets:

1. To assemble regularly to partake of the Lord's Supper, sing hymns, pray, and edify each other through the Word of God.

2. To share the congregation's wealth for the help and comfort of the poor and needy and the fulfillment of our Lord's Commission to make disciples of all nations.

3. To deal with each other and all people with the love with which Christ loved us.

4. Not to be bound by human traditions, but only by the truth of the gospel and true apostolic teachings; exercise fully the freedom in Christ in the conduct of assemblies and the performance of service to Christ.[4]

This tenet-writing activity brings focus on who is head of the church and why he put his children in the church. Writing out these tenets will help any church or ongoing group or class, large or small.

A mission statement is an enduring statement of purpose that distinguishes one business from another. It identifies the scope of operation. General Motor's Saturn Division drafted the following mission: "Market vehicles developed and manufactured in the United States that are world leaders in quality, cost, and customer satisfaction through the integration of people, technology, and business systems and to transfer knowledge and experience throughout General Motors."[5] The mission statement at one university is: "To educate our students for Christian service and leadership throughout the world."[6] A church adopted the following mission statement: "We hold as our primary goals: To know Christ and communicate that knowledge of Him to others."[7] This statement defines where the church is headed and what it can accomplish. (Of course, the Bible also has much to say about the church's purpose.)

Determining Alternatives

Matching a congregation's internal strengths and weaknesses with external opportunities and threats is central to strategy formulation. *Matching* means lining up internal factors with external factors to formulate feasible strategies. Before matching strengths and weaknesses with opportunities and threats, leaders must identify strengths and weaknesses. Once they have analyzed these factors objectively, realistically, and critically, and once they have made a match, their next step is decision making.

Leaders must decide what objectives to establish and which strategies to pursue. Every church has limited resources, so leaders must select from among various potentially beneficial goals and strategies. Then they must prioritize these goals. In a town of thirty-five thousand adjacent to a major university in Oklahoma, a congregation's main mission is to prepare college students to go out into the world as ambassadors for the Lord. That church dedicates a large component of their budget to university outreach, and they constantly reinforce this mission. They have established programs to teach English to international students by using the Bible.

A congregation in Texas developed a different strategy for long-range planning. Their initial goal was to look at all the problems of the church for the next five years. A former staff member was appointed chair of the committee. The committee comprises members from different strata and interests within the congregation. One of their first tasks was to prepare a profile of the membership, using data from a congregational survey. They have studied research techniques and have researched a great deal of literature. They have identified several emphases of their church: evangelism, education, missions, worship, and congregational life. After their initial work, they broadened the base of what they were doing with input from the minister, other leaders in the congregation, and members selected at random. They are enthusiastic and committed to strategic planning.

Analysis like this, combined with prayer and sound judgment, lays a base for good decisions. The way Christian leaders solve problems affects what happens to them and to others with whom they live, work, worship, and socialize. If leaders generate interest in a program, their enthusiasm will soon spread to other church members.

Establishing Goals

Strategy is a set of goals and policies. At face value, this description seems simple. People have been setting goals and mapping out strategies to achieve them since childhood. However, to get an A in biology class, make a touchdown, hit a home run, learn to drive a car, graduate from college, and get a good job can be problematic without a plan.

Strategic goals involve plans for an extended period, often from five to ten years. They involve deciding where a congregation is now, where it could or should be at some point in the future, and what resources will be necessary to get it there.

Churches normally have one of two kinds of broad goals: survival goals and mission goals. *Survival goals* generally are internal—body life, membership drive, budget, and building. *Mission goals* are focused outward on opportunities for new ministries, evangelism, and community involvement. Pity the congregation that plans only for survival. They are unable to turn dreams into deeds and further expand the kingdom of God.

Never underestimate the power of dreams. On one occasion a friend complained to Henry David Thoreau, "I'll never be a success . . . apparently my values are all mixed up. I'm just a dreamer." Thoreau replied, "Don't worry about it. You've already mentioned one important value: the ability to dream. If you dream of a castle in the air, the effort you've expended need not be in vain, that's where a castle should be. Now, put a foundation under it."

The foundation of every dream of accomplishment, of every vision for the Lord's church, is a well-defined, measurable program of goals. But never confuse a goal with a wish. A *wish* is a vague idea of something hoped for; it may even be something one is not working to obtain. A *goal* is a practical and effective way of changing dreams into reality. Thus goals indicate what a church is trying to achieve and become.

One morning Winnie the Pooh and Piglet were out walking. Piglet turned to Winnie and said, "Winnie, what's the first thing that you think of every morning when you wake up?" Winnie replied, "I always think, 'What's for breakfast?' What do you think of, Piglet?" Piglet answered, "I always wonder what exciting things will happen today." These are the basic dreams of most people: a breakfast dream or an excitement dream. The breakfast dream is about maintenance; the excitement dream is about vision. Transformational leaders know they have to have a dream of what exciting things can be in the church if they expect to accomplish anything.

Introspection

Transformational leaders assess their own strengths and weaknesses and their members' strengths and weaknesses. An idea seldom gets launched unless the leader endorses it—not even an idea backed by a "product champion." Leaders must sanction the idea because they decide where the congregation is going.

Introspection also allows church leaders to get in touch with God. God makes it clear that he has goals and objectives for his people. To Jeremiah was said, "Before I formed you in the womb I knew you, before you were born I set you apart; I appointed you as a prophet to the nations" (Jer. 1:5). Later God informed Jeremiah of his plans to give hope and a future (29:11). Goals must result from the leaders' thoughtful introspection and openness to God's plan for them or for their church.

Once leaders and members know through faith what God desires for them, then they must recognize him as their power source for accomplishing goals and objectives. "In his heart a man plans his course, but the Lord determines his steps" (Prov. 16:9). Once strategies are formulated and implemented, God produces the results (see 1 Cor. 3:6).

Achievement

To clearly and concisely define expected achievements, transformational leaders state what they hope to do about their environment. Thus, they assign priorities. They develop a written plan and set target deadlines.

Just think of how many deadline-oriented schedules went into the 1984 Los Angeles Olympics (the first Olympics to turn a profit) or the 1996 Atlanta Olympic Games. Without deadlines, the events would be disastrous. Deadlines create challenges for response. They also reveal the sincerity of leaders about goal accomplishment. In fact, a sincere desire to achieve a goal and be accountable for it may be the real difference between goals and wishes.

Adherents of positive living and success motivation claim there is no limit to what may be achieved when a goal is fueled and sparked by sincere desire. They point to people with disabilities who undertake incredible challenges like climbing a mountain, skiing, or wheeling themselves across the country. Achievement is goal-driven.

Becoming

Positive thinkers believe people turn desires into reality. Yes, attitudes do influence actions, but attitudes alone cannot accomplish plans. People have very little power over spiritual circumstances. Consider: "This is what the Lord says: 'Cursed is the one who trusts in man, who depends on flesh for his strength and whose heart turns away from the Lord. He will be like a bush in the wastelands; he will not see prosperity when it comes. He will dwell in the parched places of the desert, in a salt land where no one lives'" (Jer. 17:5–6).

God's Word sharply contrasts those who attempt to be all that they can be by trusting self, and those who attempt to become what God leads them to become. "But blessed is the man who trusts in the Lord, whose confidence is in him. He will be like a tree planted by the water that sends out its roots by the stream. It does not fear when heat comes; its leaves are always green. It has no worries in a year of drought and never fails to bear fruit" (17:7–8).

Here's a related thought about achieving and becoming: "The size of your goal reflects the size of your God." Your concept of God determines what you ask for and what you receive. God can do more than we could possibly think or request. "Therefore I tell you, whatever you ask for in prayer, believe that you have received it, and it will be yours" (Mark 11:24).

141

Clearing the Path to the Goals

A person's goals determine his or her task motivation. Like time management, the more that is on a person's plate, the better organized he or she is and the more that person can accomplish. The collegiate athlete who excels on the football field and in the classroom during the fall season may slack off in the off season. Hard goals result in greater effort than easy goals, and specific goals result in higher effort than no goals or more generalized goals.[8] Research generally supports these propositions so long as the goals are accepted by those for whom they are intended. Thus transformational leaders are concerned with setting clear, challenging, and specific goals for their churches.

Path-goal motivation builds on the relationship between tasks and goals, between people's behavior and their goal attainment/need satisfaction. The basic postulate of this motivational theory is that a leader's function is to set important goals for or with followers and clear their paths to those goals. For example:

- "Teach me to do your will, for you are my God; may your good Spirit lead me on level ground" (Ps. 143:10).

- "Make level paths for your feet and take only ways that are firm. Do not swerve to the right or the left; keep your foot from evil" (Prov. 4:26–27).

- "Make level paths for your feet." (Heb. 12:13).

Church members must perceive that the paths to the goals are level and that they can achieve their goals. If the goals are attainable, the usual results are satisfaction, higher performance, and personal and congregational growth. "Strategy is a human construction; it must in the long run be responsive to human needs. It must ultimately inspire commitment. It must stir an organization to successful striving against competition. People have to have their hearts in it."[9]

Christians will commit themselves to a church, a pastor, or a group of leaders who are directing them along a particular path. The hope is that, even more, they will "commit themselves to their faithful Creator and continue to do good" (1 Pet. 4:19).

Changing the Future

Two churches illustrate the importance of carefully analyzing the environment, checking the vision, and setting goals. The first developed an internal growth strategy; the second, a turnaround strategy.

Change by an Internal Growth Strategy[10]

Houston's Second Baptist Church is one of the nation's largest churches and has a Sunday morning attendance of twelve thousand plus a campus that covers thirty-two acres. In 1984, however, it was simply a conventional church on a large plot of land. A new pastor, H. Edwin Young, had just been hired. He studied the demographics of the area and discovered that closeby were thousands of young families and single people new to Houston. He sold his vision of a growing church to his congregation and persuaded them to pledge more than $17 million needed for new physical facilities. The church borrowed over $26 million for additional construction costs.

Church members were dispatched to study office management techniques at Xerox and IBM, parking and people skills at Disney World. Young changed and varied religious services to fit particular needs of the people attending. Sunday morning services remained traditional, but a Sunday evening service was added that caters to a mostly singles crowd. On Wednesday nights, separate services were offered, one traditional and one with religious rock music.

Today, computers regulate mood lighting during church services. Shuttle buses bring latecomers in from outlying parking decks. Parking attendants empty the church's numerous parking lots every Sunday in half an hour. Billboards and television advertisements invite people to visit this "Fellowship of Excitement." An information desk is staffed with cheerful attendants. Aerobics classes are held daily beginning at 6 A.M. A restaurant offers two types of food: the regular Sinners Menu and the low-calorie Saints Menu.

This revolutionary change came about because Christian leaders were willing to use their God-given initiative "to dream the impossible dream" and to formulate a strategy to get them there. Fifteen years ago few churches were willing to try what this church did. But today more than twenty thousand churches have memberships of at least two thousand. In fact, some five thousand congregations have memberships of more than four thousand.

More and more Christians are so bored with traditional churches that they stay home. Successful churches follow a very simple strategic process:

- Successful churches see a major opportunity in America's expanding demographic niches: the seniors and the younger, educated two-earner families.

- Successful churches ask what these "potential customers" need and want in a church.

- Successful churches focus on the individual's spiritual wants.

- Successful churches focus on the individual's need for a freely chosen but close community.

- Successful churches try to satisfy the desire of affluent younger people to be put to work and to hold positions of responsibility in the church.[11]

Leaders of these successful churches recognize that marketing action, not just knowledge, is required in this turbulent, competitive, fast-changing decade. Compare these successful churches with GM's Saturn, Ford's Explorer, or Nissan's Altima. The external marketing strategies of these car companies have gobbled up market shares. The Christian world is called to do no less.

Change by a Turnaround Strategy

The U.S. Catholic church has been trying to overcome stagnant revenues and steadily rising costs. The Archdiocese of Chicago has taken the following steps:

1. Sold assets of $6.2 million.

2. Restructured archdiocese offices and laid off fifty employees to save $1.5 million.

3. Required all parishes to submit three-year budgets and quarterly financial reports.

4. Established a local clergy advisory board of business leaders in each parish.

5. Devised repayment plans for loans made to parishes and began charging interest on those loans.

6. Increased tuition at parochial schools.

7. Raised the assessment each parish pays the archdiocese from 6.5 to 10 percent of its annual revenues.

8. Consolidated parishes and schools in the archdiocese.

9. Encouraged church members to increase their giving.

10. Began marketing the services of the church to new groups including young adults.[12]

Planning for change met with some resistance, but Cardinal Joseph Bernardin maintained that there was little choice. He emphasized that to "fulfill our mission, we have to have the resources."[13]

A well-defined mission and clear goals are essential to an organization's success. Businesses can easily measure sales, profits, market share, and return on investment. But goals of not-for-profit organizations are value-laden, and this makes them harder to measure. Therefore, leaders must learn to deal with conflict in order to implement their strategies (chap. 13). They must formulate and implement strategies in ways that capitalize on the strengths of the church leaders, regardless of the size of the congregation. But leaders must recognize, avoid, and/or solve conflicts or potential conflicts.

— — —

Pause to Reflect

1. Consider the five questions listed near the beginning of this chapter that will help your church decide what to do about the future. Why would Christian leaders shy away from determining answers for such questions?

2. Interpret Luke 14:28–33. Why is it important to think about implementing strategy before or during the formulation process?

3. Discuss the relationship of personal preference to choice of vision and strategy. Why is it important to deal with the personal values implicit in alternatives people choose or decisions they make?

4. Review the current goals of your congregation. Are they survival or mission goals? How can you turn the previously established goals into deeds and further expand the kingdom of God? What new goals need to be set?

5. Check a concordance for Scripture passages that are pertinent to the word "level." Do you agree that the role of a Christian leader is to smooth or make level the path to goal accomplishment in a church? Explain.

13

TRANSFORMATIONAL CONFLICT

Conflict is a disagreement about beliefs or goals, a discord between two or more people, usually ending in confrontation. Conflict may range from mild disagreement to a complete breakdown of a relationship. Conflict is beneficial if it helps accomplish organizational goals. It is disruptive and destructive if it destroys or eliminates those attempting needed reform. To effectively implement strategy, Christian leaders must deal with conflict and its sources. Congregational stress is often a natural outgrowth of change and conflict. Both are ever-present. Thus the potential for stress is inevitable.

The Charles E. Fuller Institute of Church Growth and Evangelism in Pasadena, California, has developed "The Berry Bucket Theory." This is a constructive pastoral leadership model that helps to explain certain congregational tensions.

Picture two shelves with two buckets of berries on each. On the bottom shelf, in the left bucket, are the Senior Formerberries—those people who have been in the church for a long time, provide the major income in the church, and exercise control over budgetary matters. They have clout. In the other bucket on the bottom shelf are the Junior Formerberries—children of the Senior Formerberries or those reared in the church.

On the top shelf, in the left bucket, are the Senior Newberries—those individuals older than the pastor who have come into the church within the last several years. In the right bucket are the Junior Newberries—those younger than the pastor who have recently come into the church.

If the active Newberries are comparable in number to the active Formerberries, a time of delicate balance (at best) or crisis (at worst) will take place. Here is the key to understanding this tension: Senior Formerberries expect the pastor to receive instructions, not to give orders. He or she is the chaplain, not the commander. Junior Formerberries see the pastor as the one who makes things happen. They hope for strong leadership and are most likely to be supportive of new ideas and programs.

Because the agendas of the two groups are different, berry battles (or turf conflicts) may begin. Polarization during this time is common. Some berries on both shelves make it through this period; others grow apathetic and move to a different congregation. Disillusioned berries may feel they have been stomped on or that they are being allowed to rot. They have been denied the mechanisms of church change. They lose faith in the leaders of the church (i.e., the farmers of the orchard).

> Helping bring together the Formerberries and the Newberries can seem endlessly time consuming. However, it is absolutely necessary. Until pastors form relationships with the more tenured members, they will not be able to lead the church effectively through either lasting growth or change.
>
> Those relationships never come quickly. Because of this, the most productive period in a given pastorate usually will come after several years—and probably at least one survived leadership crisis. Ministries that build significant churches often last more than a decade.
>
> To survive that decade or more with aplomb requires a pastor to know from which bucket a berry comes.[1]

From which bucket has the leadership of your congregation been picked? Is the leadership cloned? Is there a leadership problem in the congregation? Can you hear winds of discord whistling through your orchard?

Conflict should not exist either in or between churches. Rather than fight one another, Christians should rejoice when others are winning people to Christ and unite to fight Satan. As someone has said, "The fruit of Christian unity grows out of our union with Christ."

Sources of Conflict

Most Christians dislike conflict. They expect their church to be a community of reconciliation and wholeness. Many have not discovered the power of the negative and feel that all conflict is un-Christian.[2] Some people think they can promote peace by never mentioning conflict. But conflict is here to stay. Potential misunderstandings result in stressful conflicts every day. Congregations with a history of evangelism or benevolence sometimes threaten to divide without discussing their differences.

Some of the most common sources of conflict include human aggressiveness, competition for limited resources, clashes of values and interests, role-based conflict, drives for power acquisition, poorly defined responsibilities, introduction of change, and the organizational climate.[3] These categories of conflict remind me of the Sharks and the Jets, two rival gangs in *Westside Story*. They fought with misguided passion for their "territory," and they clashed over misunderstandings due to different socioethnic backgrounds.

When Herbert W. Armstrong died in 1986, the Worldwide Church of God had one hundred thousand members and $200 million in annual income. Eight years later, turmoil over doctrine had seriously eroded both funds and followers. The erosion had perhaps been gradual. New leaders changed their standard on many of the doctrines that made them unique, shifting from rigid teachings to mainstream Christianity. This resulted in crisis and upheaval among the members.

It should be noted that "what causes fights and quarrels" are the "desires that battle within" people (see James 4:1). Selfish personal desires and passions are the true sources of all organizational conflict. And humanity will be destroyed if it keeps on "biting and devouring each other" (Gal. 5:15).

Three sources of conflict stand out in a church: communication, structure, and selfishness.

Communication Conflict

Communication conflicts often result in misunderstandings and produce stress. Three common sources of misunderstandings are semantics, lack of clarity, and too many links in the communication chain.

Semantics is the study of word meanings and focuses on the relationship between words and their effect on people. Semantics does not refer to dictionary definitions of words. Rather it supports the idea that meanings are in people. If one wants to know what a word means as a certain person uses it, one must ask the person for the definition instead of consulting a compendium of meanings. In the O. J. Simpson trial, Salvadorian Rosa Lopez said, upon cross-examination, that her comments, "If you say so, sir" meant "yes," while "I don't know, sir" meant "no."

A person who learns English as a second language often adheres to a word's strict definition. Attempts at translation produce misunderstandings. The native speaker communicates via words packed with subtle meanings. And the student of English is often left confused—or even offended or angry in worst-case scenarios.

Transformational leaders select their words carefully in stating policies, instructions, directions, or orders. People think, feel, and act according to the images they allow their nervous system to create. They react to the world according to how they symbolize it. Transformational leaders respond sanely to others' words and with tolerance for differences. They thereby reduce stress and improve the congregational climate.

Lack of clarity suggests inadequate and unclear communication. Accurate and correct information is especially necessary in word instructions. The less detail given or the more ambiguous an instruction is, the more inaccurate detail members will supply and the more stressful the relationship will become. Transformational leaders plan communication paths that lead to understanding. They encode the words carefully. They do not expose their listeners to a barrage of words or lose them in a jargon jungle of word confusions. They put things in a lay person's language.

Too many links in the communication chain mean too many people through whom a message passes. If there are too many links and the receiver is far from the sender, there is more likelihood for misunderstandings. As the message travels down the chain, it will change, details will drop out, new details will be added, some things will be made more important, and some will become less important. The message will seldom arrive at its destination in the same context it began. The game "Gossip" or "Telephone" is a good example of what happens as communication travels from one person to another. A group sits in a circle and passes a message via whispers. By the time the message reaches the last person it has been altered significantly.

People's ideas, attitudes, and beliefs cause message distortion. The careless use of words or a reliance on wrong words to convey a meaning can result in a loss of understanding. And the more distorted a message becomes, the more stressful people become who recognize they are dealing with incomplete information.

These three sources of communication conflict (semantics, lack of clarity, and too many links in the communication chain) often put listeners in an ambiguous position because they do not fully understand what is expected. Most church members create enough stress for themselves and each other without leaders creating undue tension with inadequate instructions, nonlistening attitudes, and so forth.

Transformational leaders use several techniques to reduce communication stress. They provide recognition for jobs well done, help followers with their problems, provide adequate information on how to perform a task, and explain reasons for changes. They are open with their followers and keep them informed of what is happening.

Structural Conflict

Structure refers to the organizational factors a leader can control. These include size, goals, objectives, participation, responsibility, clear lines of authority, and homogeneity or heterogeneity of staff. Any of these factors, and a myriad of others, can create congregational stress. For example, if mission, authority, or responsibility are obscure, members will not know what is expected. Conflict will arise because of an incompatibility of expectations. The result will be stress.

Part of the daily wear-and-tear on congregational health and performance can be traced to dubiousness and conflict. What can be done about such pressures? The transformational leader observes these ten recommendations:

1. Do not overreact to crises. Scale down emotional reactions. Anger, panic, and frustration are inappropriate.

2. Do not take things personally. Criticism should relate to behavior and not the individual.

3. Do not worry about things that are beyond your control. Do everything possible to remedy an unsatisfactory situation. But once it is out of your hands, there is nothing more to worry about.

4. Learn to recognize personal tension symptoms. Recognize when emotional reserves are being taxed.

5. If possible, opt for a complete change of scene. Take a short vacation.

6. Discover diversions on the work scene. Go to the library and read; do knee bends and arm exercises in the office; socialize with colleagues.

7. Do not overorganize uncommitted time. Create a flexible schedule that fosters creativity and give in to a spur-of-the-moment impulse. Such behavior improves performance.

8. Rotate your "mind tires." Change the nature and pattern of how the work load is accomplished.

9. Tackle someone else's problem. Help others cope with their seemingly intractable difficulties.

10. After a mental workout at the office, put the body to work. Use sports, hobbies, or odd jobs to provide a much-needed reprieve from the problems at hand.[4]

Transformational leaders do everything possible to reduce communication stress and structural stress. They plan recreational activities with their followers—golf, tennis, table games, and other social events where laughter abounds. They recognize that the real culprit of conflict is selfishness; and the father of selfishness is Satan (see James 3:13–16).

Selfish Conflict

Selfishness probably begins at birth and ends at death. It is the mark of the spiritually uncontrolled person: "Me before you, always." "I'm the center of the universe." "I want what I want, because I want it." Such are the attitudes of selfishness. There is a joke on college campuses that asks, "How many freshman girls does it take to screw in a light bulb?" Answer: "One. She holds the bulb and the world revolves around her." Taken to an extreme, the selfish person does what the self wants, when the self wants, how the self wants, even if it hurts someone else.

Satan nurtures this selfish philosophy through slogans like these: "Watch out for Number One." "I owe it to myself." "It may cost more, but I'm worth it." "The most important person is me." These slogans are reminiscent of the "me" generation of the 1980s. They seem reasonable and logical on the surface, but they are impossible to reconcile with the biblical admonitions to be a good servant, to put others first, and to look to the needs of others.

Yet without exception when conflict exists within a congregation, it can be traced to a selfish spirit in one party, perhaps in both parties. Someone is not yielding body, mind, and spirit to God. God is not in control, for love does not insist on its own way (see 1 Cor. 13).

Transformational leaders pursue those things in life that enable them to be better servants. They do not place themselves at the center of the universe. Paul outlined the way to selfless living in these words: "Therefore, I urge you, brothers, in view of God's mercy, to offer your bodies as living sacrifices, holy and pleasing to God—this is your spiritual act of worship. Do not conform any longer to the pattern of this world, but be transformed by the renewing of your mind. Then you will be able to test and approve what God's will is—his good, pleasing and perfect will" (Rom. 12:1–2).

Paul also spoke about three "selfs"—body, mind, and life. Christians are called to yield all three (see Rom. 15:1–3; Col. 3:2). In doing so, one's life becomes a glory to God, which is spiritual worship. When one seeks to know and to respond to heavenly things, one proves the will of God by demonstrating God's goodness in one's own life.

The transformational leader recognizes that the critical key to avoiding conflict and getting members involved in productive activities is to help them see the importance of learning to serve (see John 13:1–7). The true servant—the selfless person—gains excitement and inspiration from making others happy and successful.

Results of Conflict

Conflict that results in open hostility can destroy successful churches and end friendships. A small congregation in Arizona went through a terrible split. Members disagreed on whether to care for orphans personally or institutionally. Friendships became so strained that those who believed in institutional support of orphans started another congregation. A third of the members joined this new church, while another third stayed at the old church. Worst of all, though, the remaining third dropped out of church entirely. The number of members was already so small that the split seriously crippled the work of both churches and was a black eye for them in the community.

After studying the situation for a year, a new preacher began to explore the possibility of getting the two congregations together. He invited a group from both factions to his church building to discuss reconciliation. Both groups had a very positive exchange and agreed to continue discussions. However, within a week after the meeting, he was severely chastised by the old guard (the Senior Formerberries) for even letting "those people" in the building. Twenty-five years have passed, and the two congregations are still split, still weak, and still in turmoil.

Negative Results of Conflict

Conflict can have at least three negative effects on members:

1. Conflict magnifies faults and weaknesses in others. Amidst conflict, people seek to justify their position and win the dispute. In attempting to "prove" my stand, I discredit your views. I focus on your life to show up additional faults and weaknesses to add support for my feelings and opinions. This only damages our relationships and weakens our organization's productivity.

2. Conflict creates divisions within the organization. Unresolved conflict is the cause of every church split, divorce, or labor strike (see Matt. 12:25). Division tears apart both large organizations and individual relationships and eventually destroys them.

3. Conflict wastes energies on nonproductive activities. Conflict leaves people physically and emotionally drained and consumes a great deal of "thinking time."[5]

Positive Results of Conflict

Conflict does not always have to end in hostility and fist-in-face confrontation. Disagreements can be beneficial.

1. Disagreement can lead to individual and organizational changes that ultimately produce improvements (see Prov. 27:17).

2. Disagreement can reveal the need for change. Mature leaders or managers welcome disagreement because it forces them to evaluate their own beliefs and make positive changes where needed (see Prov. 18:15).

3. Disagreement can help make people more tolerant of opposing views. Disagreement can become an excellent teacher of tolerance. Learning to accept differing viewpoints without developing hostile reactions is another mark of the mature leader (see Prov. 23:12). The effective manager learns to "agree to disagree." In doing so, one also learns to avoid developing a critical attitude even when others are critical and exhibit hostility toward him or her.[6]

When leaders can learn to agree to disagree, they will begin to see the value of Paul's statement: "If it is possible, as far as it depends on you, live at peace with everyone" (Rom. 12:18).

Confrontation

Change and conflict can lead to confrontation. Sometimes the only way to resolve disagreement is to approach it head on, face to face, with the individual or individuals involved.[7]

At an offsite Oklahoma church meeting a number of years ago, a group of individuals gathered to discuss the work of the church and its minister. Most of those present were open with their opinions of the ineffectiveness of the preacher and his work. The next morning at a local institution, the office manager, who was a member of the same congregation but not present at the meeting, confronted one of the informal leaders of the meeting. He asked, "Why are you trying to run off our preacher?" Several weeks later that same leader was told by the church elders that a certain member had left the church because he and others were trying to get rid of the preacher.

These same elders had sanctioned the original meeting and some were in attendance. The only way to deal with the issue was face-to-face with each person who felt the meeting leader had wronged the person who left the church. To compound the situation for this group leader, he was at that time under consideration to become a deacon, waiting approval of the congregation. Leaders of the church asked him to withdraw his name from consideration because of the ill feelings generated from the meeting that they approved. (It was three years before he was allowed to serve as a deacon, and even then some had not forgotten the above incident.)

When Christians Sin against One Another

The New Testament gives Christians an approach for handling confrontation successfully. Christ's model for reconciliation advises people to try working out differences privately; if this fails, they should take the matter to the elders and then to the entire church (Matt. 18:15–20). (See Box 13.1)

Box 13.1

A Scriptural Approach to Confrontation

1. Deal with facts, not guesses or hearsay (Deut. 19:15). Conflict provides an excellent opportunity to serve others (Matt. 5:40–41).

2. Make the initial confrontation in private between you and the person involved (Prov. 25:7–10; Matt. 18:15).

   a. Be committed to resolving the conflict quickly. The longer it continues, the more difficult it is to resolve.

   b. Take the initiative in confronting those involved. Do not wait for those involved to approach you.

3. If the other person involved refuses to resolve the conflict, take someone with you and try again (Matt. 18:16). Even though hostility and anger may be present, avoid angry arguments (Prov. 14:29).

4. If the person continues to resist resolving the conflict, you may need to dissolve the relationship (Matt. 18:17).

5. If the other person is willing to repent and correct the problem, forgive him or her and continue the relationship—no matter how often conflicts continue to occur (Luke 17:3–4).

SOURCE: Adapted from M. Rush, *Management: A Biblical Approach* (Wheaton, Ill.: Victor, 1987), 212–15.

When churches can work toward peace, remembering they have been reconciled to Christ, harmony can result (2 Cor. 5:18–19).

When the Church Has Problems

Corinth was "sin city." The Corinthian church was a problem church. Check the conflicts: divisions (1 Cor. 3), sexual immorality (5; 6:12–20), lawsuits (6:1–11), and abuse of spiritual gifts (12–14). And there were cliques: the Paul, Apollos, Cephas, and Christ parties (1:10–13). Paul took three decisive actions to confront these problems:

1. He appealed to them in Christ's name to cooperate with one another.

2. He defined himself and announced that he was a minister and missionary, not a politician or party leader.

3. He pointed out that only Christ had died for the church.[8]

Christian leaders may assist with conflict management, but only Jesus can reconcile and make friends of enemies.[9]

When Christian Employees and Employers Disagree

The book of Philemon is a study in confrontation. Here is how Paul went about solving the issue:

1. He started on a positive note by using positive words (vv. 1–3).

2. He affirmed the other involved party's positive character qualities (vv. 4–7).

3. He based his approach on love and gentleness (vv. 8–9).

4. He made a request (vv. 9–16).

5. He was willing to be personally responsible to help right the wrong (vv. 17–18).

6. He anticipated a positive response to the confrontation (vv. 19–22).[10]

Change and conflict must be accepted as continuing results of people living, working, and worshiping together. Resolution of conflict by confrontation is a sensible solution for a more productive organizational environment, particularly during periods of change. Transformational leaders guide any energies being wasted in conflict into productive accomplishment of goals.

— — —

Pause to Reflect

1. The chapter contends that conflict is beneficial if it contributes to accomplishing goals. Do you agree or disagree? Why?

2. One result of conflict is open hostility that can destroy successful churches and end friendships. Have you observed this behavior? Discuss.

3. This chapter discusses three sources of conflict within the church. In your opinion, is one of these sources potentially more dangerous than the others? Explain.

4. Ultimately, it seems that both change and conflict lead to confrontation. Do you agree with this conclusion? Discuss.

5. Matthew 18:15–20 is often quoted as the scriptural approach to confrontation. Do you agree or disagree? Have you seen conflict handled diplomatically so that both sides end not only in a solution but also as friends? Describe the situation.

14

STRATEGIC IMPLEMENTATION

Once established, strategies must be put to work. Strategy implementation implies action—mobilizing members and leaders. This requires personal discipline, commitment, and sacrifice. But implementation is worth the effort because unimplemented strategies serve no purpose.

Strategy implementation is designed to achieve results. It hinges on four possible relationships between Christian leaders and church members. (See box 14.1.) These relationships depend on how well the leader understands the members' needs, wants, and abilities, and how well the members understand the leader's plan. Either group may choose to understand or not to understand. When either group chooses not to understand, they are working at cross purposes.

To facilitate strategic implementation, transformational leaders think in terms of action. They consider the following actions for change:

1. Examine the internal and external forces that require a change.

2. Diagnose the reasons for change.

3. Determine an appropriate intervention to introduce change.

4. Examine the constraints and limitations that may inhibit change.

5. Identify the performance objectives and outcomes.

6. Apply methods to implement change.

Box 14.1

IMPLEMENTATION RELATIONSHIPS BETWEEN CHRISTIAN LEADERS AND CHURCH MEMBERS

	Members do not understand the plan.	Members do understand the plan.
Leaders do not understand members' needs, wants, and abilities.	**Failed Implementation** Power and authority are the only available approaches.	**Partial Implementation** Participation and education are possible approaches.
Leaders do understand the members' needs, wants, and abilities.	**Partial Implementation** Motivation and selling are possible approaches.	**Full Implementation** Requires full use of the change process.

Adapted from A. J. Rowe, R. O. Mason, K. E. Dickel, R. B. Mann, and R. J. Mockler, *Strategic Management: A Methodological Approach,* 4th ed. (Reading, Mass.: Addison-Wesley, 1994), 483.

7. Provide means for evaluating the effectiveness of implementation and feedback mechanisms to correct the implementation if required.[1]

Transformational leaders attempt to reach a state of mutual understanding. They know that for comprehension, one needs openness and listening (attention), suspension of judgment, congruence (agreement), and feedback (reaction). Therefore, they focus attention on their messages, motivate their listeners, tailor the information to their audience, talk about familiar and understandable things, repeat the important points in their message, and use illustrations to achieve understanding.

In order to develop confidence, reliance, expectation, and hope, transformational leaders develop communication policies of openness, honesty, and trust. They encourage people to be credible sources. They improve the two-way flow of information and promote good listening habits. They are empathetic and recognize that listening is an active process involving meanings, feelings, and cues. They are responsive to what is heard, read, and seen. They believe that feedback is helpful and that they are responsible for it. They know how to give and receive constructive criticism. They place a high priority on understanding. These measures build bridges between Christian leaders and church members and provide answers to communication problems.

Strategy implementation impacts everyone. It may be thought of in three phases: structuring for strategy, controlling for success, and focusing ministry efforts.

Structuring for Strategy

The successful functioning of the church requires much more than drawing an organizational chart or describing well-designed jobs. It is more than deciding who performs what tasks or who works with whom. It is more than identifying the main trends of organizational structure in modern management theory. Transformational leaders set into motion an organization that works efficiently and effectively toward its desired end—the salvation of souls.

Certainly the church is not a business entity, although often it must operate as one. Religious groups with worldwide ministries must remember that the church is a body with a distinct head, Jesus Christ (Eph. 1:22–23). The New Testament presents at least six models of the church:

1. *The church is a society subordinate to no other and lacking nothing.* It has structures, rights, offices, and power. There are three primary functions—teaching, sanctifying, and governing.

2. *The church is a communion between the horizontal and vertical dimensions of spiritual life.* Its goals are both spiritual and supernatural, leading people into communion with God.

3. *The church is an outward sign, instituted by God to give grace.* It links the church of today with the church of the New Testament and bears witness to the true nature and meaning of grace as a gift from God.

4. *The church is a herald.* It has received an official message and is commissioned to pass that message to others.

5. *The church is a servant to all people.* Its mission is to help all, wherever they are, and promote their reconciliation to God.

6. *The church is a community of disciples.* As such, it calls Christians to suffering and renunciation, to a new life in Christ. Its goal is to disciple people.[2]

Whichever structure is adopted, one basic reality must be accepted: Jesus Christ is the head of the church (Eph. 1:22–23; 4:15; Col. 1:18).

> If we are a body and Jesus is our head then organizational structures and leadership functions should vary significantly from forms and functions appropriate to any other kind of organization—even those institutions ordained by God for his Old Testament people. . . . In the New Testament the people of God are organically related to Jesus as a body is to its head. Principles from the Old Testament in which the people of God were associated with one another in a national institution or in tribal institutions, hold no normative parallels for our understanding.[3]

Following this analogy, Christians are members of a living organism (1 Cor. 12:27). Each member is linked to every other member intimately, and each has a certain function to perform (Rom. 12:4–8; 1 Cor. 12:12–31; Eph. 4:11–13). Christians are members of the body, not an enterprise, institution, or industry, and are expected to grow (Eph. 4:14–16; Heb. 5:12–14). Any church not growing has disconnected itself from its head (Col. 2:18–19).

In addition, the church exists to carry out the continuing mission of Christ (Acts 1:8).

> Wherever believers walk, Jesus' presence should be felt. The more Christians grow and mature into his likeness, the more his body will respond as he did to meet human needs and to accomplish the goals of God in the world.
>
> Jesus is present.
>
> Leaders do not need to organize "programs" to make his presence felt. Instead they need to concentrate on the growth that brings members to maturity and Christlikeness, confident that Jesus will express himself through them in a dynamic world. Because Jesus is with them, they can touch the world around them as Jesus Christ touched his world.[4]

The church is an organism expected to grow and minister to others. Transformational leaders place an emphasis on service in all planning, organizing, motivating, and controlling activities. They recognize they are responsible for feeding Jesus' lambs, taking care of his sheep, and feeding his sheep (see John 21:15–23). For only then can the church be structured strategically for godly ministry.

Controlling for Success

Strategic control determines whether an organization's strategies are successful in reaching its goals. If strategies are failing, then controls are typically modified so goals may be achieved.

In some ways, strategic control is similar to the control exercised at a dam. The engineer controls the water flow needed for the community below. Too much water encourages uncontrolled growth; too little withers growth.

Although "control" is generally discussed as budgeting, strategic control is much broader than simply controlling budgeted expenditures. Two factors are pivotal: establishing policies and allocating resources.

Establishing Policies

Policies are rules or guidelines that express the limits within which actions occur.[5] These rules also may take the form of contingent decisions for resolving conflict between or among goals. Policies guide the thinking, decision making, and actions of followers in strategic management. Policies may be segmented into two categories—strategic policies and implementation policies.

Strategic policies guide the strategic planning process in an organization. Issues involved in setting policies for a congregation include scope of the congregation's activities, congregational image, fundamental goals/ objectives, societal/community responsibility, and congregational orientation.

Implementation policies guide the strategy implementation process.[6] Among the issues involved in implementing policies are type of structure, leadership styles, motivation systems, coordination techniques, and evaluation systems.

Whatever the policies, transformational leaders assume flexibility and do not etch operational rules in concrete. They are consistent with the congregation's environment, internally and externally.

Allocating Resources

Strategy implementation also consists of allocating resources according to goal priorities. The process typically involves reviewing budgets, revising program scheduling, initiating strategic planning, planning personnel load, and setting objectives. The ultimate decision is who gets how much. Thus two issues stand out:

- What budgets and programs are needed by each group to carry out its part of the strategic plan;

- How to focus people's energies on achieving organization-wide objectives as opposed to just carrying out assigned duties.[7]

How well these two issues are handled determines whether an organization is results-oriented and directed toward strategy accomplishment or is bogged down and wandering off the path.

All ministry groups of a congregation must have the resources, both human and financial, they need to carry out their programs. Here are some examples of resource allocation issues:

1. How many extra dollars to allocate to a department trying to rebuild and reposition itself after a period of decline and weakness.

2. How much to budget for advertising and promotion of evangelistic efforts.

3. What extra resources it will take to assimilate a newly acquired computer and software system and establish effective reporting measures and financial controls.

4. What extra research and study efforts will have to be made to establish a church growth program.

5. What additional resources it will take to bring a new ministry to fruition on schedule.

6. What are the resource allocation implications of shifting from a grow-and-build strategy to a maintain-and-hold posture.

7. What it will cost to build a distinctive competence in providing support services to the community.[8]

How well strategists resolve such decisions determines success. Transformational leaders shift resources in support of strategic change.

Focusing Ministry Efforts

Critical tasks and key activities are linked directly and clearly to strategy implementation activities. Matching structure to strategy provides valuable linkage. Most ineffective and unsuccessful organizations have low member involvement and interest and lack performance results.[9] Restrictions such as these commonly plague congregations:

1. Their general meetings are large and formal.
2. Their leaders and members have little candid interaction.
3. Their leaders participate little in departmental/divisional meetings.
4. Some of their members are not personally familiar with others, thus reducing the warmth and openness of the interaction.
5. Their members feel that leaders have little interest in their ideas.
6. Their members feel little influence upon the congregation.

Effective and successful organizations have high member involvement and good results. These congregations have these characteristics in common:

1. Their members are encouraged by other members to be involved in the work of the congregation.
2. Their basic unit for action is a small group, and the optimum size is twelve to twenty people.
3. Their leadership holds ultimate responsibility for the congregation's various functions.
4. Communication flow is sustained by having committees and departments united by common members and leaders.
5. Face-to-face interaction within groups is the basic mode of operation.
6. Group meetings are warm, close, and candid with feelings freely expressed as opposed to formal meetings where standard rules for motions and discussions are employed.
7. There is a free flow of communication between leaders and individual members.
8. The congregation sustains a minimum number of organizational layers.
9. Members recognize that the leadership has an attitude of acceptance and support.

Transformational leaders look inward, analyzing whether they are promoting effective growth or hindering excellence. True, a congregation may grow in spite of its leadership. But a congregation with absentee leaders (absent physically, mentally, or spiritually) cannot sustain growth, nor can a congregation with a structure that does not follow strategy. Organizational structure should flow from decisions about strategic direction; but the existing structure determines what the organization can actually do.[10] When the structure of a church is out of sync with the members, it is little wonder they do not demonstrate loyalty to the leadership. And it is little wonder that ministry efforts suffer.

For effective strategy implementation, the transformational leader masters the art of communication (chap. 15).

— — —

Pause to Reflect

1. Read the scriptural texts (Eph. 1:22–23; 4:15; Col. 1:18) that describe Jesus Christ as the head of the church. What do these texts mean to you and to the members of your congregation? What are the implications for Christian leaders?

2. Review this year's budget at your church. How are resources allocated? Who makes and/or approves the decisions about who gets how much? Is your process viewed as fair and equitable? Why or why not?

3. Compare the characteristics of an effective church described in this chapter with your church. How do they compare? How are they different? What are some things that could be done to make your church even more effective than it already is?

4. Compare your congregation's strategy implementation processes with those of other congregations within your denomination (or of similar congregations). What have you learned that can be applied to your church's strategic planning and implementation? What is the role leaders must play in this process?

5. Discuss the following statement: "Spiritual leaders must learn to feed Jesus' lambs, take care of his sheep, and feed his sheep. Only then can the church be really structured strategically for godly ministry." Do you agree? Why? What lessons do you see for Christian leadership?

15
TRANSFORMATIONAL COMMUNICATION

A football player once described the tactics of his high school coach. Before the game, the coach would inspire the team. He would talk to them about the smell of victory. Then he would describe what it was like to win and hear the roar of the crowd, to see the sparkle in a girlfriend's eye, to be congratulated by classmates in the hallway at school. The player said at the end of these pep talks they not only imagined victory, but they could smell, feel, and taste it. And they would go out to win the game.

The transformational leader uses communication as a tool to respond to challenges. No group, not even a church, can exist very long without good communication. Yet, communication is one of the least understood processes of interpersonal relationships. It involves the intentions of the speaker and the impressions of the hearer.

What Is Communication?

Communication involves one person transmitting information about something to another person, or vice versa. Although sending and receiving are essential, they do not adequately describe the importance of interpersonal communication.[1]

The best way to communicate to a person is through a person. The best person to use is one who is intimately related to you. That is what God did. He went beyond general revelation to speak more personally and fully to people through the prophets, and then he climaxed his communication and spoke to us in his Son (Heb. 1:1–3). He continues this incarnational type of communication to the world through Christians—who are intimately related to him (John 17:18; 20:21). Christ became flesh and "explained" the Father to the world (John 1:14–18). Now we have this same treasure (truth about God) in our earthen vessels and have the same responsibility to "explain" it to our world (2 Cor. 4:5–7).[2]

Communication is the essence of all personal and spiritual relationships. It is the focal point for transformational leaders, central to control and survival, and essential for followers. Much of Jesus' communication was comprised of dialogue with others. He often used inductive teaching methods such as questions, parables, and rhetorical thought. These prompted questions and answers. This inductive teaching manner may have been the key to his effectiveness as a communicator.

A Definition

For our purposes we adopt the following definition: *Communication is the sending and receiving of messages, the sharing of ideas and attitudes.* The word *messages* refers to the interpersonal side of communication. *Ideas* stress an intrapersonal view of communication. *Attitudes* overlap intrapersonal and interpersonal communication and suggest the importance of nonverbal communication. Successful communication results in understanding between sender and receiver.

Through communication people process information, test ideas, exchange opinions, and achieve consensus on decisions. Through communication they develop interpersonal relationships and form subgroups from a large number of individuals. Communication is the organizing medium for the transformational leader.

Communication Goals

For communication to be productive, those involved must see some reason for interaction. The most obvious goal is to be heard. There are, however, other goals that precede and succeed this vital goal. Here are five goals of communication:

Communication goal #1: To gain the receiver's attention. The sender wants the other person to listen to what he or she says. Imagine the frustration the receiver might experience when speaking before a group that is not paying attention. The speaker might as well be talking to a wall.

Communication goal #2: To achieve understanding. A transformational leader presents ideas or messages in a manner acceptable to the needs of the members. He or she makes sure the members structure ideas in their minds the same way the leader had originally framed them. The transformational leader knows that communication is basically a process of exchanging meanings. To attain understanding, the sender and receiver must perceive the purpose of the exchange, recognize whether the purpose is being achieved, and help each other achieve the purpose. Otherwise, there is no real need to communicate.

Communication goal #3: To gain acceptance of ideas. While acceptance may not be essential to getting others to do what the leader wishes; it is helpful for the long-run life of the group. Clearly, members are inclined to maintain satisfying relationships if they believe in their leaders and what they are doing. If either acceptance or agreement is impossible, a corollary goal should be to prompt the listener to think.

Communication goal #4: To gain productive action. Not only do transformational leaders want followers to listen to them, understand what they say, and accept their ideas; they also want followers to do what they suggest. Action is one way to check communication results. It is, in fact, the main criterion for speaking or writing. In an advertising campaign, an ad is written to produce results—to increase sales, promote an event, win a vote, or attract prospective customers. A successful ad increases those numbers. If market research has discovered an unfulfilled need, no response to an advertising campaign indicates a failure to communicate.

Communication goal #5: To strive to maintain good relationships with others. Friends understand one another much more quickly than opponents. When a transformational leader develops satisfying relationships, members are more likely to listen to what the leader says and respond as the leader desires.

Unfortunately some leaders operate as a board of directors. They think they can meet like politicians in smoke-filled rooms, making policy decisions and handing down edicts. But this excludes members from participation, at times rejecting or even ignoring their suggestions. Transformational leaders must avoid this nonproductive behavior and enter into congregational settings where communication and planning can take place.

Communication and Task Situations

It is impossible to discuss communication without relating it to task situations. Although a church is not a business in the traditional sense, it still has tasks to perform. Consequently, communication should be explored in terms of flows, networks, interactions, and feedback.

Communication Flows

Communication is often described as information flowing vertically or horizontally—up and down, back and forth. We can also contrast one-way and two-way flows. Two-way communication has an important advantage in decision making: those who have to carry out a proposal have an opportunity to react to it and contribute to the decision. But one-way communication also has its advantages: speed, simplification, and orderliness. Nonetheless, two-way communication is more valid since it allows for more accurate transmission of information.

Vertical communication involves messages that flow up and down an organizational hierarchy. Downward communication involves directives, policies, procedures, instructions, goals, or objectives. Leaders tell others what to do or pass on information needed to perform a job or service. They may use announcements, memorandums, Post-it™ Notes, or voice mail. However, if the communication is unclear, followers do not respond in the way leaders wish. And if it is limited, people will give only minimal compliance. Downward communication is a one-way process and can be stifling since people feel they have no say about how things are done.

Upward communication involves members' relaying information to their leaders. This type of message flow provides feedback. Therefore, it is two-way and, as a general rule, improves morale. People feel as though they have a voice in how things are done. Leaders who listen and observe their followers find many implicit messages being sent upward. Examples are poor attendance, boring preacher, meaningless lessons, and lack of interest in programs and plans. From such information, leaders can rectify ineffective practices, jump-start lifeless activities, and take other important steps to breathe new life into tired practices. Thus, upward communication benefits both a congregation and its members. Transformational leaders ensure that their communication lines are open, encouraged, and frequent. They not only keep their ears to the rail, but also they keep their eyes open for the train!

Both upward and downward communication are related to formal structures. Lines connect the various units within a church's hierarchy. Systems of responsibility and explicit delegations of duties are clearly drawn. Because of this high formality, some congregations try to establish more informal atmospheres. The Bible seems to favor communication in a "body" structure or a "vineyard" structure rather than a pyramidal structure. Transformational leaders, therefore, create a climate of acceptance, warmth, and listening rather than communicating authority and power.

Horizontal communication is usually the strongest flow of information because it allows for message exchange among people on the same level of authority. It typically leads to better understanding among members than vertical communication. Good horizontal communication includes task coordination, problem solving, information sharing, and conflict resolution. Additionally, horizontal communication provides a good opportunity to banish certain communication barriers by downplaying status.

The grapevine is communication that is fast and selective, and has churchwide influence. Vertical and horizontal communication are considered formal types of communication because they follow a chain of command on most organizational charts. A great deal of communication flows outside these formal channels and without official sanction. This is referred to as the grapevine, rumors, or gossip. It creates an informal structure that departs from formal tasks and hierarchy and develops its own channels of communication and dependence. I-heard-it-through-the-grapevine communication is strong, and it is here to stay. Transformational leaders know who passes on information. They understand how the grapevine works well enough to influence and use the grapevine network by supplying accurate data. They also use the grapevine to keep current on what members are thinking and saying.

Communication Networks

Every group develops its own structure and pattern of communication. These patterns connect the senders and receivers to a functioning social organization and are called networks. *Networks show who talks to whom.* Group size affects these communication networks. Members have fewer chances to speak in groups of twelve than in groups of five. Members feel threatened and inhibited in large groups. This is why discussion diminishes as group size increases. The distribution of participation also varies. The gap between the participator and the other group members grows as size increases.

The transformational leader develops a one-on-one network with various church members. This involves visiting with members professionally or socially, speaking with them at church assemblies, and doing things with them—Little League, soccer, football, cheerleading, theater. Whatever the situation, the transformational leader should allocate significant time to developing "a network of cooperative relationships" among both members and outsiders. In these networks "the nature of the relationships varies significantly in intensity and in type; some relationships are much stronger than others, some much more personal than others, and so on. Indeed, to some degree, every relationship in a network is different because it has a unique history, it is between unique people, and so forth."[3]

Networks often help leaders implement their agenda. That is, transformational leaders marshal their "interpersonal skills, budgetary resources, and information to influence people and events in a variety of direct and indirect ways."[4]

Communication Interactions

A person's behavior affects those in the group. One who chooses not to participate or communicate encourages other members to remain uninvolved. On the other hand, the member who gets involved encourages others and improves group interaction.

Two styles of interaction can influence a group: the peacemaker and the democratic group member. A *peacemaker* gets a consensus and keeps people together. A *democratic group leader* tries to include everyone in a discussion. By learning to be sensitive to the participation and interaction level of a group, the transformational leader discovers potential trouble spots. Knowing that the interaction skills of group members vary, the transformational leader emphasizes brevity, objectivity, and listening. This builds bridges, soothes hurt feelings, increases effectiveness, and solves problems before they get out of hand.

Communication Feedback

Feedback determines levels of understanding. Poor feedback saps a church's vitality, and problem-solving ability suffers. Group interaction is the communicative feedback provided by and for the members. Therefore, *feedback* refers to the responses a person makes to others. For example, one individual asks a question and someone responds to that question, comments, or expands upon another's suggestion. Each member then influences and is influenced by others. The terms *interaction* and *communication* are often used synonymously. There are two basic types of feedback: positive and negative.

Positive feedback reinforces and stimulates. A university president gave positive feedback when he wrote this note to faculty and staff:

Dear Friends,

We made it! We've just experienced what is possibly the most exhilarating yet most intense week of the school year on a university campus. Months of planning, times of refreshing and refueling, intense scholarship, and "plain-old" hard work have resulted in an excellent beginning for the 1994–95 year. I have seen countless demonstrations of love in action during the past 10 days. Thank you. [5]

Negative feedback counteracts and neutralizes. The university president who made the following pronouncement to faculty in one of his colleges can be certain his listeners will not continue to perform at high levels with motivation:

> Half of you people are vocational and worthless. The other half know absolutely nothing of the real world. Your research is of no value to anyone in business. Therefore, in the future all released time for research is to be funded only by extramural grants or restricted funds. If you don't like that, you know where the door is. We were looking for faculty when we hired you, and we can find others to take your place. However, don't all of you resign at the same time![6]

Groups use both positive and negative feedback to regulate their progress toward consensus decisions. Members tend to reinforce each others' acceptable behavior but punish deviant behavior.

Verbal feedback must be helpful to be useful. That is why feedback needs to be very specific. If recipients of feedback are to be helped, they need to understand what is said, be willing to accept it, and be able to do something about it. Trust must exist between leaders and followers before a message is accepted. The same is true of nonverbal feedback. Although it is very relevant, nonverbal behavior often seems vague and nonspecific.

A congregation in Nashville decided it needed more educational facilities. There was a vacant building on the property that was the old auditorium with a basement. Findings of an architectural study revealed that this building could be completely gutted inside. A three-story educational building would be the result, with some thirty-three thousand square feet of space. In order to communicate the need to the members, one Sunday morning all the adult classes toured the existing children's facilities. They found small, cramped rooms in some of the oldest parts of the building. It was difficult at best to teach in these circumstances. After clearly showing the need and allowing members to experience the situation firsthand, congregational dinners were held. It was estimated that the total project would take $1.5 million. The congregation was prepared with repeated announcements and bulletin articles. A multimedia presentation was given before the special collection. With such communication and backing from the leaders, the people felt they were a part of what was being done. And in one day, members gave a third of the amount needed. Amazing results can be generated if people understand

and support a project. That kind of clarity only comes through precise, frequent communication.

Transformational leaders use all available feedback to enhance their communication skills and abilities.

Recognizing Barriers to Communication

Communication difficulties result from both real and imagined problems. A *communication barrier* is anything that blocks the message flow so that a receiver does not get the intended message. When a breakdown occurs between the sender and receiver, nonproductive communication is the cause. New and better communication is needed to correct the problem. The transformational leader identifies communication barriers and works diligently to overcome them.

Nonproductive communication may occur because people do not want to communicate, they do not provide feedback, they fail to listen, or they try to show off their knowledge. Becoming aware of potential communication barriers is the starting point in coping with breakdowns. Anticipating, preventing, or easing them is the next logical step. Some common communication problems are "allness," bypassing, ambiguity, and status.

Allness

Allness is a tendency people have to believe that whatever they say about a particular subject is all there is to say about that topic. The person who says, "Don't confuse me with the facts; I already know what I want to know on this subject," is suffering from allness. It is a common affliction among many church leaders, especially ministers.

Transformational leaders remember that many particulars are left out of everything they say, hear, read, or write. There is always more information than what is presented. There is always an "et cetera"!

Bypassing

Bypassing is the tendency not to recognize that one word can have different meanings and that different words can have the same meaning. For example, when people refer to death, they use a whole gamut of words—"passed," "asleep in the Lord," "gone on before," "sleeping until Judgment Day," "ceased to be," or even phrases like "kicked the bucket" and "dead as a doornail." Yet all these phrases refer to the same thing.

Misunderstanding results when a leader assumes a church member is using words the same way he or she would use them. Communication breakdown is likely when people project their meanings into someone else's words. Whenever possible, find the most precise term to communicate meaning; avoid euphemisms. In the 1988 presidential debates, both Bush and Dukakis accused each other of "questionable judgment." What they really questioned was the other's competence and patriotism, yet each cloaked his accusation in vague language.

Transformational leaders look to people for meanings instead of to words. They are sensitive to the way words are currently used. Meanings are in people, not in words.

Ambiguity

Ambiguity, like bypassing, results because words mean different things in different contexts. One church leader said to a committee, "I know this person very well and cannot recommend him too highly!" What does that mean?

A mother asked her child to say grace, but the child did not know what to say. "Just say what Mommy says," replied the mother. Bowing her head the little girl prayed, "Dear God, why did we ever invite these people to lunch?"

The transformational leader learns to spot statements that can have several meanings and asks the speaker to clarify, paraphrase, or confirm. He or she asks for specific examples to avoid conflict and confusion.

Status

Communication problems also result from an involvement of different people's egos, status relationships, or positions. Status can be measured by job/profession, titles, offices, desk sizes, parking spaces, home location, car, degrees, spouse's position, and so forth. The two major status determinants are probably the nature of a person's work and the size of his or her paycheck. Dissatisfaction ensues when one person or group perceives another as out of line. Communication problems often arise, and the status ladder must be realigned to reduce the perceived inconsistencies.

The transformational leader works toward overcoming anything that interferes with his or her relationship with members. Even Jesus said, "There is only One who is good" (Matt. 19:17).

Listening to Discover Barriers

Good communication is at best a difficult process. Almost any serious effort to improve communication will have beneficial results. One of the best ways for the Christian leader to start improving communication is to become aware of communication problems. Normal communication often results in partial misunderstanding. Thus decisions must be made as to how large a margin of difference in understanding can be tolerated. Then, the leader must learn to cope with the problems.

When overcoming most barriers, very few verbal or nonverbal communication tools rival effective listening (see James 1:23–24). In fact, if more leaders were aware of the need for effective listening, they could probably double their knowledge and success. Unfortunately, many seem to have trouble paying attention to others. Research indicates most people experience a 75 percent loss of information within forty-eight hours. And what is worse, as ideas are communicated from one person to another person and etc., they are distorted by 80 percent. (Remember the telephone/gossip game?) Based on these figures, one might question a person's memory. However, it is difficult to remember what was not heard in the first place. Perhaps that is why many people seem to invent stories to tell others (while others take notes). Or why many people cannot remember the name of a person they were just introduced to five minutes ago.

The transformational leader becomes an effective listener, a person who is genuinely interested in what the other person is saying. Such a leader is a motivator. Members are usually more committed to a leader who is interested in their ideas and in them personally. Most people want to be heard. If the leader shows a willingness to listen to other's ideas, the speaker will reciprocate. "There is a time to be silent and a time to speak" (Eccl. 3:7). And sometimes silence speaks louder than any words.

Active Listening

Effective listening requires practice. Active listening relates to hearing, understanding, and responding as the message sender intended. Transformational leaders hear and react to the needs stated by their members. They practice the art of listening. Thus they are sought-after, trusted friends.

People often pretend to pay attention when they are not really listening. They may make eye contact, smile, and nod their heads knowingly, but their minds are on another subject. Others listen to every word until the speaker uses terminology that causes them to become so detached that they lose contact with what is actually being said. They become emotionally deaf. Other people let their egos get in the way. They think only about what concerns them. They are not interested in a statement unless there is something in it to enhance their status. Others are just lazy. They do not want to take the time or expend the energy it takes to listen.

Listening is the key to solving ethnic tensions as well: between the Arabs and Israelis, Protestants and Catholics in Northern Ireland, the

Serbs and Croats in former Yugoslavia. Warring factions are so wrapped up in their own agendas, they turn a deaf ear to the valid objectives of the opposition. On the other hand, active listening was a key to solving a problem between two ethnic groups in the infant church in Jerusalem (Acts 6:1–7). One group felt that their widows were being discriminated against in the distribution of food. So the apostles wisely listened to their complaint, worked out an acceptable solution, and settled the dispute. Showing love via active listening can bind Christians together in a common faith.

Transformational leaders understand the messages they receive. It is possible to hear but not actually receive a transmitted message. Two simple tools can be used to improve active listening skills immediately: confirmation and clarification. Confirmation helps one understand exactly what was said and why. For example: "So, are you saying you would be willing to . . . ?" Or, "It sounds like you are feeling some anger over this situation." It is especially helpful to someone who disagrees with the message or is being asked to become committed to a particular program. Whenever there is doubt about what is being sent or meant, one should confirm the message. They should make sure they know what was said and why before taking action. After all, if members do not have time to get it right the first time, when will they have time to do it over?

When a person does not understand a message or is not certain about a speaker's motives, he or she should ask for clarification. For example, "I do not believe I understand what you are saying. Tell me more." "Why do you think that?" "Why do you feel this way?" Or, simply, "Oh?" Transformational leaders make sure they understand what their members mean. Thus they have more motivated, committed members than leaders who do not listen. And they are more apt to have needs met or problems solved.

Prescriptions for Better Listening

Many opportunities arise every day to listen, confirm, respond, question, and clarify thoughts not understood. Transformational leaders work to become better listeners. They concentrate, work at listening, keep an open mind, take advantage of thought speed, listen for total meaning, and are sensitive.

The first mandate is to concentrate, that is, to force attention, to focus on the subject. To learn how to give undivided attention to what a speaker says, leaders must learn to control environmental conditions. They must neither yield to distractions nor tolerate or create interferences. If interruptions do occur, they should not be allowed to upset the situation. Leaders should take them in stride and return attention to the speaker.

Transformational leaders do not pretend to pay attention, but they try to develop a sincere interest in the ideas being communicated. They find purpose in every listening situation. They learn to adjust to various listening situations and to different speaking rates. In short, they work at listening and get actively involved with what is happening. An active listener can aid the speaker by creating a nonthreatening climate. Transformational leaders are neither critical, evaluative, nor moralizing. Instead, they develop a climate of equality, understanding, acceptance, and warmth.

An open attitude is also important. One can become overly emotional by reacting to certain words, but it is possible for a leader to learn to temper enthusiasm by not getting overstimulated about certain subjects. Avoiding arguments and not criticizing a speaker's delivery before the idea has been fully developed will also help to maintain emotional stability.

One thinks as much as six times faster than the average person speaks. Transformational leaders take advantage of the thought-speaking time difference to make mental summaries and increase their attention span. They also review what is heard and seen. They focus on the nonverbal as well as the verbal by noticing all cues. They use thought speed for productive listening, not daydreaming.

Transformational leaders listen for total meaning. Both the content and tone of a message are necessary for complete understanding of what a speaker means. Thus several skills are important: listening for main ideas as well as facts, identifying supportive elements, and analyzing the message's basic elements. It also helps to find a natural link between the questions asked and the responses received. The primary objective of listening is to listen in depth. One must learn to respond to the feeling or attitude underlying the message and become involved with the speaker's message and actions.

Sensitive listening can assist leader-member relationships. When tone is more important than content, the listener should respond in a manner that is sensitive to the feelings of the person communicating. Sensitivity can be thought of as the ability to predict what others will feel, say, or do. The transformational leader's sensitivity creates a supportive climate. It allows one to detect and cope with communication barriers. It also gives the communicator greater satisfaction.

Nonverbal Communication

Nonverbal communication has much to do with the way Christian leaders perceive and respond to members. Ability to communicate is much more than the ability to speak. Body language is another technique to achieve understanding among people. Success also depends on interest, competence, sincerity, trustworthiness, and sensitivity to the feelings of others. Nonverbal communication must match the words expressed. No one can accept a grudging apology.

> "Body language" is not a 20th-century phenomenon. The Bible talks about it. The "right hand of fellowship" from James, Cephas, and John communicated approval of Paul and Barnabas and their ministry to the Gentiles (Gal. 2:9). Greeting one another with a holy kiss was a meaningful way of expressing concern for others (1 Cor. 16:20). The look that Christ gave Peter spoke powerfully though silently (Luke 22:61). The act of washing another's feet says something concrete about servanthood (John 13:1–18). Lifting up the hands was a silent symbol of one's worship of and dependence upon God (1 Tim. 2:8).[7]

Tone and inflection of voices, facial expressions, body positions, and gestures speak very clearly. Jesus' silence during his trial, his weeping for Lazarus, his sleeping in the boat during a storm, and his turning over the tables in the temple courtyard all speak volumes nonverbally. Such nonverbal expressions significantly affect sending and receiving messages. The specific signals that alert individuals as to what to send or how to receive are cues. In a mime, an actor communicates a message and a variety of emotions without speaking a single syllable. Communication that incorporates verbal and nonverbal elements is chock-full of meaning at many different levels.

Cues

Nonverbal cues are signals that do not require a person's concentrated efforts. These cues may be intentional or unintentional. The expressions of feelings, emotions, and attitudes are nonverbal and can rarely be concealed from others. Messages frequently consist of intentions that are logically inconsistent with the verbally professed statements. That may be why some preachers, for example, practice cues and even include hand motion comments in their outlines. Sincerity is probably the key to all communication cues. Forgetting oneself and focusing on others helps one to make natural, graceful cues.

If people have difficulty communicating their thoughts and feelings by verbal symbols, they will communicate by means of nonverbal symbols. This is sometimes called "body language." Remember:

- Leaders cannot not communicate. Nonverbal cues go out constantly: facial muscles tighten, eyes dart, bodies turn away, voices sound bored.
- Listeners pay more attention to nonverbal communication than to spoken language. If leaders' words say one thing and their body

language signals something else, people value the nonverbal more than the verbal communication.

Research indicates only 10 percent or less of a message is transmitted by words. Most of a message is nonverbal—tone of voice, facial expression, and body motion. It is no wonder members pay more attention to what leaders do than what they say. (A church member expects that the pastor will not just "talk the talk, but walk the walk.") Ralph Waldo Emerson's statement is still true: "What you are speaks so loudly I can't hear what you say."

Body Motions

Kinesics, the study of body motions, concerns five primary areas: the face, gestures, posture, body type, and physical attractiveness. Each of these areas provokes certain actions from other people and may assist or impede communication.

The face is the most visible indicator of emotions and feelings. With more than one hundred possible expressions, the face accurately reflects one's feelings toward others and provides feedback on others' comments. Perhaps the part of the face most likely to yield information is the eyes. Rolling one's eyes, for example, says a lot, and it may be different in different situations. When communicating with others or establishing or maintaining relationships, the transformational leader increases eye contact—but does not stare. Contact needs to be broken every so often. Sometimes people look at a person's forehead if it is hard to keep focusing on the person's eyes.

Gestures can express one message or an entire language. Although the hands are most prominent, the whole body can send a message. Successful ministers confirm that members send nonverbal messages of acceptance or reflection of messages by folding or unfolding their arms, leaning forward or reclining in their chairs, crossing or uncrossing their legs, or checking the time. (When a parishioner takes off his or her watch and waves it in the air, it is time to quit preaching.) Gestures can be large, expansive, assertive, and outgoing; or they can be limited, self-protective, and close to the body. But, as with mimes, every movement has a meaning.

Posture also provides information. The way one sits, stands, walks, or lies down expresses feelings, interest, involvement, or tension. Body language as well as physical barriers can be used to get rid of time-wasting office guests. A leader may rise and remain standing when someone enters his or her office; this makes the visitor reluctant to sit and signals that this will have to be short. Holding a pen or pencil at the ready implies someone is about to write something important and is eager to get on with it. A raised eyebrow sometimes signals irritation, disbelief, a desire to get back to the business at hand, or a tell-me-more attitude. Posture tells whether one wishes to include or exclude other people in one's thoughts or conversations, whether one is open or closed to certain ideas. It expresses whether one is warm toward certain people, whether one likes or dislikes certain ideas, whether one can become emotionally involved. Posture also says something about one's role and status in certain groups. Standing erect versus slouching may indicate an appropriate pecking order in North American culture.

There are three general body types: ectomorph (frail, thin, and tall), endomorph (fat, round, and short), and mesomorph (muscular, athletic, and tall). Most people stereotype one of these physiques. Research suggests that ectomorphs are tense, suspicious of others, nervous, pessimistic, and quiet. Endomorphs are talkative, old-fashioned, sympathetic, weak, dependent, and trusting. Some researchers contend endomorphs encounter negative prejudice in job interviews and promotional decisions. And, in fact, a number of endomorphs are taking their employers to court and charging them with job bias. Mesomorphs are stereotyped as handsome, adventurous, mature, and self-reliant. Look at the models used in advertising to appreciate this stereotype; at least 90 percent are mesomorphs. King Saul was "an impressive young man without equal among the Israelites—a head taller than any of the others" (1 Sam. 9:2).

Anyone can exhibit characteristics of all three groups. Transformational leaders do not let societal attitudes affect the way they relate to each of these types of people. Christ was so much the common person that he could disappear into a crowd. He had no form or comeliness to recommend him (see Isa. 53). He was not good looking, yet he was able to exhibit warmth, love, anger, disdain, and a host of emotions and attitudes with his less desirable body type. He did not scare little children; they were drawn to him.

In today's world, however, physical attractiveness is a factor in nonverbal communication. Body color, smell, hair length, and clothing influence the quality and quantity of communication among people. Based solely on physical appearance, many people make decisions about dating, courtship, and marriage, not to mention hiring and firing. For example, it is believed many business managers put people through testing programs during interviews to weed out weak candidates, and then they hire the tallest person. However, one does not have to be physically attractive to be either an effective leader or communicator. Mother Teresa is not beautiful; Ross Perot is not attractive or tall. Yet both are excellent communicators. Such an index is the world's standard. While others may judge by looks, God searches the heart (1 Sam. 16:7).

Unfortunately, many excellent church leaders have not been respected or have been ignored because they do not resemble Robert Redford, Christian Slater, Alec Baldwin, Meryl Streep, Rachel Hunter, or Jaclyn Smith (to name a few). Americans tend to overemphasize the externals. Yet, President Lincoln would not have looked good on television. President Taft's weight exceeded three hundred pounds. How would he appeal to today's voters? How would voters react to Franklin Delano Roosevelt in a wheelchair?

Jesus pointed out that the inhabitants of Jerusalem did not go to the desert to listen to John the Baptist because of his looks, location, or stature (Luke 7:24–28). They went because of his passionate message and plea. The transformational leader does not relegate people to the pew and keep them out of leadership opportunities because of their appearance, mannerisms, physical limitations, or ungraceful words.

Space

Spatial relationships (proxemics) also affect the quality and quantity of communication among people. Distances between persons (arrangement of furniture in homes, classrooms, and offices) may enhance or stifle understanding. A person sitting behind, beside, or away from the desk may convey different messages, depending on where they are sitting.

Personal space varies among nationalities. Americans, who tend to talk at arms' length, mark off a generous amount of personal space in which to operate. However, members of some other nationalities customarily interact within inches of each other. That is why one may find Americans backing up when speaking to Arabs.

Space is often referred to as territory; this assumes certain ownership rights of an area without any legal basis. Examples of territory might include a certain chair in a classroom, a certain parking space, a certain easy chair at home, or a certain pew at church. Anyone who invades this territory is apt to be treated with suspicion or exasperation. Territory can be employed to convey an aura of power. Some church leaders' offices may be viewed almost as shrines by easily impressed visitors. Or, they may have a boomerang effect—some may see a quest for power or a waste of church budget. The transformational leader uses space to enhance communication, not to indicate power.

— — —

Pause to Reflect

1. This chapter makes a case for the idea that communication is the essence of all personal and spiritual relationships and that the church would not exist very long without good communication. Do you agree or disagree? Discuss.

2. Five communication goals are set forth in this chapter. In your experience, which of these is the most difficult to achieve? Why? What steps have you or those around you taken to overcome obstacles to effective communication?

3. Feedback determines the level of understanding in any conversation. How may a church's vitality and problem-solving ability be enhanced or suffer because of feedback or a lack thereof?

4. This chapter asserts that few verbal or nonverbal communication tools rival effective listening for overcoming communication barriers. Do you agree or disagree? Discuss and give examples.

5. The point is also made that nonverbal communication has much to do with the way leaders perceive and respond to others. How are people constantly communicating information about themselves? Describe one of your experiences where nonverbal behavior sabotaged the verbal.

16

STRATEGIC EVALUATION

The final stage in the strategic leadership process, after formulation and implementation, is evaluation. Three fundamental activities must be performed to effectively assess a church's strategies:

1. The congregation must review the internal and external factors upon which its current strategies are based. Key questions to ask (see SWOT analysis in chap. 10) include: Are internal strengths still strengths? Are internal weaknesses still weaknesses? Are external opportunities still opportunities? Are external threats still threats?

2. The congregation must measure performance. Strategists should examine planned versus actual progress being made toward achieving stated goals and objectives.

3. The congregation must implement corrective actions (or contingency plans) as needed to improve its internal and external strategic positions.

Strategy evaluation is a critical stage in the strategic leadership process because internal and external factors do change. Successful churches anticipate and adapt to changes quickly and effectively. Major changes in the underlying bases of a strategy may not impact current performance until it is too late to avoid or capitalize upon the event or trend. Therefore, alternative strategies should be considered whenever key internal and external factors change significantly.

Strategy evaluation is needed because success today is no guarantee for success tomorrow! In fact, success generally renders ineffective the behavior that brought it about. Success always creates new and different problems.

This chapter discusses measuring strategy, implementing strategy, and contingency planning.

Measures of Performance

Measures of performance evaluate the success of implementation. The most commonly used measures of strategic performance are strategic plans, the long-range plan, budgets, performance appraisals, policies and procedures, and statistical reports.[1] Many organizations employ measures of performance even more comprehensive than these. In fact, the list is almost endless.

One particular technique that may be employed is the *strategic audit*. The general format of such analysis follows this twofold pattern: determine the organization's current position in terms of its mission, goals, objectives, policies, and hierarchy of strategies; and ascertain the firm's strengths, weaknesses, opportunities, and threats.[2] (See box 16.1.)

Strategy evaluation should provide a true picture of what is taking place in a congregation. Although evaluation should not dominate decisions, it should foster mutual understanding, trust, and support. Likewise, in spite of the long, preceding list, an evaluation should not be cumbersome and restrictive. It should be simple and useful. There is no one ideal strategy-evaluation system. The larger the congregation, the more elaborate the system; the smaller the congregation, the simpler the system.

Tests for Strategy

Once strategies have been formulated and implemented, they must be evaluated. The best-known set of criteria may be summarized under six categories: internal consistency, environment consistency, appropriateness, risk acceptability, duration of commitment, and workability.[3] Before studying these six categories, read carefully the Clio Community Church case in box 16.2. (Note: The Clio Community Church is a compilation of a number of congregations in various locales. It is fictitious and for illustrative purposes only.)

Box 16.1

A Strategic Audit

LEADERSHIP

Mission/Goals

1. Has the congregation identified its mission? If so, is it appropriate?
2. What is its mission? What are its goals?

Objectives

1. Does the congregation have strategic objectives?
2. What are they?

Grand Strategy

1. What is it? How good is it?

Congregational Strategy

1. Is the congregation seeking a niche? Is this action appropriate?
2. Does the congregation have a plan for growth? How good is it? What type of growth does it seek? How appropriate is it?
3. Does the congregation know what its ministry is?
4. Is the congregation's strategy sound?
5. Is the congregation's basic action strategy appropriate to the community, the state, the nation, the world?
6. Does the congregation have a strategic advantage? What is it? How good is it?
7. Is the congregation an innovator or an imitator? How appropriate is this strategy?

FUNCTIONAL STRATEGIES

Planning

1. Does the congregation have objectives and plans to reach those objectives for each of its major ministry areas? How good are those plans and objectives?
2. Does the congregation have a plan or does it take a haphazard approach?
3. Do the plans meet the evaluative criteria?
4. Are planning and feasibility studies performed? How good are they?
5. How are planning and control coordinated? How well?

Organizing

1. What is the division of labor? What procedure exists for establishing roles?

   a. How are roles established? Is this procedure appropriate?

   b. Is there any evidence that members are dissatisfied with their tasks? If so, what impact does their dissatisfaction have?

2. How is authority distributed?

   Is the distribution of authority correct for this congregation? If not, what distribution would be better?

3. What is the structure?

   a. How do size, technology, environment, geographic factors, informal organization, leadership prerogatives and philosophy, and strategy affect the congregation's structure? What impacts do these effects have?

   b. Could the congregation be better structured? If so, what structure would be more appropriate?

Leading

1. What is the dominant leadership style of the congregation? Of its leaders? Are these styles appropriate?

2. Should some change be made in the distribution of authority?

3. What is the climate of the congregation? What impact does this climate have on morale?

4. How do the leaders motivate the members? Is this method appropriate?

5. Would recognition be a useful form of motivation in this congregation?

Communicating and Decision Making

1. Does the congregation have a communication strategy, policies, and so on? Are they satisfactory?

2. Does the congregation use appropriate decision techniques? To what extent are decisions determined by social relations?

OTHER CONSIDERATIONS

Leaders and Key Members

1. Are leaders providing the necessary leadership?

2. Are leaders performing the management functions?

3. Rate the leadership. What criteria was employed to do so?

4. What impact does internal dissension have on the congregation?

5. What changes in leadership have occurred recently? How do they affect morale and/or performance?

6. How do value orientations affect leaders' decisions? What impact do leaders' value orientations have?

7. Is the leadership keeping up with changes in the environment, management techniques, and the like?

8. Have leaders been making the correct strategic decisions?

9. What impact does a family-emphasis ministry have on the congregation?

10. Is there a teacher-training program in the congregation? If so, how good is it?

Overall Performance

1. Does the congregation use appropriate human resources, and social and environmental performance measures?

2. How good is the congregation's performance in these areas?

Box 16.2
The Clio Community Church
A Strategy Evaluation Problem

Nestled just four blocks from the downtown area, Clio Community Church (CCC), established in 1970, is within close proximity to shopping areas, office complexes, and numerous governmental offices. The building was renovated in 1985 following a $1 million fundraising drive. Today, it houses a five hundred-seat auditorium, twenty classrooms, several large meeting rooms for multipurpose use, a gymnasium, and a commercial kitchen. The facilities are accessible to the disabled, and ample parking is available.

The CCC leadership consists of a board of elders (eleven members, of which five are women), thirty-two ministry leaders, two ministers (a senior pastor and a youth/college minister), two full-time office personnel, and 450 members. The elders have strong, diverse backgrounds that include extensive professional, business, and community service experience. The majority have expertise in finance and law. The ministry leaders include: a medical doctor, a nursing home administrator, a shopping center manager, several teachers (university, elementary, and community college), secretaries, a stockbroker, a social worker, managers in various local businesses and government, and entrepreneurs. Committees include: Finance and Fundraising; Long-Range Planning; Personnel; Benevolence; Membership; Building and Grounds; Education; Music and Worship; Marketing, Communications, and Advertising; Special Services; Music; and Youth and College. CCC's mission is to thrust its collective energies into evangelizing the community for Jesus Christ by every means possible.

CCC PROGRAMS AND SERVICES

Programs and services are divided into three major categories.

- Elementary Day Care. CCC provides state-licensed child care before and after school hours and during the summer. Child care is provided from 6:30 a.m. until school begins and after school until 6 p.m. The cost is twenty dollars for the morning and twenty-five dollars for the afternoon session. This includes a breakfast or afternoon snack, tutoring, and other activities. Summer day care is provided for a ten-week period, nine hours per day, for one hundred dollars per week, including breakfast, snacks, and lunch. In addition, child care is available during school holidays. Summer programs focus on cultural and environmental awareness and community service. Program offerings depend upon the availability of staff personnel.

- Youth Development. A variety of programs and activities are available for middle/high school and college-age students. Classes are held in martial arts, cooking, art, dance, and other recreational activities. Special health programs stress exercise, self-esteem building, and nutrition. Other activities focus on goal setting and problem solving. Basketball and volleyball tournaments are standard offerings.

- Special Community Services. Special services available to the community include: prenatal care, crafts, cooking, wardrobe, personal growth, and leadership classes; advocacy courses that cover sexual harassment, affirmative action, and discrimination; seminars on diverse topics such as balancing work and family, substance abuse, and book reviews. When possible, seminar series are linked to worship services to attract new members. Follow-up is a necessity when such occurs.

DEMOGRAPHICS

Between 1985–95, the population of Clio declined by 11 percent, from 140,000 to slightly under 125,000. This was approximately the same level as the city's 1960 population. Two universities and a community college are also located in the city; their enrollment figures have been flat for the past two years—reflecting the reduction.

The decrease can be attributed primarily to the aerospace industry crisis. Major employers moved their operations out of state, taking many residents from the area. However, both population and employment levels have begun to increase as new employers from diverse industries relocated to Clio. Residential housing construction has experienced a boom in the last year. Forecasts indicate that the area is on the road to economic recovery, but the recovery will be slow.

THE PROBLEM

In late 1993, CCC developed its initial budget for 1995, indicating short-fall of slightly more than ten thousand dollars. The elders recognized that they could not continue operating as they had in the past. If CCC was to avoid "red ink," it would either have to raise revenues from fundraising activities or cut its level of service. The elders realized that CCC's environment had changed, and to prosper, they would have to differentiate themselves from other organizations and churches with programs and/or services that met unfilled community needs.

Through most of the mid-1980s and early 1990s, CCC flourished in spite of an unfavorable local economic environment. Its facilities were renovated and its programs expanded. However, several problems are becoming evident.

As 1995 approached, the elders viewed the deteriorating, although not yet critical, budget situation and realized that some action was required to avoid cutting its services. Newer evangelical churches, potential complications in depending on tithes from members, the need to niche-market its programs, decreasing numbers of experienced volunteers, and other problems all need to be addressed if CCC is to continue to serve its members and community effectively.

THE PROPOSED SOLUTIONS

To solve or at least alleviate the perceived budgeting problems, the elders targeted four functional areas for increased controls: operations, marketing, finances and budgets, and human resources.

First, ministry leaders reviewed their areas in terms of heightening productivity and quality. Any system could be improved to streamline efficiency and encourage promptness. Those in charge of special services were asked to implement a fee structure for future workshops/seminars. *Second*, those in charge of CCC's marketing and advertising focused on regulating sales, prices, costs, and market share in an effort to try to control opinions about CCC's services. *Third*, all committee chairs adopted a zero-base budget. Each person involved was required to justify each element of the budget, regardless of whether there was money for a given activity in last year's budget. *Fourth*, the personnel committee members were asked to develop a system to specify, monitor, and control employee performance, appraisals, compensation, etc.

Test #1: Internal Consistency

Is the strategy internally consistent? Internal consistency refers to the cumulative impact of individual policies on goals. In a well-worked-out strategy, each policy will fit into an integrated pattern. These strategies must reflect not only the current but the evolving elements within the organization. Some specific questions to ask about a church's internal consistency would include:

1. Is the strategy consistent with internal strengths, objectives, and policies of the church?
2. Does the strategy conflict with other church strategies?
3. Does the strategy exploit strengths and avoid major weaknesses?
4. Is church structure consistent with the strategy?
5. Does the strategy contribute to the church's performance?
6. Will the strategy produce new administrative problems?
7. Does the strategy fit spiritual values and philosophy?

Is the strategy at Clio Community Church (see box 16.2) internally consistent?

Test #2: Environmental Consistency

Is the strategy consistent with the external environment? Does it make sense with respect to what is going on outside the organization? Strategy must reflect not only the current but the evolving elements in the environment because these elements open up opportunities and/or pose threats. Several questions to ask about environmental consistency include:

1. Is the strategy acceptable to church members?
2. Is the strategy in consonance with the brotherhood?
3. Does the strategy give the church a competitive advantage?
4. Are forecasts on which the strategy is based credible?
5. Is the strategy in conformance with biblical guidelines?

Is the strategy at Clio Community Church (see box 16.2) consistent with the external environment?

Test #3: Appropriateness

Is the strategy appropriate in light of the available resources? Resources include both spiritual and physical forces. Spiritual forces include the Father, Son, Holy Spirit, and prayer. Physical forces include money, competence, facilities, and member loyalty. What are the critical resources?

Is the proposed strategy appropriate for available resources? Does the proposed strategy achieve balance between strategic goals and available resources? Strategists must decide how much to commit to opportunities currently perceived and how much to keep uncommitted in reserve. Illustrative questions of appropriateness include:

1. Does the church have the spiritual commitment to carry out the strategy?

2. Does the church have sufficient capital to successfully implement the strategy?

3. What will be the financial consequences associated with capital allocation to the strategy?

4. Is the strategy appropriate with respect to the existing and prospective physical facilities?

5. Will the strategy use the physical facilities to capacity?

6. Are there identifiable and committed leaders to implement the strategy?

7. Do the leaders have the necessary skills and knowledge to make the strategy successful?

Is the strategy at Clio Community Church appropriate in light of the available resources?

Test #4: Risk Acceptability

Does the strategy involve an acceptable degree of risk? Each congregation must decide its own comfort zone with risk. The risk spectrum ranges from no risk to a situation where survival is at stake. Three qualitative factors assist evaluation of risk inherent in a strategy: (1) the amount of resources appropriated, though the continued existence or value is not assured; (2) the time span to which resources are committed; and (3) the proportion of resources committed to a particular course of action. Here are some specific questions about risk:

1. Has the strategy been tested with appropriate analysis (materially and spiritually)?

2. How large a portion of capital and leadership is tied to the strategy?

3. Does the strategy detract from the church's main mission?

Does the strategy at Clio Community Church (see box 16.2) involve an acceptable degree of risk?

Test #5: Duration of Commitment

Does the strategy have an appropriate time horizon? Viable strategy reveals not only what is to be accomplished but also when the goals will be achieved. The longer the time horizon, the greater the range of alternatives. Goals must be established far enough in advance to allow the church to adjust to them. Here are some specific time-related questions:

1. Is the strategy appropriate for the present and prospective positioning of the church?

2. Is the strategy in agreement with the church's stage within the life cycle?

3. Is the strategy being rushed (especially if it involves major change)?

Does the strategy at Clio Community Church (see box 16.2) have an appropriate time horizon?

Test #6: Workability

Does the strategy work? If a strategy will not work, there is little reason for implementing it. Some illustrative questions relative to the workability of strategy and its implementation include:

1. Can the strategy be implemented efficiently and effectively?

2. Is there commitment by the leaders to assure the proper implementation of the strategy?

3. Is the timing appropriate?

4. Does the church culture need changing?

Does the strategy at Clio Community Church (see box 16.2) work?

Does the proposed strategy pass these six tests for strategy? If so, the church has the right strategy for itself. Although these criteria do not guarantee success, they are valuable for giving leaders the time and room to maneuver. And these key questions also provide many decision-making opportunities. Unacceptable answers may alert the church either to change strategies or to take corrective and preventive actions. What would be the best decision for Clio Community Church? Do they have the appropriate strategy to handle their budgetary crunch?

Contingency Planning

Regardless of how carefully strategies are formulated, implemented, and evaluated, unforeseen events can make a strategy obsolete. To minimize the impact of newly discovered weaknesses and/or threats, transformational leaders develop contingency plans to support their formal plans. A contingency plan is an alternate plan that can be put into effect if certain events do not occur as expected. It acts as a safety chute if the main parachute does not open. Such contingency plans, however, should be compatible with current strategy as well as economically feasible. They also should be subject to evaluation.

Transformational leaders remain flexible in their strategic planning, especially given society's rapidly changing conditions. In fact, changes of the magnitude occurring globally require leaders to embrace new ways of remaining flexible.

> It is difficult to overcome inertia barriers by fostering a new way of thinking in the midst of so much turmoil. The do-nothing solution that seemed so right in the past is a difficult life preserver to sacrifice when one is afloat in the vast, cold ocean. But it is necessary to overcome these mental barriers in order to reposition the firm with ease. . . . Flexible firms must be willing to hang loose. Being flexible means being willing to create flexible systems wherein people (the differentiating factor) are given autonomy to change their organization and its focus.
>
> For many firms, however, time is running out.[4]

May God forbid that time runs out on his congregations because leaders fail in their willingness to adapt, within biblical bounds, to the needs of their memberships. Christian leaders can sharpen their strategic responses to Satan and the world. Such actions may require taking risks and abandoning the mediocre. Certainly it will require getting members out of their pews, refocusing a strategic posture, applying analytical techniques to a variety of strategies, and constantly studying and praying.

Transformational Strategy

This book calls for transforming the church through leadership and strategy. In summary form, here are seven steps in strategic planning:

1. Form a dream team.
2. Clarify the mission and tenets.
3. Gather the appropriate data.
4. Create a strategic vision.
5. Identify strategic needs/issues.
6. Devise an action plan to manage the needs/issues.
7. Monitor progress.

Following these steps will enable the emulator to provide sustained, proactive, initiatory leadership in the church. The adherent will be on the way toward creating a needed revolution within the kingdom. The proponent will transform and be transformed.

One last step is necessary in this strategic transformation: motivation (chap. 17).

— — —

Pause to Reflect

1. Conduct a situational analysis of your church. What are the key internal and external factors? What is presently contributing to any uncertainty surrounding your church?

2. Analyze what you consider to be the key alternatives for your church to pursue in the future. What crucial questions should you ask in order to test your strategic alternatives?

3. Review the multiple questions asked in this chapter about strategic analysis. Are there other questions you can think of that your church should consider? If so, what?

4. Comment on this statement: "Leaders must remain flexible in their strategic planning, especially given the rapidly changing conditions in society." On a scale of 1 to 10, with 10 being the highest, how flexible is your church's leadership? What are some of the contingency plans that your church has ready in case the adopted strategy is not working as originally planned?

5. Comment on this statement: "A church's ability to cope with the dynamic environment of our world is one of its most important determinants of success or failure." Do you agree or disagree? Why? How can the environment be influenced to impact a church's success potential?

17
TRANSFORMATIONAL MOTIVATION

Here are five statements by leaders who understood the power of motivation:

"We have nothing to fear but fear itself" (Franklin D. Roosevelt).

"Ask not what your country can do for you but what you can do for your country" (John F. Kennedy).

"Winning isn't everything. It's the only thing" (Vince Lombardi).

"Follow my example, as I follow the example of Christ" (Apostle Paul).

"You will be my witnesses in Jerusalem, and in all Judea and Samaria, and to the ends of the earth"(Jesus Christ).

These five were leaders by who they were, by what they said, and by what they did.

A great deal has been written about motivation. Theories have been proposed and corollaries applied. However, when motivation yields either negative or neutral results, many practitioners say the theory is good but, in practice, it is irrelevant or not workable. The fault may be in poor application. This chapter studies the proper application of motivation theory within the church.

Motivational Theory

There are two ways to look at motivation. The *traditional* view defines motivation as a process of directing people to action in order to accomplish a desired goal. According to this view, leaders motivate their followers to achieve goals and objectives. The second view looks at motivation as creating a state of tension and disequilibrium that causes the individual to move in a goal-directed pattern toward need satisfaction and equilibrium. As you see, both of these ways of viewing motivation center on goal achievement, whether driven internally or externally.

An *internal drive*, or intrinsic motivation, allows church leaders and members to express their skills and talents. They achieve satisfaction because the work is gratifying in and of itself. Church members find their mission so interesting that motivation comes from within.

A widow decided to build a mansion in San Jose, California. It cost her $5 million when laborers worked for fifty cents a day. The mansion has *one hundred-fifty* rooms, *thirteen* bathrooms, *two thousand* doors, *forty-seven* fireplaces, and *ten thousand* windows. On the day she died, she had already bought enough materials to have continued building for another eighty years. What motivated her to build such a house?

The year was 1918, and the owner was Sarah Winchester. Her husband had amassed a fortune by manufacturing and selling rifles. After he died of influenza, she moved to San Jose. Because of her grief and her long interest in spiritism, she sought out a medium to contact her dead husband. The medium told her, "As long as you keep building your home, you will never face death."

Sarah believed the spiritist. She bought an unfinished seventeen-room mansion and started expanding it. The project continued until her death at age eighty-five. Today that house is more than a tourist attraction. It is a silent witness to the internal motivation process and the fear of death that holds millions of people.

An *external drive*, or extrinsic motivation, is induced from an outside force. Someone provides an external, tangible reward to get something accomplished. Often the reward is money. Churches usually use intrinsic motivation—recognition, leadership position, love, satisfaction. Sometimes churches use extrinsic motivation—money, a nice home, a corner office, a Sunday School Teacher of the Year award.

Most human motivational systems are based on the belief that people can be led to expend energy in a desired direction if they are offered the proper reward or are threatened with punishment. Most business organizations are based on that premise. The reward system might include promotions, salary increases, and prestige. The punishment system would withhold promotions, raises, and recognition. In the church, the ultimate reward is heaven; the punishment, hell.

Many of the human relations problems in business and the church may be due to narrow definitions of rewards and punishments. The reward-punishment system is intrinsically sound. However, it fails to consider the multiplicity of people's responses. If so, motivational attempts in the church must make study and worship so challenging and exciting that fellowship is its own reward.

There is a fable about a dog who bragged about his great running skill when chasing other animals. Then one day, a rabbit challenged him to a race. With ease the rabbit outran the dog. The other animals began to laugh. The dog excused himself by saying, "You forget that I was only running for fun. He was running for his life!"

Motivation affects everything one does. It determines the way Christians serve God—halfheartedly out of obligation, or zealously out of gratefulness for his saving grace. Because motivation is concerned with the whole person and with personal behavior, transformational leaders view motivation as being related to activities both in and out of the church. That is, they explore human needs, task motivation, and goal setting.

The Hierarchy of Human Needs

Everyone needs something, but different people need different things. Church leaders have certain needs, and members have others. Sometimes these needs mesh, but often they do not. Needs are requirements necessary for work or social satisfaction; but it is the unsatisfied needs that motivate a person's actions. Many people have attempted to explain the range of needs. Psychologist Abraham H. Maslow ranked all human needs into the following hierarchy of needs: basic, security, social, esteem, and self-actualization.[1]

Basic Needs

The most basic needs are physiological. These include the needs for oxygen, water, food, and maintenance of body temperature. A person does not search for much else in life when these elements are not provided. It may be impossible to teach a starving person the steps of salvation, for example, until he or she has been fed (see James 2:14–20). World Vision, a Monrovia, California-based international relief and development agency, understands this principle; it strives first to meet the physical needs of suffering people, then to minister to their spiritual well-being.

Security Needs

Once basic needs are satisfied, safety or security demands emerge. These include the avoidance of sources of anxiety or fear such as the fear of falling, loud noises, flashing lights, bodily injury, illness, and pain. Such needs are often coupled with the security needs of an organized, orderly, predictable environment. The church can meet security needs through the doctrine of grace and the promise of a home after death (see 1 John 5:11–12).

A pastor baptized a man into a church. The person had been through eight weeks of training before joining the church, some of it with the pastor. But as they were stepping into the baptistry, the pastor called him by the wrong name, even though he was wearing a name tag. How secure would you feel in such a situation?

Social Needs

When the safety/security needs subside, social needs arise. These belongingness or love needs include friends, a sweetheart or spouse, children, affectionate relations with others, or a place in a chosen group. These needs encompass both giving and receiving love. One of the strongest desires human beings have is to belong and be accepted by others. But this feeling of belonging consists of more than mere membership in a group such as a Bible class. It is acquired by participation. When someone contributes to the group, the group recognizes the contribution as worthwhile. Thus the transformational leader enhances human relations by involvement (see Gal. 6:10).

Esteem Needs

Once the social needs have been met, esteem needs appear. These include the need for high self-regard and respect for others. All people need love, support, and respect. These needs may be met by self-estimations of strength, confidence, and freedom, and by others' recognition of a person's status, prestige, reputation, importance, or competence.

A university professor uses "door prizes" to motivate students. The prize is only a candy bar, but it has the appeal of having students attend class because they never know when their name will be selected. It also is another way of giving students self-esteem. The self-concept is the most important factor in relations with others. It comes from significant others who have loved (or not loved) the person (see 1 John 4:7–12).

Self-Actualization Needs

Once esteem needs are satisfied, the need arises for self-actualization—doing what one is fitted for, fulfilling one's potential, and becoming everything one is capable of becoming. Included in this category are the needs for creative expression and contribution to worthwhile objectives (see 1 Cor. 14:12; 2 Cor. 8:7). Also, discovering the spiritual gifts and talents of the congregation helps leaders plan for the future.

Any or all of these five needs, from the most basic to the highest level, may be satisfied through social, human contact with others in the church. That is why transformational leaders arrange their congregation's environment so members can achieve personal goals by directing their efforts toward goals. They create opportunities for members to satisfy their basic needs, provide growth opportunities for them to exercise their potential, recognize accomplishments, or coach them to overcome their weaknesses (see Rom. 12:1–8).

Persons and the Needs Hierarchy

Maslow studied various groups to determine how people attain goals. He identified characteristics of healthy persons and characteristics of difficult people.

Healthy Persons

Maslow concluded that healthy, happy people demonstrate ten characteristics:

1. Clearer, more efficient perceptions of reality;
2. More openness to experience;
3. Increased integration, wholeness, and unity of the person;
4. Increased spontaneity, expressiveness, full functioning, aliveness;
5. A real self, a firm identity, autonomy, uniqueness;
6. Increased objectivity, detachment, self-transcendence;
7. Recovery of creativeness;
8. Ability to fuse concreteness and abstractness;
9. Democratic character structure; and
10. Ability to love.[2]

These characteristics of self-actualization are ideal goals for which to strive. Leaders who possess these characteristics can be invaluable to others. Centuries earlier the apostle Paul described such individuals as those who are productive, progressive, powerful, and positive.

For this reason, since the day we heard about you, we have not stopped praying for you and asking God to fill you with the knowledge of his will through all spiritual wisdom and understanding. And we pray this in order that you may live a life worthy of the Lord and may please him in every way: bearing fruit in every good work, growing in the knowledge of God, being strengthened with all power according to his glorious might so that you may have great endurance and patience, and joyfully giving thanks to the Father, who has qualified you to share in the inheritance of the saints in the kingdom of light (Col. 1:9–12).

Difficult People

Every organization has its share of unhealthy, immature people. These are problem people. The church is no different. These difficult people are a nuisance and may threaten the well-being of a group. These seven patterns of difficult behavior are disruptive or frustrating:

1. Hostile-aggressives—people who try to bully or overwhelm by bombarding others, making cutting remarks, or throwing tantrums when things do not go their way.

2. Complainers—individuals who gripe incessantly but never try to do anything about the situation, either because they feel powerless to do so or because they refuse to bear the responsibility.

3. Silent-unresponsives—people who respond to every question or plea for help with a yes, a no, or a grunt.

4. Super-agreeables—individuals who are always very reasonable, sincere, and supportive but either do not produce what they say they will or act contrary to the way you expected them to act.

5. Negativists—people who deflate others' optimism by responding to any project proposal with "It will not work" or "It is impossible."

6. Know-it-all experts—"superior" people who believe and want others to recognize they know everything about everything.

7. Indecisives—individuals who stall major decisions until the decision is made for them or who will not let go of anything until it is perfect—in other words, never.[3]

Even Complainers do not always complain and Indecisives sometimes make decisions. In business, such problem employees are often encouraged to quit or are fired. Should the church "fire" them, too? (All people are probably "problem people" to an extent.) Recognizing such behavior patterns of these people sets the stage for taking effective action. In the church, these problem people, if they learn the importance of the doctrine of submission and become God-motivated, can become above-average members.

A church member told a new minister, "We don't want you to believe everything you've heard about this church, because we aren't as bad as some people have said." To which another member promptly replied, "Nor as good either!" It always helps to see ourselves as others see us.

Motivation Theory and Leadership

Motivation theory has two significant implications for leaders: the role of unsatisfied needs for motivation and the role of goal setting for motivation.

Unsatisfied Needs

The underlying principle of need theory is this: *Once a need is satisfied it can no longer motivate behavior.* Church leaders cannot offer members fulfillment of needs that have already been met. However, just because a certain need is satisfied does not mean the person will never have to satisfy that need again.

Even though they cannot motivate behavior, satisfied needs can create problems. Satisfied needs can produce boredom, laziness, or sloppiness, aggravating problem people. Unsatisfied needs produce leaders' worst headaches. Unsatisfied needs result in frustration, conflict, or aggression. They can lead to gradual decline by promoting division and quarreling and by blurring the goal. Thus, transformational leaders direct their efforts to reducing tensions arising from unsatisfied needs or blocked goals.

Goal Setting

In addition, motivation theory teaches that a person's conscious goals are the primary determinants of task motivation. This theory suggests that hard goals result in greater effort than easy goals, and specific goals result in higher effort than no goals or more generalized goals. These propositions are generally supported by research, so long as the goals are acceptable. Therefore, transformational leaders set clear, challenging, and specific goals for their congregations.

The relationship between tasks and goals, between people's behavior and their goal attainment/need satisfaction, is called the *path-goal theory of motivation.* The basic postulate is that a leader's function is to set important goals and clear the paths to those goals. Three factors are involved:

1. *Church members must perceive that they can achieve the goals.* Intrinsic rewards must exist, and they must be distributed selectively in accordance with individual needs.

2. *Church members must see that intrinsic and/or extrinsic rewards are the result of specific behaviors.* There must be a perceived connection between their behavior and the rewards or punishments they receive.

3. *Church leaders must make judgments about which paths are high performance and which are low performance.* These judgments must be clear.[4]

The path-goal approach emphasizes the Christian leader's role in maximizing motivation to achieve goals. It provides insight as to the relationship between action and goal attainment and the relationship between satisfaction and performance.

In both strands of motivational theory (human needs and tasks/goals), there must be a concern for what God does for people through Christ and in them through the Spirit. God's working in people provides powerful and compelling reasons for acting according to his will. His children are reached by the love of God "as his forgiving and transforming work is done in us, and new attitudes and values are formed which enable and impel us to become better people."[5]

Action Guides for Motivating Self and Others

Church leaders must understand human motivation and apply their understanding to human relationships within the church. Otherwise, theories are just theories. Wherever and whenever human relations is a problem, it is up to the leader to correct it.

Transformational leaders begin by examining their own motives. They recognize their motives, so they can seek to motivate others. They learn the motivational level of each follower so they can assume the role of a shepherd. They know the importance of knowing "the sheep by name" and being able to lead them to "green pastures" (see John 10; Ps. 23). In essence, people work to satisfy needs. Transformational leaders know that to motivate members, they must satisfy their needs.

Consider some general motivational expectations for personal and member needs.

Personal Needs

A recent study of 251 people in various organizational settings suggests a surprising level of consistency in motivational practices.[6] Subjects were asked to describe an incident of what they believed to be a time when another person or persons motivated them. Results showed that 61 percent of the motivators come from an external source; they owe their power to a source outside themselves. Among these *external motivators* are the following:

- Example/role model
- Coworker's and friend's encouragement
- Superior's encouragement
- Confidence and trust from others
- Praise and verbal encouragement
- Approval and recognition by others

On the other hand, *internal motivators* originate in the individual's cognitive nature. The motivator appears to come from within the individual, though it is often promulgated from outside the person. In other words, when someone appears to be "responsible" and anxious to achieve certain "goals/objectives," the actual initiator may be a role model or the organizational culture. Among these internal motivators are the following:

- Responsibility and organizational goals/objectives
- Monetary rewards or promotions
- Goals/objectives and work itself
- Competition and self
- Fear or security

Women are more likely than men to be motivated by interpersonal exchanges. Men are more likely than women to be motivated by tangible motivators—a raise in pay, a well-spent 9 A.M. to 5 P.M. day, or a title that attributes positional power, titles like usher, greeter, treasurer, or deacon. Women are more likely than men to be motivated by intangible motivators—a friend's smile and encouragement or love and acceptance from peers. The limited research now available (more is needed) suggests that women and men respond somewhat differently to particular motivational attempts.

Leaders must understand the wants and needs of their followers if they are to lead. Does the following story sound familiar?

Church leaders adopt a program of expansion, hire an architect to design new facilities, approve the plans, send the plans to contractors for bids, accept a bid, and begin a fund-raising drive. Church members have had no input; they ignore appeals for money and respond minimally to the program, sometimes with hostility. The leaders cannot understand what has gone wrong and assume that they need a better motivational technique.

What these leaders need is open communication, and the church needs leaders who will communicate with church members and learn their goals.

Member Needs

Members of any organization, including a church, have at least five needs:

Members have a right to know precisely and accurately what is expected of them. They want clear descriptions, delineations of authority, and responsibility. Transformational leaders listen to this need because members who are involved and know what is expected are usually more satisfied than those who are uninvolved or are kept in the dark.

Members need to be involved in a task. They may be involved in designing the task or in establishing goals/objectives. Members are not just numbers, not just cogs in a machine. They have ideas about how things should be done and questions about why certain things are done the way they are. They want to be involved. Transformational leaders motivate members by asking them for help in setting goals.

Members need feedback on how they are doing. One university professor attends two different churches—one she feels at home in socially, and one in a poorer, minority neighborhood were she is needed more. Unrecognized members are often marginally committed and alienated from the congregation and the leadership. They may even go to another congregation. Transformational leaders recognize achievements or progress toward goals. When necessary, they revamp their communication systems to provide feedback.

Members need help from leaders and guidance in improving skills. Transformational leaders know that most of the time spent interacting with members deals with advising, guiding, coaching, counseling, and training. They see themselves as teacher, judge, specialist, generalist, planner, coordinator, organizer, motivator, and evaluator.

Members need rewards when they do something well. The rewards may be internal or external, but the most important ones seem to be intrinsic. The transformational leader attempts to satisfy the members' needs.

Leader Needs

Leaders also have certain needs. Here are six ways in which the needs of these high-achievers differ from the needs of other members:

Leaders are more concerned with achieving success than avoiding failure. They concentrate their energies on maximizing strengths and taking advantage of opportunities rather than minimizing weaknesses and warding off threats. Transformational leaders give close attention to the realistic probabilities for success and prefer situations where there is clear criteria for their success.

Leaders prefer situations they can influence and control rather than outcomes that depend on chance. Peak performers often dislike seeing anything wasted and a tendency to become angry over inefficiency. They have a high regard for self-discipline and are often intolerant toward those they perceive as undisciplined. They prefer clear-cut individual responsibility so that if they do succeed, that fact can be attributed to their own efforts. Thus transformational leaders typically have preferences for competent-but-difficult work partners over congenial-but-incompetent ones.

Leaders are future-oriented and can wait on outcomes expected to yield positive results. An important component of this future orientation is vision, an ability to see the big picture. However, with this seeming strength of character, many leaders also demonstrate tendencies of being unable to relax on holidays and vacations, of becoming annoyed when others are late for appointments, and of thinking about work-related matters outside the office.

Leaders have a long-standing pattern of working hard to be at the top of their chosen profession. They are able to stay on course despite the obstacles. In addition, these superleaders create structures that harness the energies of others. Transformational leaders monitor the activities of the group, learn from mistakes, and improve performance of the organization.

Leaders must be willing to take risks. Many would-be leaders are not great leaders because they are too risk-averse. Paul, Elijah, Jonah, Moses, Abraham, and Jesus were risk takers. Risk means that a decision has clear-cut goals and good information available, though future events and alternatives are subject to change. Enough information is available to allow the leader to estimate the probabilities of success or failure. Using these probabilities, transformational leaders determine which likelihood is more desirable for their congregation. Unfortunately, many potentially "star" programs never get off the drawing board in churches because their leaders are not risk takers. They will deal only with projects of certainty.

Leaders are motivated by their love for God and humanity. They are self-confident and independent, able to make decisions, and enjoy managing others; but they also are confident in God, seek to find God's will, delight in obeying God, and are God-dependent. Transformational leaders take on the mantle of the servant-leader (see Mark 10:43–45).

Motivational Plans

Leaders need to be prepared with a plan. Church members have needs that must be satisfied, and the leader is the key person in motivating members by satisfying their needs. They must bring out the best in people. Here are twelve motivational techniques, each with one main goal, that bring out the best in people.

1. Expect the best from people.
2. Make a thorough study of the other person's needs.
3. Establish high standards for excellence.
4. Create an environment where failure is not fatal.
5. If people are going anywhere near where the leader wants to go, climb on other people's bandwagons.
6. Employ a mixture of positive and negative reinforcement.
7. Recognize and applaud achievement.
8. Employ models to encourage success.
9. Appeal sparingly to the competitive urge.
10. Place a premium on collaboration.
11. Build into the group an allowance for storms.
12. Take steps to keep personal motivation high.[7]

These twelve techniques appeal to internal drives, interests, and values. Because church members bring different personalities and aspirations to church assemblies, they react differently to motivational attempts. For too long church leaders have cajoled, coached, and threatened members into a "salvation by works." Church members have responded by defending their freedom in the Lord and resented such approaches.

The transformational leader understands what members want from their church leaders and realizes that fear is seldom an effective tool for continuing self-motivation. Love is the answer to all real motivation! What would the church be like today if every leader believed: "The only thing that counts is faith expressing itself through love" (Gal. 5:6)?

— — —

Pause to Reflect

1. This chapter suggests that there are two ways to view motivation and that both are centered on goal achievement. Which of these two

views is true of what motivates you, and which are you most likely to use on others? Discuss.

2. The needs of both leaders and followers apparently are requirements necessary for work or social satisfaction, but only the unsatisfied needs motivate our actions. Do you agree or disagree? What are your needs? Discuss.

3. Motivational theory suggests that a person's conscious goals are the primary determinants of task motivation. Do you agree or disagree? How have you seen this work in a church setting?

4. Motivation is possible and a congregation's psychological needs can be met by a transformational leader using the necessary skills. Do you agree or disagree? Explain.

5. Twelve general techniques of motivation that bring out the best in people are listed in this chapter. Which of these are more important—based on your experience—than others for motivating Christians? Discuss.

Part Four
TRANSFORMING THE
CHRISTIAN LEADER:

Guaranteeing the Future

Revival, revitalization, transformation. Seldom experienced phenomena in the church today! Why? Is the price too high? Are there too few to pay the price of transformational leadership? Walter Lippman wrote, "For every right that you cherish, you have a duty which you must fulfill. For every hope that you entertain, you have a task that you must perform. For every good that you wish to preserve, you will have to sacrifice your comfort and ease. There is nothing for nothing any longer."

David told Araunah the Jebusite, "I will not sacrifice to the Lord my God burnt offerings that cost me nothing." It is not a stretch to conclude: As people who are to offer their lives as living sacrifices, holy and pleasing to God, Christians should be willing to pay the price of serving. The problem with being a living sacrifice, of course, is that people keep crawling off the altar.

Our prayer must be the words of the psalmist: "Revive us, and we will call on your name. Restore us, O Lord God Almighty; make your face shine upon us, that we may be saved" (Ps. 80:18–19).

Nehemiah provides a formula for Israel's revival or revitalization in his day: Read God's Word, rejoice in God's mercy, repent of and confess sins, and resolve to follow God (Neh. 8–10). Unfortunately, within a decade the Israelites broke all their promises.

Chapters 18 and 19 suggest a twofold model for guaranteeing the future of the twenty-first-century church: creating trust and commitment within the Christian community. Actions can be taken after transformation and revitalization to ensure that Christians do not break their promises. After all, God "has given us the Spirit as a deposit, guaranteeing what is to come" (2 Cor. 5:5). Then in a closing summary, chapter 20 provides the affirmations necessary for transformational leadership.

To have great Christian leaders, the church must foster transformational leadership. Both members and leaders need to move beyond "name-calling, scapegoating, a distaste for diversity, and an intolerance for debate and contemplation."[1] These three chapters should help individuals take responsibility for their own lives, set priorities, clarify values, and achieve goals. The twenty-first-century church depends upon the willingness of members and leaders to assume a transformational attitude. May each be willing to pay the price required.

The Challenge of Transformational Leadership

I. Transforming Christian Leadership: Recognizing the Need for Revitalization
  1. Transformational Leadership

II. Transforming Leadership Theory: Understanding What Christian Leadership Is Really About
  2. Power and Influence
  3. Strategic Leadership
  4. Traits of Leadership
  5. Initiatory Leadership
  6. Leadership Behavior
  7. Possibility Leadership
  8. Situational Leadership
  9. Visionary Leadership

III. Transforming Leadership Strategies and Practices: Responding to the Challenge
  10. Strategic Analysis
  11. Transformational Change
  12. Strategic Formulation
  13. Transformational Conflict
  14. Strategic Implementation
  15. Transformational Communication
  16. Strategic Evaluation
  17. Transformational Motivation

IV. Transforming the Christian Leader: Guaranteeing the Future
  18. Trust
  19. Commitment
  20. Affirmation

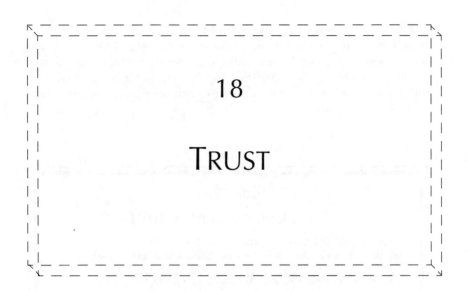

18

TRUST

Transformational leaders create an environment of trust. Trust is often referred to as confidence, reliance, expectation, and hope. Trust involves an element of blind faith. It is the firm belief in the honesty, truthfulness, justice, or power of another person. Leaders generate and sustain trust by demonstrating constancy, congruity, reliability, and integrity.[1]

Openness, honesty, trust, and continual communication pay off in lower turnover and higher morale. But winning the respect of employees, developing mutual feelings of trust between management and the work force, and opening clogged lines of communication are the kinds of accomplishments most managers hope for but few achieve. The same is true in the church. That is why transformational leaders create climates conducive to spiritual productivity. Healthy, trusting relationships encourage people to achieve their full potential. (See box 18.1.)

The Risk in Trusting

Trusting is risking. If people lived in a risk-free environment, there would be little need for trust. "You, too, have been called to go out on a limb a time or two. You know the imbalance that comes from having one foot in your will and one foot in his. You, too, have sunk your fingernails into the bark to get a better grip. You know too well the butterflies that swim in the pit of your stomach when you realize change is in the air.[2]

Mistrust develops when the limb of trust is cut. If church members trust their leaders to feed them spiritually and protect them, and if that trust is betrayed, it will be very difficult to regain that trust or use any motivation technique to move the congregation to higher ground. Neither leaders nor members can really trust each other until the other demonstrates their trustworthiness.

Box 18.1

The Development of Trust

Judgments an individual makes about how much and in what ways she or he trusts a new leader may be differentiated accordingly:

CHARACTER-BASED SOURCES OF TRUST

1. *Integrity.* Perceptions of honesty in the relationship, moral character, and basic honesty.

2. *Motives.* Perceptions of the other's intentions, commitment, posture, and agenda.

3. *Consistency of Behavior.* Perceptions of reliability and predictability.

4. *Openness.* Perceptions of leveling with someone and being honest in discussing problems related to the organization and relationship.

5. *Discretion.* Perception that the other person would not violate confidences or carelessly divulge potentially harmful information.

COMPETENCE-BASED SOURCES OF TRUST

1. *Specific Competence.* Perceptions of competence in the specialized knowledge and skills required to do a particular job.

2. *Business Sense.* Perception of a more generalized competence than expertise in a specific area; experience base, common sense, wisdom.

3. *Interpersonal Competence.* Perception of competence in working with people; people skills.

Adapted from J. J. Gabarro, *The Dynamics of Taking Charge* (Boston: Harvard Business School Press, 1987), 103–8.

Leader A lacks trust in Group B because of loose talk regarding a confidential matter by B several years back. A tries to hide his attitudes about Spiritual Issue X when communicating with B. Leader A hides his attitudes by evasive, compliant, or aggressive communication. Immediately, A assumes B disagrees about X. The long-term result is that B disregards most of what A has to say. The risk is too high to trust A.

A preacher in a church of 250 members is grappling with the issue of women in leadership roles. The preacher occasionally takes a jab at women who assert leadership outside the home. His comments discourage professional women. They either disregard his comments or disregard them as patronizing. Result: The church weakens its ability to attract and hold professional women, who are one of its greatest resources.

Other examples of sensitive topics abound: AIDS, divorce, homosexuality, unwed mothers, alcoholism and drug abuse, and insensitive comments by church leaders. Some congregations are very issue-oriented, and these issues have credible advocates on both sides. The one who makes the first move toward reconciliation and trust incurs the highest risk level and often reaps the greatest rewards.

Credibility and Trust

Trust, confidence, and credibility are very similar. The important thing to remember about factors influencing credibility is that they vary as a function of each specific situation. Modern research has identified several dimensions of interpersonal trust or credibility factors—expertise, reliability, intentions, dynamism, respect, competence, and objectivity. Deciding whom to trust is a complicated task based on a variety of cues—talking speed, gestures, body language, physical appearance, similarity of other person to oneself, comfortableness with the other person.[3] Trust cuts across all social arenas and is the glue that cements good social and working relationships.

Transformational leaders are viewed as credible sources because they combine moral character with goodwill and good sense. As a result, they are perceived as intelligent, reliable, and interested in their members. Such trust is built carefully and patiently.

Patience

Trust cannot be achieved overnight. Trust is built slowly and reinforced over time. And it is always a two-way street! If leaders want the members' trust and respect, they in turn must trust and respect the members. Leaders must trust followers first. The initiative begins at the top.

However, this requires character and strength. Nontrusting behaviors result in unproductive rifts and are ungodly traits.

Patience is especially critical in a church environment. In a society seeking instant answers and instant trust, patience is needed more than ever.

> Be patient, then, brothers, until the Lord's coming. See how the farmer waits for the land to yield its valuable crop and how patient he is for the fall and spring rains. You too, be patient and stand firm, because the Lord's coming is near. Don't grumble against each other, brothers, or you will be judged. The Judge is standing at the door!

> Brothers, as an example of patience in the face of suffering, take the prophets who spoke in the name of the Lord. As you know, we consider blessed those who have persevered. You have heard of Job's perseverance and have seen what the Lord finally brought about. The Lord is full of compassion and mercy (James 5:7–11).

Most people consider any betrayal of trust as an egregious violation. Once damaged, trust is very difficult to repair. In fact, it often takes longer to rebuild trust than it did to establish it. Couples who go through counseling due to one partner's infidelity often talk of the time it takes to restore trust in the unfaithful partner.

Congruence

Research into patient, credible, trusting climates suggests that people trust those who provide them with congruent information. That is, most people prefer individuals with whom they have agreement and harmony. They seek reinforcement from situations that substantiate their attitudes, beliefs, and values. When confronted with opposing viewpoints, they often distrust the person and the information.

Cognitive dissonance theory affirms that people avoid others who hold attitudes, beliefs, or values dissimilar to their own. They are uncomfortable with them. They often view dissimilar individuals as untrustworthy.

The same theory of cognitive dissonance asserts that the existence of inconsistency motivates people to reduce it so that consistency can be restored. If there is tension between leaders and members because of distrust and inconsistency, one or both individuals/groups will try to reduce the tension to restore trust and consistency. For example, a minister who was dismissed for refusal to follow the elder's job description of his ministry went to several of the church members trying to find support to validate his position and self-worth.

In other words, the search for congruence—the "process"—enables one to grow in character and trust. The tension, however, will always remain because balance, like perfection, is an ideal state; it can never become reality. Achieving this equilibrium is not so important as the process itself—the steps one takes and what happens along the way.

According to balance theory, people tend to organize their perceptions in consistent and comfortable ways. They prefer balance to imbalance, congruence to incongruence. Suppose that leaders tell the members that the congregation will be introducing a change in the care-group structure and operations. Balance theory looks for three attitudes: the members' attitude toward leaders, the members' attitude toward the change, and the members' perception of the leaders' attitude toward the change. According to balance theory, there will be a balanced system (or triad) if the members have a positive attitude toward the change and toward the leaders, and if the members believe the leaders favor the change. (See box 18.2.)

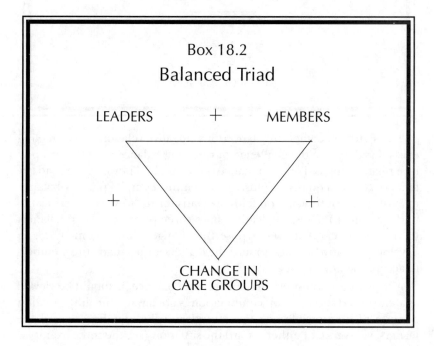

Box 18.2
Balanced Triad

LEADERS   +   MEMBERS

+   +

CHANGE IN
CARE GROUPS

However, this comfortable system can become unbalanced if the members distrust any of the three possible relations (leaders/members, leaders/change, or members/change). (See the three examples in box 18.3.)

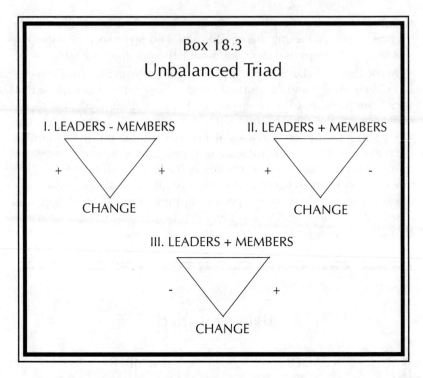

Box 18.3
Unbalanced Triad

I. LEADERS - MEMBERS

II. LEADERS + MEMBERS

+   +

+   -

CHANGE

CHANGE

III. LEADERS + MEMBERS

-          +

CHANGE

The system becomes unbalanced if a negative relationship or feeling exists. Leaders face the challenge of restoring balance by creating a positive relationship or feeling. Balance theory is also known as the triad system because it requires all pluses or two minuses and a plus for balance to exist. (Accept this rule on faith. The answer to "why" is not critical to understanding.) Thus, the leaders have three options to keep balance: tell the members that they oppose the change, allow the members to develop a negative attitude toward the leaders, or persuade the members to accept the new change.

Although two minuses and a plus create balance, it should be viewed as a short-lived success. This combination is not always a healthy situation because of the possible negative attitudes of the members toward the leaders, vice versa, or either toward the situation (see the three examples in box 18.4). No one wants to live or work very long in a negative environment.

The three positive relationships (box 18.2) represent the best type of balance to attain long-range goals, but such systems sometimes become stagnant. Thus some leaders may deliberately cause tension by creating unbalance (+, +, -) to reach a higher plateau (new +, +, + relationships).

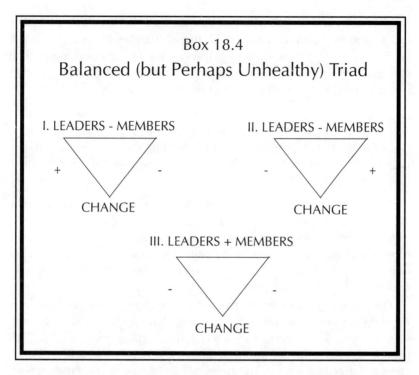

Box 18.4

Balanced (but Perhaps Unhealthy) Triad

I. LEADERS - MEMBERS

+ CHANGE -

II. LEADERS - MEMBERS

- CHANGE +

III. LEADERS + MEMBERS

- CHANGE -

Instead of introducing a needed change bit by bit, they present the entire "change package" to shock the congregation into looking with new eyes at a proposed idea.

Church members react defensively to unbalanced triads. Defensiveness is an act of protecting one's views; it may involve a somewhat hostile, emotional state of mind. Two facts often cause defensiveness:

- Defense of self-image. It is traumatic to have your image challenged, to risk losing the ability to predict, control, and know oneself. In fact, any fear of change is a basis for defensiveness. If one perceives a threat, both one's perception and subsequent behavior will be affected.

- Inability to tolerate differences in others. Although defensiveness is greater in some people than in others, it does affect the behavior of people involved in a communicative encounter. Thus it can have a very destructive, self-perpetuating cycle.

Support

How can leaders reduce defensiveness in members? Some leaders attempt to persuade members to change their ideas and/or behavior.

But this can backfire. Members may dig in their heels and defend their freedom to act or think, especially if they think they are being manipulated. This is why transformational leaders provide an open, supportive climate in their congregation. Empathy, understanding, and genuineness go a long way in reducing defensiveness.

> *Support* means showing concern for subordinates as people. It means being available and approachable. It means helping people, coaching them, encouraging their ideas, and defending their positions. It may mean socializing with them. It certainly means taking an interest in their lives and careers.[4]

One technique for showing supportive behaviors is the helping relationship. The helping relationship is a special form of temporary interaction between a helper—someone who has achieved an acceptable level of personal adjustment—and a helpee—someone who is experiencing difficulty because he or she lacks certain personal skills of adaptation, coping, and problem solving.

The primary goal is constructive behavioral change. No standard helping-skills classification system exists, but abilities such as understanding, support, and action certainly facilitate the helping relationship. With these abilities, the helper avoids judging the relative goodness, appropriateness, effectiveness, or rightness of the helpee's statements; and refrains from interpreting what the helpee might or ought to think. Instead, the helper supports the helpee's intense feeling; probes for more information; provokes further discussion and queries; or responds in a manner that assists the helpee to understand what has been said or felt.

Helpees receive support from the following reactions:

1. Description—to ask questions that are perceived as genuine, non-judgmental requests for information; to present "feelings, events, perceptions, or processes which do not ask or imply that the receiver change behavior or attitude."

2. Problem-Orientation—to communicate "a desire to collaborate in defining a mutual problem and seeking its solution," thus creating the same problem orientation in the other; the antithesis of persuasion; to imply that he or she has no preconceived solution, attitude, or method to impose upon the other; to allow the receiver to set his or her own goals, make his or her own decisions, and evaluate his or her progress—or to share with the sender in doing so.

3. Spontaneity—to express guilelessness; natural simplicity; free of deception; having a "clean id"; having unhidden, uncomplicated motives; straightforwardness and honesty.

4. Empathy—to express respect for the worth of the listener; to identify with his or her problems, share his or her feelings, and accept his or her emotional values at face value.

5. Equality—to be willing to enter into participative planning with mutual trust and respect; to attach little importance to differences in talent, ability, worth, appearance, status, and power.

6. Provisionalism—to be willing to experiment with one's behavior, attitudes, and ideas; to investigate issues rather than taking sides on them; to problem solve rather than debate; to communicate that the other person may have some control over the shared quest or the investigation of ideas.[5]

For trusting relationships, for effective communication of ideas, for win-win compromises, and for effective solving of problems, transformational leaders provide a supportive climate for the membership.

Respect and Trust

The preceding ideas of trust, risk, credibility, and support are age-old topics. Yet for most churches, adherence to these principles would result in a radical shift in the way a congregation is managed. This book encourages a move away from any approach that centers all power and responsibility at the top but favors a system in which every member is involved in guiding the congregation. Such an approach is based on patience, a spirit of mutual trust, and forbearance. It is based on the servanthood-leader model of Jesus, who showed respect for his followers by serving them. It also is based on the assumption that most members prefer to function as adults and not spiritual babes (see Heb. 5:12–14). In brief, this approach exemplifies the leader's respect for his or her membership.

Transformational leaders remember that members are their most valuable resource. They believe that each member is filled with unlimited creative potential and yearns to fulfill that potential. Such leaders empower members to put their ideas into practice without going through a cumbersome bureaucratic approval system. When such respect and mutual trust are present in a congregation, there is little that stands in the way of successful programs of involvement, growth, and evangelism.

Trust is the glue that holds the church together. Trust in God, in our leaders, and in humanity is essential to survival. Furthermore, trust in God is the anchor in an uncertain, risky environment. And closely related to trust is commitment (chap. 19).

— — —

Pause to Reflect

1. Trust is often referred to as confidence, reliance, expectation, and hope. How is trust equated with blind faith? Read Hebrews 11 and discuss the relationship between trust and faith.

2. In a risk-free environment, there would perhaps be no need for having a chapter dealing with trust. However, this is not a perfect world. Why is trusting another person risky? How do *you* go about developing source credibility?

3. Research indicates that people avoid other people who hold attitudes, beliefs, or values dissimilar to their own. What impact does this have on the church?

4. This chapter uses balance theory to explain congruence. How have you seen this theory work in your own experiences? Discuss its relevance in the church.

5. This chapter states that the primary goal of building supportive relationships is constructive behavioral change. Do you agree or disagree? Discuss.

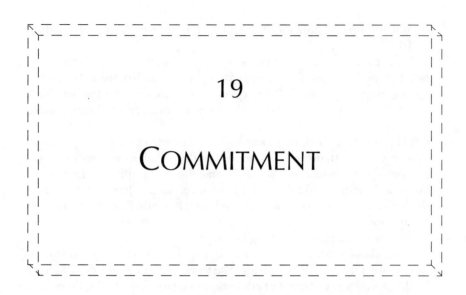

19

COMMITMENT

High above Niagara Falls, a man is rolling a wheelbarrow with two hundred pounds of dirt back and forth on a tight rope. After completing the trip safely several times, he asks the crowd, "How many of you believe I can roll a person across in this barrel?" One observer excitedly shouted, "I know you can do it!" The tight rope walker responds, "All right, sir, you're first." The observer leaves in haste.

How many leaders and followers respond this way to the mission of the kingdom? The key to commitment is trust (see chap. 18)—trust in God, in one another, and in church leaders. There is little question that God requires commitment by his people. His Son, Jesus, said:

> If your right eye causes you to sin, gouge it out and throw it away. It is better for you to lose one part of your body than for your whole body to be thrown into hell. And if your right hand causes you to sin, cut it off and throw it away. It is better for you to lose one part of your body than for your whole body to go into hell (Matt. 5:29–30).

Doing God's will is more important than mere eyes or hands. He calls us to get in the wheelbarrow. *That* is real commitment!

On another occasion Jesus told a rich young ruler to "sell your possessions and give to the poor. Then come, follow me" (Matt. 19:21). It would seem that if money stands between God and his children, the wealth should be immediately sacrificed in order "to get eternal life" (Matt. 19:16).

Many members resemble Peter. They try to walk on water with a half-hearted commitment. They are caught up in the work of their church but are not caught up in God. That explains why some church members work so hard and are enthusiastic about building attendance for Vacation Bible School, but they are often disappointed when the number of visitors do not keep coming to church after VBS has ended. These members' commitment to growth drops like a stone after the initial drive. They need sustaining power. Fortunately for Christians, there is comfort in the story of Peter; although he abandoned Christ three times, Jesus brought him through a growth process and affirmed his self-worth. Despite our human frailty, God gives us more than one opportunity to demonstrate whole-hearted commitment to his kingdom work.

Many church members are only playing church—not really involved, not really caught up in the spirit of the work, and not really dedicated to God. Consider the statement addressed to a large crowd of followers:

> "If anyone comes to me and does not hate his father and mother, his wife and children, his brothers and sisters—yes, even his own life—he cannot be my disciple. And anyone who does not carry his cross and follow me cannot be my disciple" (Luke 14:25–27).

In God, there can be no halfhearted commitment, no middle ground, no neutral territory. It is all or nothing!

> He who doubts is like a wave of the sea, blown and tossed by the wind. . . .
> He is a double-minded man, unstable in all he does (James 1:6, 8).

> "No one can serve two masters. Either he will hate the one and love the other, or he will be devoted to the one and despise the other. You cannot serve both God and money" (Matt. 6:24).

Christians must submit to God's will, be loyal to his Son and Word, allow the Spirit to work, take time to be holy, and become involved, working for his church (see Matt. 25:14–30; Rom. 12:1–2).

Yet why are so many Christians careless, indifferent, and lukewarm about their service and leadership? Why are there not more who are faithfully and loyally serving God? Why are more not seeking God with their whole heart and building their goals around his priorities? Why are there so many pew sitters, uninvolved and uncommitted? Why will so few get in the wheelbarrow?

The main reason more Christians are not committed to the Lord and supportive of his church is that they do not, or cannot, trust their leaders' vision, communication, and/or motivational attempts. This statement may seem too bold. Yet if we are committed to Christ, our commitment to his church is implicit.

Commitment to the Lord is commitment to his church. However, commitment to the church is not necessarily commitment to the Lord. This paradox raises an interesting question: What is the church? Is it a mechanistic unit of people such as Grace Bible Church, University Methodist Church, or Southern Hills Church of God in Christ? Or is the church a universal organism, the living bride of Christ? If it is only a particular congregation, what distinguishes it from the Lions, Rotary, or Kiwanis organizations?

Members and prospective members come to a church with certain needs, desires, skills, and abilities. They expect (and rightly so!) to find a spiritual environment where they can use their abilities and gifts and satisfy their needs. When a church provides the means for people to satisfy their desires in the Lord, commitment is enhanced. When the leadership is not dependable and fails to provide growth opportunities, the commitment level wanes.

For our purposes, we may define commitment as the relative strength of an individual's identification with and involvement in a particular organization.[1] Committed members believe in and accept the organization's goals and values; they are willing to work for the organization; and they want to maintain membership in that organization. Transformational leaders influence members to become involved. They call them by name, showcasing their talents, gifts, and interests.

Redesigning the Church

Churches must often redesign some of their characteristics and behaviors in order to improve the perceptions of church members toward their leaders, or vice versa. Churches can do this in four ways: by changing the people, by changing the church, by changing the interface between members and leaders, and by individualizing the church.[2]

Changing the People

Change is what a church is about—changing people's knowledge, emotions, skills, and their eternal destiny. Jesus wanted to be about his Father's business; he wanted to change people for the better, to give them wellness and a new life and hope.

Changing the Church

Your church cannot and should not eliminate or control all differences in people. The church must allow a wide repertoire of performance for achievement of objectives. Transformational leaders are flexible. Their ultimate focus remains on the quality of spiritual life for the members. But they might take specifics to increase commitment; for example, they might modify their goals, structure, and work design.

Goal modification. Goals should reflect the collective desires of the membership. But as society, communities, and members change, so too do their collective objectives. When this occurs, transformational leaders modify congregational goals.

Structure modification. Most churches have fashioned themselves after business organizations—leaders at the top, members at the bottom. Churches should abolish this hierarchy by using teams, task forces, liaison roles, and by integrating roles.

Work-design modification. Many members seek satisfaction directly from church work. Their internal work motivation and church involvement increases when their tasks are enriched in some way. How can churches enrich tasks? Current research by organizational theorists and practitioners recommends providing widened jobs, social support, continuous learning, participation in decision making, and meaningful relations between members' secular jobs and the outside world.[3]

Changing the Interface between Members and Leaders

A congregation may need to make both formal and informal adjustments to encourage member participation. In fact, leaders may need to work very hard at system changes that nurture interaction between members and leaders. A summary of some strategies that could be used to change the leader-member interface include growth through task accomplishment, leadership style, and organizational development.

Growth through task accomplishment. Leaders must consider each person's aspirations and values in order to use tasks to enhance growth and development. They must identify the skills and experiences necessary to reach a target and identify the necessary sequence of tasks to build required skills and experiences. More specifically, leaders should:

1. Select jobs that provide changes that are large enough to "stretch" the individual's skills and abilities, yet small enough to be manageable.

2. Consider lateral, developmental, cross-functional moves as well as promotions.

3. Allow enough time to master the job, but not so much that the job becomes routine.

4. Consider jobs that complement or supplement, not merely duplicate, previous experiences.

5. Plan alternative moves or sequences (contingency plans), since it is unlikely that all scheduled activities will take place as projected.[4]

Of course, some people enjoy routine and mastery; it defines who they are. One church member taught four-year-olds for thirty-five years; another was head of the teacher's workroom for more than twenty years.

Growth through leadership styles. What role should leaders play? Seldom, if ever, is only one leadership style recommended. The focus is typically on matching leadership style to the situation (see chap. 8). One such technique for matching style to situation recommends the identification of the maturity level of members (in terms of their willingness and ability to set goals and accept responsibility for goal achievement).[5] Low-maturity members are appropriately led with an autocratic, closely supervised style. Highly mature members are appropriately "led" by a highly delegative, *laissez faire* style.

Growth through organizational development. The various procedures and techniques developed to open an organization's climate have been collectively labeled organizational development (OD). Some examples include team building, diagnosis and feedback, development of interpersonal skills, and mirroring. The focus of OD is the collective set of member values and attitudes evidenced in the way people work together, confront conflict, and cope with change.

Individualizing the Church

A congregation may try to change its members to make them fit the present structure or make internal changes to try to fit the congregation to the members. There is not much research evidence to suggest either approach is successful. The option left is to individualize the church. Because members differ, it makes sense to make a congregation as flexible as biblically possible. The more options available and the more easily these are matched to membership differences, the more likely a congregation is to adapt to change. Some ways to individualize a congregation include:

1. Determining what kinds of behavior the congregation desires.
2. Figuring out what outcomes each member values.
3. Making sure the desired behavior is achievable.
4. Linking the desired outcomes to the desired performances.
5. Analyzing the total situation to eliminate conflicting expectancies such as conflicts between group norms and congregational requirements.
6. Making sure outcomes offered are large enough to motivate significant behavior.

7. Checking the system for equity.[6]

By treating individuals differently it is possible to get them to behave in the same way.[7]

Leaders will not have successful congregations if they do not take their members seriously. When leaders treat members with respect, members will increase their involvement in a system of continual improvement. To do this, leaders must somehow eliminate their supply of negative words and phrases. They must leave behind their frustrations and must change their value-starved attitudes of contempt. If they do not develop a trusting, respectful climate, leaders can expect a downward spiral in congregational morale, growth, and support. Commitment to the church, to the Lord, to the leaders, and to one another will reach new lows.

Transformational leaders are people of faith. They recognize that God does not work where there is doubt, unbelief, and a lack of commitment—because a lack of faith and commitment limits our blessings from God (see Ps. 78:22, 41, 57; Matt. 9:29; Heb. 11:6). They get into the wheelbarrow and let God carry them because of his balancing skills.

God calls for transformational church leaders for the twenty-first century. Now is the time to accept the challenge. Are you ready?

— — —

Pause to Reflect

1. One definition of commitment is doing the will of God. Read 1 Samuel 15. What does it say about obedience to God's will? Contrast obedience and commitment.

2. Another definition of commitment is the relative strength of an individual's identification with, and involvement in, a particular organization. Read 1 Peter 4:12–19. What does it say about suffering and involvement with the church? Contrast persecution and commitment.

3. This chapter proposes that the main reason more Christians are not committed to the Lord and supportive of his church is that they do not trust their leaders' vision, communication, and/or motivational attempts. Do you agree or disagree? Discuss.

4. Four alternatives for redesigning a church are discussed in this chapter. In your opinion, which of the four would be the most difficult to implement in your church? Why?

5. By treating individuals differently, it is possible to get them to behave in the same way. Do you agree or disagree? Why? Discuss a time when you saw this principle in action.

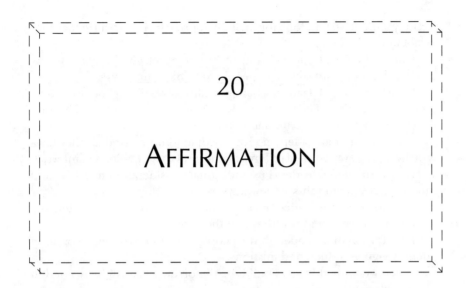

20

AFFIRMATION

"Of making many books there is no end, and much study wearies the body" (Eccl. 12:12). This statement could easily be said about Christian leadership books. Or, one might glibly say, "Now all has been heard; here is the conclusion of the matter" (Eccl. 12:13), knowing that there will certainly be more to come. However, this "making many books" should be encouraging. For in today's knowledge society, with emphasis on the learning organization, leaders and followers must always be growing in knowledge.

When John spoke well of Demetrius, he said, "You know that our testimony is true" (3 John 12). When the angel showed John the river of the water of life, John said, "These words are trustworthy and true" (Rev. 22:6). In both cases, he declared his affirmation firmly and positively.

Similar affirmations can be made of transformational leadership as discussed in the previous chapters. The following is a summary of the attributes of God's transformational leaders.

Summary

Chapter 1: Transformational Leadership

Transformational leaders employ the style that best suits the situation they face. They do not approach every situation in the same way. They restudy a situation and look for the best approach. They realize that style is not as important as results.

Transformational leaders inspire others to excel, give others individual consideration, and stimulate people to think in new ways.

Transformational leaders change reality by building on followers' need for meaning. They focus on values, morals, and ethics. They are proactive and encourage human potential.

Transformational leaders motivate people to do more than they envision by raising awareness of different values and transcending self-interests.

Transformational leaders give individual consideration to others and stimulate people to think in new ways.

Transformational leaders change markedly, and for the better, the people and organizations with which they work.

Transformational leaders bind people together around a common identity—goals, values, and missions.

Transformational leaders build for tomorrow what will be needed in the kingdom at that time.

Transformational leaders use their initiative to lead people to a closer and more intimate relationship with God. Leaders are open to his transformation so they may in turn transform others.

Chapter 2: Power and Influence

Transformational leaders use their power to empower others.

Transformational leaders provide members with the knowledge, skills, information, resources, and support to accomplish goals.

Transformational leaders give people credit for being able to think, reason, plan, and implement those plans.

Transformational leaders increase their referent power by being fair, developing credibility, building morale, and communicating respect.

Transformational leaders strengthen their legitimate power base through consistency, gentleness, kindness, openness, and patience.

Transformational leaders use a servant-leader model to get others to accept ownership and accountability for the well-being of the church.

Chapter 3: Strategic Leadership

Transformational leaders engage in strategic planning.

Transformational leaders focus their strategies, provide congruence between the strategy they set and the strategies set by others, and are prepared for the future.

Transformational leaders establish an environment that consistently encourages innovation and growth.

Transformational leaders focus on what to do next. They know that organizational development is never-ending.

Transformational leaders recognize the tell-tale signs of decline. They regroup, replan, restructure, or rethink as needed.

Chapter 4: Traits of Leadership

Transformational leaders create a vigorous relationship between leaders and followers.

Transformational leaders recognize and appreciate the worth and dignity of each person. They strive to understand human relations and respect others. They understand their own feelings and frustrations and accept others' feelings and frustrations. They are open, friendly, and hospitable.

Transformational leaders exhibit expertise or competency in those areas that significantly improve their social skills.

Transformational leaders realize that people need to be needed. They provide proper recognition.

Transformational leaders believe people have unlimited potential and value. They communicate this understanding to those individuals via warmth and openness.

Transformational leaders develop trusting relationships.

Transformational leaders exhibit the highest standards of moral and intellectual honesty.

Transformational leaders typically have greater analytical ability and can see broad problems and complicated relationships.

Transformational leaders excel at communicating ideas, motivating others, and understanding what others are communicating.

Transformational leaders have faith in God and in themselves.

Transformational leaders are emotionally stable and mature.

Transformational leaders have a broad range of interests and abilities. They also have healthy self-concepts, are self-assured, and have respect for others.

Transformational leaders can understand incoming data, convey ideas, and inspire others.

Transformational leaders are neither defeated by failure nor overjoyed with victory.

Transformational leaders strive to "reach unity in the faith and in the knowledge of the Son of God and become mature, attaining to the whole measure of the fullness of Christ" (Eph. 4:13).

Transformational leaders are the epitome of these traits: social, moral, mental, personality, and maturity.

Chapter 5: Initiatory Leadership

Transformational leaders rise up and begin anew the work the Lord has delegated.

Transformational leaders employ a rational approach toward anticipating, responding to, and altering the future.

Transformational leaders use their initiative to incorporate change to meet the realities of the marketplace and to meet the changing needs of Christians and non-Christians alike.

Transformational leaders use new models of vision, communication, and motivation.

Transformational leaders actively compete for leaders, souls, members, funds, and a new strategic initiative.

Chapter 6: Leadership Behavior

Transformational leaders focus on using the skills and ideas of others to formulate, implement, and evaluate strategy.

Transformational leaders rely on strategic visions, communication, decisions, and motivation to accomplish their work.

Transformational leaders contribute to commitment, loyalty, involvement, and satisfaction of followers.

Transformational leaders are considerate, consultative, participative, consensual, and collaborative.

Chapter 7: Possibility Leadership

Transformational leaders are dreamers—visionaries. They lead and manage by vision.

Transformational leaders use an integrative thinking style. That is, they bridge both hemispheres of the brain.

Transformational leaders discover ways to involve others in creating dreams for the future, at least how the situation will be different in two, five, and ten years down the road.

Transformational leaders know the importance of helping others work toward their goals.

Transformational leaders fortify their congregations with a positive climate for ministry and mission.

Chapter 8: Situational Leadership

Transformational leaders find their power in the Word, in prayer, and in obedience.

Transformational leaders are concerned with task roles, delegating tasks to those whose talents and interests will further the kingdom.

Transformational leaders have a servant's heart and a sensitive heart.

Transformational leaders pray with Solomon: "So give your servant a discerning heart to govern your people and to distinguish between right and wrong. For who is able to govern this great people of yours?" (1 Kings 3:9).

Transformational leaders consistently practice these functions: communicating effectively and responding creatively and innovatively; setting priorities; possessing a results orientation, an empathetic attitude, and a supportive attitude.

Transformational leaders clearly explain the goals and procedures designed to accomplish those goals.

Transformational leaders know that people are not mind-readers. They recognize how vital communication is in order to make effective decisions.

Transformational leaders are interested in results. They want to be measured by what they do, not by who they are.

Transformational leaders work to ensure that they stick closely to performance expectations, not only to get better results but also to maintain higher levels of morale and production.

Transformational leaders couple effectiveness with efficiency by allowing God to arrange the parts in the body just as he wants them to be.

Transformational leaders are innovative. They are willing to begin again, introduce something new, and be creative.

Transformational leaders decide what is to be done and in what sequence. They articulate priorities.

Transformational leaders do not get caught in the activity trap. They realize that they sometimes can accomplish more by doing less.

Transformational leaders question every program that uses time, energy, and money.

Transformational leaders project themselves into their members' personalities. They exercise their intuition to predict how certain information will affect people and whether it will be understood, accepted, rejected, or ignored.

Transformational leaders remain accessible while holding onto their own beliefs, standards, and expectations. They are sensitive and sincere.

Transformational leaders transform situations for the good of the kingdom.

Chapter 9: Visionary Leadership

Transformational leaders create a compelling picture of the future.

Transformational leaders grasp the vision's challenge, commit to the mission, and implement the goals that will accomplish the mission and fulfill the vision.

Transformational leaders have faith in their dream, their ability, and God's power to bring dreams into reality.

Transformational leaders have the ability to think and plan, plus a sense of being called by God.

Transformational leaders put words to their visions and share them with others, for either the day-to-day accomplishment of good works or the achievement of greatness.

Transformational leaders create a vision, communicate that vision to others, coach others to create visions, and build support for the achievement of these visions.

Transformational leaders become communication champions. They consistently articulate the vision so that it is a recognizable, discernible, driving force in congregational activity.

Transformational leaders communicate faith, hope, and optimism.

Transformational leaders' statements show commitment and conviction. Their verbal statements match their nonverbal behavior.

Transformational leaders use metaphors, parables, and pictures to provide an image for their vision.

Transformational leaders maintain a vision by defining the vision specifically, expressing it so other people understand it, and repeating it.

Transformational leaders take a new vision for a church and systematically develop a blueprint that will marshal and motivate the people who will make the dream come true.

Transformational leaders "dream the impossible dream."

Chapter 10: Strategic Analysis

Transformational leaders position their congregations so they take advantage of the opportunities that present themselves and avert threats from the environment.

Transformational leaders understand their opportunities and threats. They are able to identify where they can be most effective.

Transformational leaders understand their strengths and weaknesses. They identify their distinctive competencies.

Transformational leaders make effective use of SWOT analysis. They know how to use their strengths to compensate for their weaknesses, approach opportunities, and avoid threats.

Chapter 11: Transformational Change

Transformational leaders do everything possible to ensure effective communication.

Transformational leaders follow certain communication rules to gain compliance with their decisions.

Transformational leaders provide accurate and detailed information as early as possible regarding any change to be implemented, and allow time for acceptance of the change.

Transformational leaders are "entrepreneurial," they sharpen and champion the vision, put the dream on display, tell the story of the church's history, link members together, and shape the church's environment.

Transformational leaders are agents of change. They are the difference between a vitalized and deteriorating organization.

Chapter 12: Strategic Formulation

Transformational leaders plan for the future. They know they have to have a dream of what exciting things can be done in the church if they expect to accomplish anything.

Transformational leaders rely on environmental analysis to provide pertinent information.

Transformational leaders start thinking about implementation when they begin forming a strategy.

Transformational leaders know that what needs to be done is critical to deciding what to do.

Transformational leaders deal with the values implicit in how people choose paths.

Transformational leaders honestly assess themselves and their members in terms of strengths and weaknesses.

Transformational leaders recognize they cannot go anywhere until everyone knows exactly where they are going. Thus they assign priorities. They develop a written plan and set target deadlines.

Transformational leaders are concerned with setting clear, challenging, and specific goals for their churches.

Chapter 13: Transformational Conflict

Transformational leaders select their words carefully in stating policies, instructions, directions, or orders.

Transformational leaders respond sanely to others' words and with tolerance for differences. They thereby reduce stress and improve the congregational climate.

Transformational leaders plan communication paths that lead to understanding. They encode the words carefully. They do not expose their listeners to a barrage of words or lose them in a jargon jungle of word confusions. They put things in a lay person's language.

Transformational leaders provide recognition for jobs well done, help followers with their problems, provide adequate information on how to perform a task, and explain reasons for changes.

Transformational leaders are open with their followers and keep them informed of what is happening.

Transformational leaders do all that can be done to reduce communication stress and structural stress.

Transformational leaders recognize that the real culprit of conflict is selfishness.

Transformational leaders pursue those things in life that enable them to be better servants. They do not selfishly place themselves at the center of the universe.

Transformational leaders recognize the critical key to avoiding conflict and getting members involved in productive activities is to help them see the importance of learning to serve.

Transformational leaders guide energies being wasted in conflict into productive accomplishment of goals.

Chapter 14: Strategic Implementation

Transformational leaders think in terms of action.

Transformational leaders know that for comprehension, one needs attention, suspension of judgment, agreement, and feedback.

Transformational leaders focus attention on their messages, motivate their listeners, tailor the information to their audience, talk about familiar and understandable things, repeat the important points in their message, and use illustrations to achieve understanding.

Transformational leaders develop communication policies of openness, honesty, and trust.

Transformational leaders improve the two-way flow of information and promote good listening habits.

Transformational leaders are empathetic and recognize that listening is an active process involving meanings, feelings, and cues.

Transformational leaders are responsive to what is heard, read, and seen. They believe that feedback is helpful and that they are responsible for it.

Transformational leaders know how to give and receive constructive criticism. They place a high priority on understanding.

Transformational leaders set into motion a congregation that works efficiently and effectively toward its desired end—the salvation of souls.

Transformational leaders emphasize service in all planning, organizing, motivating, and controlling activities.

Transformational leaders assume flexibility and do not etch operational rules in concrete.

Transformational leaders shift resources to support strategic change.

Transformational leaders look inward, analyzing whether they are promoting effective growth or hindering excellence.

Chapter 15: Transformational Communication

Transformational leaders recognize the importance of communication and learn to use it as a tool to respond to challenges.

Transformational leaders present ideas or messages in a manner acceptable to the needs of members. They make sure the members structure ideas as originally framed.

Transformational leaders develop satisfying relationships with others.

Transformational leaders ensure that their communication lines are open, encouraged, and frequent. They not only keep their ears to the rail but their eyes open for the train!

Transformational leaders create a climate of acceptance, warmth, and listening rather than communicating authority and power.

Transformational leaders understand how the grapevine works in order to supply accurate data. They use the grapevine to keep current on what members are thinking and saying.

Transformational leaders develop a one-to-one network with various church members. They allocate significant time to developing "a network of cooperative relationships" among both members and outsiders.

Transformational leaders emphasize brevity, objectivity, and listening.

Transformational leaders use all available feedback to enhance their communication skills and abilities.

Transformational leaders identify communication barriers and work diligently to overcome them.

Transformational leaders remember that many particulars are left out of everything one says, hears, reads, or writes. There is always an et cetera.

Transformational leaders look to people for meanings instead of to words. They are sensitive to the way words are currently used.

Transformational leaders learn to spot statements that can have several meanings and ask the speaker to clarify, paraphrase, or confirm. They ask for specific examples to avoid conflict and confusion.

Transformational leaders work toward overcoming anything that interferes with their relationship with others.

Transformational leaders become effective listeners, persons genuinely interested in what others are saying.

Transformational leaders hear and react to the needs stated by their members. They practice the art of listening.

Transformational leaders work to become better listeners. They concentrate, work at listening, keep an open mind, take advantage of thought speed, listen for total meaning. They are sensitive. They make sure they understand what their members mean.

Transformational leaders find purpose in every listening situation. They get actively involved with what is happening.

Transformational leaders are neither critical, evaluative, nor moralizing. Instead, they develop a climate of equality, understanding, acceptance, and warmth.

Transformational leaders take advantage of the thought-speaking time difference to make mental summaries and increase their attention span. They also review what is heard and seen. They use thought-speed for productive listening, not daydreaming.

Transformational leaders listen for total meaning. They focus on the nonverbal as well as the verbal by noticing all cues.

Transformational leaders are aware of the nonverbal ways of reacting to situations. They understand what others are experiencing and their circumstances.

Transformational leaders increase eye contact—but do not stare—when communicating with others or establishing or maintaining relationships.

Transformational leaders do not let societal attitudes affect the way they relate to people. They do not relegate people to the pew and keep them out of leadership opportunities because of their appearance, mannerisms, physical limitations, or ungraceful words.

Transformational leaders use individual space to enhance communication, not to indicate power.

Chapter 16: Strategic Evaluation

Transformational leaders develop contingency plans to support their formal plans.

Transformational leaders remain flexible in their strategic planning.

Transformational leaders form the appropriate "dream team" to create a strategic vision for their church.

Transformational leaders conduct the appropriate situation audit and clarify the mission and tenets.

Transformational leaders identify strategic needs and issues. They devise an action plan to manage the needs and issues.

Transformational leaders monitor and evaluate progress.

240

Chapter 17: Transformational Motivation

Transformational leaders view motivation as being related to activities both in and out of the church.

Transformational leaders explore human needs, task motivation, and goal setting.

Transformational leaders enhance human relations by involvement.

Transformational leaders arrange their congregation's environment so members can achieve personal goals by directing their efforts toward ministry goals.

Transformational leaders create opportunities for members to satisfy their basic needs, provide growth opportunities for them to exercise their potential, recognize accomplishments, and coach them to overcome their weaknesses.

Transformational leaders direct their efforts toward reducing any tensions arising from unsatisfied needs or blocked goals.

Transformational leaders set clear, challenging, and specific goals for their congregations. They motivate members by asking them for help in setting goals.

Transformational leaders examine their own motives to motivate others. They learn the motivational level of each follower so they can assume the role of a shepherd.

Transformational leaders recognize the importance of knowing "the sheep by name" and being able to lead them to "green pastures."

Transformational leaders listen to the members' needs for clear descriptions, delineations of authority, and responsibility.

Transformational leaders revamp their communication systems to provide feedback.

Transformational leaders know that most of the time spent interacting with members deals with advising, guiding, coaching, counseling, and training. They realize they are a teacher, judge, specialist, generalist, planner, coordinator, organizer, motivator, and evaluator.

Transformational leaders attempt to satisfy the members' needs. They recognize achievements or progress toward goals.

Transformational leaders give close attention to the realistic probabilities for success and prefer situations where there is clear criteria for their success.

Transformational leaders typically have preferences for competent-but-difficult work partners over congenial-but-incompetent ones.

Transformational leaders possess the capacity to monitor the activities of the group, learn from mistakes, and improve performance of the organization.

Transformational leaders take on the mantle of the servant-leader.

Chapter 18: Trust

Transformational leaders create an environment of trust that is conducive to spiritual productivity.

Transformational leaders combine the elements of good sense, good moral character, and good will to be viewed as credible sources. They are perceived as intelligent, reliable, and interested in their members.

Transformational leaders know that members are their most valuable resource. They believe that every member is filled with unlimited creative potential and hungers for fulfillment of that potential.

Transformational leaders empower members to put their ideas into practice without going through a cumbersome approval system. They provide a supportive climate for the membership.

Chapter 19: Commitment

Transformational leaders influence members to become involved. They call them by name, showcasing their talents, gifts, and interests.

Transformational leaders are flexible. Their ultimate focus remains on the quality of spiritual life for the members.

Transformational leaders modify congregational goals and objectives as society, communities, and members change.

Transformational leaders are people of faith. They recognize that doubt, unbelief, and a lack of commitment frustrates God's working. They are willing to let God carry them beyond what they can physically see.

Conclusion

"What shall we conclude then?" (Rom. 3:9).

Transformational leaders are transformed by God so they can transform their followers and the church. The result in followers is a heightened level of confidence and outcomes. This transformation is achieved by Christian leaders through any of the following interrelated ways:

1. Making members aware of the importance and values of certain rewards and how to achieve them.

2. Helping members look beyond self-interest to see "the big picture" for the sake of the church.

3. Helping members go beyond a focus on minor satisfactions and to search for self-fulfillment.

4. Helping members understand the need for change, both emotionally and intellectually.

5. Investing in members a sense of the urgency of change.[1]

Transformational leaders serve as a release mechanism for the motivation that is in all Christians to serve God and others.[2] In essence, is that not what Jesus did with his disciples? He transformed a dysfunctional group of misfits into a committed team of followers who "turned the world upside down" (Acts 17:6, KJV). Should transformational leaders do any less for the kingdom today?

Christian leaders must work toward becoming more transformational. To that end, check your transformational leadership characteristics in Box 20.1. Then, if necessary, re-read this book. Or, develop an action plan you think will help you develop in the desired direction. God will provide both growth and reward (see 1 Cor. 3:5–9).

Grace and peace.

Box 20.1
Becoming a Transformational Leader

Directions: Indicate the extent to which you possess each transformational characteristic listed below, using a 1–5 scale: (1) very below average, (2) below average, (3) average, (4) above average, or (5) very above average.

Transformational Characteristic	Degree to Which You Possess the Attribute				
1. Strategic thinker	1	2	3	4	5
2. Ability to empower others	1	2	3	4	5
3. Initiative	1	2	3	4	5
4. Formulate and implement strategy	1	2	3	4	5
5. Positive mental attitude	1	2	3	4	5
6. Servant's heart	1	2	3	4	5
7. Visionary	1	2	3	4	5
8. Identify competencies	1	2	3	4	5
9. Willingness to change	1	2	3	4	5
10. Ability to handle conflict	1	2	3	4	5
11. Effective communicator	1	2	3	4	5
12. Clarify mission and tenets	1	2	3	4	5
13. Skilled motivator	1	2	3	4	5
14. Ability to inspire trust	1	2	3	4	5
15. Ability to gain commitment	1	2	3	4	5

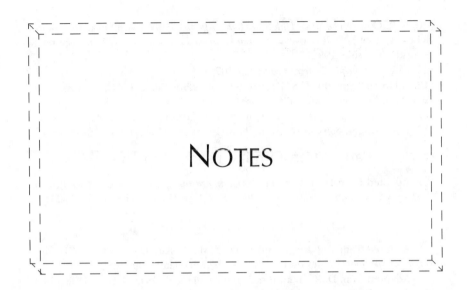

Notes

Preface: New Eyes for Leadership

1. See T. J. Peters, "Restoring American Competitiveness: Looking for New Models of Organizations," *Executive*, 2 (2), (1988): 103–9; and T. J. Peters, *Thriving on Chaos* (New York: Harper & Row, 1987).

2. T. P. Faase, "Toward a Model of Research for Participative Church Planning," *Review of Religious Research*, 31 (1), (1989): 82–93.

Chapter 1: Transformational Leadership

1. Adapted from J. M. Kouzes and B. Z. Posner, *The Leadership Challenge* (San Francisco: Jossey-Bass, 1987).

2. Adapted from S. R. Covey, *Principle-Centered Leadership* (New York: Simon & Schuster/Fireside, 1992), 287.

3. Adapted from B. M. Bass, *Leadership and Performance Beyond Expectations* (New York: Free Press, 1985), 11.

4. P. M. Senge, *The Fifth Discipline: The Art and Practice of the Learning Organization* (New York: Doubleday/Currency, 1990), 13.

5. Adapted from N. M. Tichy, "Revolutionize Your Company," *Fortune* (December 13, 1993): 114–18.

6. Tichy, 115.

7. Ibid., 118.

8. Adapted from N. M. Tichy and M. A. Devanna, *The Transformational Leader* (New York: Wiley, 1986), 50.

9. Ibid.

10. S. R. Covey, *The Seven Habits of Highly Effective People* (New York: Simon and Schuster, 1989); S. R. Covey, *Principle-Centered Leadership* (New York: Simon & Schuster/Fireside, 1992).

11. Covey, *Principle-Centered Leadership,* 107–8.

12. Adapted from the U.S. Department of Labor Secretary's Commission on Achieving Necessary Skills, *What Work Requires of Schools: A SCANS Report for America 2000* (Washington, D.C.: U.S. Government Printing Office, 1992).

13. J. A. Conger, *Spirit at Work* (San Francisco: Jossey-Bass, 1994), 182–3.

Part 2: Transforming Leadership Theory

1. Adapted from D. R. Conner, *Managing at the Speed of Change: How Resilient Managers Succeed and Prosper Where Others Fail* (New York: Villard Books, 1993), 7.

Chapter 2: Power and Influence

1. Adapted from V. P. Richmond and J. C. McCroskey, *Organizational Communication for Survival* (Englewood Cliffs, N.J.: Prentice-Hall, 1992), 92.

2. Adapted from D. R. Hampton, *Management* (New York: McGraw-Hill, 1986), 320; and T. D. Daniels and B. K. Spiker, *Perspectives in Organizational Communication,* 2nd ed. (Dubuque, Iowa: Wm. C. Brown, 1991), 140.

3. M. Korda, *Power! How to Get It, How to Use It* (New York: Ballantine, 1976), 7.

4. J. A. Conger, *Spirit at Work* (San Francisco: Jossey-Bass, 1994), 73–78.

5. Ibid., 79.

6. Ibid., 74.

7. E. Harrison, "Fall of College President Stuns Students, Staff," *Los Angeles Times* (February 21, 1995): A1, A12–13.

8. J. R. P. French Jr., and B. Raven, "The Bases of Social Power" in D. Cartwright and A. Zander (eds.), *Studies in Social Power* (Ann Arbor: University of Michigan Press, 1959),150–67.

9. Adapted from J. W. Gibson and R. M. Hodgetts, *Organizational Communication: A Managerial Perspective* (New York: HarperCollins, 1991), 302–3.

10. Adapted from B. N. Lee, *Executive Excellence,* 5 (8) (August 1988): 12–14.

11. Richmond & McCroskey, 93.

12. Adapted from J. G. Bachman, D. G. Bowers, and P. M. Maracus, "Bases of Supervisory Power: A Comparative Study in Five Organizational Settings," in A. S. Ranenbaum (ed.), *Control in Organizations* (Homewood, Ill.: Irwin, 1968), 236.

13. Adapted from D. Hellriegel, J. W. Slocum, and R. W. Woodman, *Organizational Behavior,* 4th ed. (St. Paul, Minn.: West, 1986), 465–66; and T. D. Daniels and B. K. Spiker, 141–42.

14. Hellriegel, Slocum, and Woodman, 465.

15. D. E. Zand, *Information, Organization, and Power: Effective Management in the Knowledge Society* (New York: McGraw-Hill, 1981), x.

16. N. Carr-Ruffino, *The Promotable Woman* (Belmont, Calif.: Wadsworth, 1982), 30.

17. L. Anderson, *A Church for the 21st Century* (Minneapolis, Minn.: Bethany House, 1994), 225.

18. Hellriegel, Slocum, and Woodman, 466.

19. See R. K. Greenleaf, *The Servant as Leader* (Indianapolis: The Greenleaf Center for Servant-Leadership, 1969).

Chapter 3: Strategic Leadership

1. B. B. Tregoe and J. W. Zimmerman, *Top Management Strategy* (New York: Simon and Schuster, 1980), 28–29.

2. D. Foster, *Will the Cycle Be Unbroken?* (Abilene, Tex.: Abilene Christian University Press, 1994).

3. I. Abramovitz, ed., "Trends: Profit Potential," *Success* (October 1994): 10.

4. P. M. Senge, *The Fifth Discipline: The Art and Practice of the Learning Organization* (New York: Doubleday/Currency, 1990).

5. C. P. Wagner, *Leading Your Church to Growth* (Ventura, Calif.: Regal, 1984).

6. Ibid.

7. N. R. Aquino, *Business and Economic Review,* 57 (4), (July-September 1991): 18–21.

Chapter 4: Traits of Leadership

1. Adapted from a message printed in the *Wall Street Journal* by United Technologies Corporation, Hartford, Conn.

2. J. P. Kotter, *The Leadership Factor* (New York: The Free Press, 1988), 22.

3. B. M. Bass, *Bass and Stogdill's Handbook of Leadership: Theory, Research, and Managerial Applications,* 3rd ed. (New York: The Free Press, 1990), 88.

4. Ibid., 510.

5. R. R. Cueni, *The Vital Church Leader* (Nashville: Abingdon, 1991), n.p.

6. T. W. Engstrom and R. C. Larson, *Seizing the Torch* (Ventura, Calif.: Regal Books, 1988), n.p.

7. Adapted from J. O. Sanders, *Spiritual Leadership,* rev. ed. (Chicago: Moody, 1980).

8. Ibid., 50.

9. W. Kiechell III, "How Executives Think," *Fortune,* (February 4, 1985): 127–28.

10. M. Maltz, *Pscho-cybernetics* (Hollywood: Wilshire, 1964), 110.

11. Adapted from T. W. Engstrom, *The Making of a Christian Leader* (Grand Rapids, Mich.: Zondervan, 1976).

Chapter 5: Initiatory Leadership

1. Portions of this chapter were originally published as P. V. Lewis and W. C. Mitchell, "Strategic Initiative," in M. Morrison, ed., *Sparks That Leap: Essays on Faith and Learning* (Abilene, Tex.: Abilene Christian University Press, 1991), 115–26.

2. B. Heirs and G. Pehrson, *The Mind of the Organization,* rev. ed. (New York: Harper & Row, 1982), 44–45.

3. A. L. Ash, *The Gospel According to Luke, Part I* (Austin: Sweet, 1972), 99.

4. See D. Bonhoeffer, *Cost of Discipleship,* rev., (New York: Collier, 1963).

5. W. Oncken Jr., and D. L. Wass, "Management Time: Who's Got the Monkey?" *Harvard Business Review,* 52 (6), (November-December 1974), 75–80.

Chapter 6: Leadership Behavior

1. B. M. Bass, *Bass and Stogdill's Handbook of Leadership: Theory, Research, and Managerial Applications,* 3rd ed. (New York: The Free Press, 1990), 416–17.

2. Ibid., 417.

3. Ibid., 418.

4. Modified from R. Tannenbaum and W. H. Schmidt, "How to Choose a Leadership Pattern," *Harvard Business Review,* (May-June 1973): 167.

5. W. J. Reddin, *Managerial Effectiveness* (New York: McGraw-Hill, 1970), 226–27.

6. M. Rush, *Management: A Biblical Approach* (Wheaton, Ill.: Victor, 1983).

7. Reddin, 217–18.

8. See Bass, 544.

9. R. R. Cueni, *The Vital Church Leader* (Nashville: Abingdon, 1991), 25–26.

10. Adapted from Bass, 511.

11. Bass, 512.

12. J. A. Conger, *Spirit at Work* (San Francisco: Jossey-Bass, 1994), 184.

Chapter 7: Possibility Leadership

1. Workplace survey, "A Woman's Place? In Charge," *Business Week,* (February 27, 1995).

2. P. M. Senge, *The Fifth Discipline: The Art and Practice of the Learning Organization* (New York: Doubleday/Currency, 1990), 277–281.

3. M. Rush, *Management: A Biblical Approach* (Wheaton, Ill.: Victor Books, 1983).

4. C. Butz, "Jesus, the Wind Beneath My Wings," *APU Business News,* 1 (4), (February 1995): 1.

5. R. R. Cueni, *The Vital Church Leader* (Nashville: Abingdon, 1991), 57–61.

6. N. V. Peale, *Positive Imaging* (New York: Fawcett Crest, 1982), n.p.

7. Peale, 31.

8. M. Ray and R. Meyers, *Creativity in Business* (New York: Doubleday, 1986).

9. L. R. Bittle, *What Every Supervisor Should Know* (New York: McGraw-Hill, 1985), 265.

10. Cueni, 62–65.

Chapter 8: Situational Leadership

1. D. Page, "Needed: A Theology of Christian Leadership for Christian Colleges and Universities," *The Academic Scholar* (1993): 124.

2. K. G. Prunty, "Jesus: The Inner Side of Leadership," in K. F. Hall, ed., *Living Leadership: Biblical Leadership Speaks to Our Day* (Anderson, Ind.: Scripture Press, 1991), 161.

3. L. Eims, *Be the Leader You Were Meant to Be* (Wheaton, Ill.: Victor, 1975), n.p.

4. K. Mills, "Creativity Principles and Leadership," *Image,* 4 (7), (1988): 30–32.

5. Ibid., 30.

6. R. Von Oech, *A Kick in the Seat of the Pants* (New York: Harper & Row, 1986).

7. G. S. Odiorne, *MBO II: A System of Managerial Leadership for the 80s* (Belmont, Calif.: Fearon Pitman, 1979).

8. H. W. Norton, Editorial: "Could We Do More If We Did Less?" *Christian Chronicle* (August 1988), 22.

Chapter 9: Visionary Leadership

1. P. Block, *The Empowered Manager: Positive Political Skills at Work* (San Francisco: Jossey-Bass, 1987), 104.

2. N. M. Tichy and M. A. Devanna, *The Transformational Leader* (New York: Wiley, 1986), 126.

3. W. Kiechil III, "Visionary Leadership and Beyond," *Fortune,* (July 21, 1986), 127–28.

4. Adapted from R. R. Cueni, *The Vital Church Leader* (Nashville: Abingdon, 1991), 37–38.

5. J. Haggai, *Lead on!* (Waco, Tex.: Word, 1986), 27–28.

6. Ibid., 45–52.

7. Block, 105.

8. See P. Pascarella and M. A. Frohman, *The Purpose-Driven Organization* (San Francisco: Jossey-Bass, 1989), 46–47.

9. Adapted from Ibid., 51.

10. F. Smith, *Learning to Lead* (Carol Stream, Ill.: Christianity Today, Inc., 1986), 34–36.

11. P. James, *George W. Truett* (Nashville: Broadman, 1953).

Part 3: Transforming Leadership Strategies and Practices

1. S. Nash, "Living with Integrity in a Chaotic World," speech delivered to the Christian Business Faculty Association, Azusa Pacific University, October 7, 1994.

Chapter 10: Strategic Analysis

1. L. Anderson, *Dying for Change* (Minneapolis: Bethany House, 1990), 10.

2. Ibid., 46.

3. Ibid., 81–94.

4. Ibid., 102–108.

5. Barna Research Group, a full-service marketing research company in Glendale, California, conducts extensive research on how the church can meet challenges of the future. Or, the McIntosh Church Growth Network, 3630 Camellia Dr., San Bernardino, California 92404.

6. H. Weihrich, "The TOWS Matrix—A Tool for Situational Analysis" *Long Range Planning,* 15, 1982, 54–66.

7. R. Shelly, *The Lamb and His Enemies* (Nashville: 20th Century Christian Foundation, 1983), n.p.

8. Ibid., 44.

9. R. Lemmons, "New Winds Are Blowing," *Image,* 4 (10), (1988): 4, 12.

Chapter 11: Transformational Change

1. See Heather A. Haveman, "Between a Rock and a Hard Place: Organizational Change and Performance Under Conditions of Fundamental Environmental Transformation," *Administrative Science Quarterly,* 37 (March 1992), 48–75.

2. Adapted from R. Albanes, *Managing: Toward Accountability for Performance,* 3rd ed. (Homewood, Ill.: Irwin, 1981), 615.

3. Adapted from R. C. Shirley, "A Model for Analysis of Organizational Change," *MSU Business Topics* (Spring 1974), 62.

4. See C. Argyris, "Today's Problems with Tomorrow's Organizations," *Journal of Management Studies* (February 1967), 53.

5. The first six items are adapted from Anderson, 110–18; the second four items are adapted from P. V. Lewis, *Organizational Communication: The Essence of Effective Management* (New York: Wiley, 1987), 292.

Chapter 12: Strategic Formulation

1. K. R. Andrews, *The Concept of Corporate Strategy* (Homewood, Ill.: Irwin, 1987), 53.

2. Ibid., 61.

3. Azusa Pacific University, School of Business and Management (1993). Tenets.

4. Inland Valley Church of Christ, Covina, California. Directory (1994): 1.

5. Saturn Corporation, company literature (Spring Hill, Tenn.: Saturn Corporation, 1992).

6. Adapted from Abilene Christian University, undergraduate catalog (1992–94): 2.

7. Adapted from Inland Valley Church of Christ: 1.

8. E. Locke, "Relation of Goal Performance with a Short Work Period and Multiple Goal Levels," *Journal of Applied Psychology,* 67 (1982): 512–14; E. A. Locke, G. P. Latham, and M. Erez, "The Determinants of Goal Commitment," *Academy of Management Review,* 13 (1988): 23–39; and G. P. Latham and J. J. Baldes, "The Practical Significance of Locke's Theory of Goal Setting," *Journal of Applied Psychology,* 60 (1975): 187–91.

9. Andrews, 63.

10. R. G. Niebuhr, "Megachurches Strive to Be All Things to All Parishioners," *Wall Street Journal* (May 13, 1991).

11. P. F. Drucker, "Marketing 101 for a Fast-Changing Decade," *Wall Street Journal* (November 20, 1990).

12. K. Kelly, "Chicago's Catholic Church: Putting Its House in Order," *Business Week,* 65 (June 10, 1991).

13. Ibid.

Chapter 13: Transformational Conflict

1. C. F. George, "The Berry Bucket Balance," *Leadership* (1987): 52–57.
2. R. D. Dale, *To Dream Again* (Nashville: Broadman, 1981), 119.
3. A. Dubrin, *Fundamentals of Organizational Behavior–An Applied Perspective* (New York: Pergamon, 1974), 304–11.
4. Adapted from A. Uris, "How Managers Ease Job Pressures," *International Management* (June 1972): 45–47.
5. M. Rush, *Management: A Biblical Approach* (Wheaton, Ill.: Victor, 1987), 204–6.
6. Ibid., 206–7.
7. The Institute for Dispute Reconciliation, established in 1986 at Pepperdine University School of Law, provides the nation's most comprehensive training in non-litigation negotiation and mediation.
8. Adapted from R. D. Dale, *Good News from Great Leaders* (New York: Alban Institute, 1992), 95–96.
9. Ibid., 97.
10. Adapted from E. B. Habecker, *The Other Side of Leadership* (Wheaton, Ill.: Victor, 1987), 100–102.

Chapter 14: Strategic Implementation

1. J. L. Gibson, J. M. Ivancevich, and J. H. Donnelly Jr., *Organizations* (Plano, Tex.: Business Publications, 1988).
2. A. R. Dulles, *Models of the Church* (New York: Doubleday, 1991).
3. L. O. Richard and C. Hoeldtke, *A Theology of Church Leadership* (Grand Rapids, Mich.: Zondervan, 1981), 17.
4. Richards and Hoeldtke, 69–70.
5. J. B. Quinn, *Strategies for Change: Logical Incrementalism* (Homewood, Ill.: Irwin, 1980), n.p.
6. G. Boseman and A. Phatak, *Strategic Management: Text and Cases* (New York: Wiley, 1989), n.p.
7. A. A. Thompson, Jr., and A. J. Strickland III, *Strategic Management: Concepts and Cases*, 4th ed. (Plano, Tex.: Business Publications, 1987), n.p.
8. Ibid., 230.
9. R. Likert, *New Patterns of Management* (New York: McGraw-Hill, 1961), 238–39.
10. R. McGlashan and T. Singleton, *Strategic management* (Columbus, Ohio: Merrill, 1987).

Chapter 15: Transformational Communication

1. Some of the material in this chapter was adapted from P. V. Lewis, *Organizational Communication: The Essence of Effective Communication* (New York: Wiley, 1987), chaps. 1 and 3.
2. J. G. Howard, *The Trauma of Transparency* (Portland: Multnomah, 1979), 167–68.
3. J. P. Kotter, "What Effective General Managers Really Do," *Harvard Business Review*, 60 (6), (November/December 1982): 156–67.

4. Ibid.

5. R. E. Felix, "From the president," *Dateline,* Azusa Pacific University, (September 12–18, 1994), 1.

6. Source withheld to protect the innocent and avoid embarrassment.

7. Howard, *The Trama of Transparency,* 167.

Chapter 16: Strategic Evaluation

1. R. L. Daft and N. B. Macintosh, "The Nature and Use of Formal Central Systems for Management Control and Strategy Implementation," *Journal of Management,* 10 (1), (1984): 43–66.

2. J. M. Higgins and J. W. Vincze, *Strategic Management: Text and Cases,* 4th ed. (Chicago: Dryden, 1989), n.p.

3. S. Tilles, "How to Evaluate Corporate Strategy," *Harvard Business Review* (July/August, 1963): 111–21.

4. K. R. Harrigan, *Strategic Flexibility* (Lexington, Mass.: Lexington Books, 1985), 3.

Chapter 17: Transformational Motivation

1. A. H. Maslow, *Motivation and Personality* (New York: Harper & Row, 1954).

2. A. H. Maslow, *Toward a Psychology of Being* (New York: Van Nostrand Reinhold, 1962).

3. R. M. Bramson, *Coping with Difficult People* (New York: Ballantine Books, 1981).

4. Adapted from M. G. Evans, "The Effects of Supervisory Behavior on the Path-Goals Relationship," *Organizational Behavior and Human Performance,* 5 (1970): 277–98.

5. M. L. Rudnick, *Christian Ethics for Today: An Evangelical Approach* (Grand Rapids, Mich.: Baker, 1979), n.p.

6. P. V. Lewis, W. J. Mitchell, and M. Lewis, "Motivational Practices: A Student-Generated Critical Incident Method," *Proceedings of the Academy of Management—Southwest* (1989): 130–34.

7. A. L. McGinnis, *Bringing Out the Best in People* (Minneapolis: Augsburg, 1985).

Part 4: Transforming the Christian Leader

1. Adapted from J. B. Rosener, "To Have Great Leaders, Citizens Must Foster Great Leadership," *Los Angeles Times* (March 26, 1995): D2.

Chapter 18: Trust

1. W. Bennis, *On Becoming a Leader* (Reading, Mass.: Addison-Wesley, 1989), 160.

2. M. Lucado, *God Came Near* (Portland: Multnomah, 1987), 40.

3. S. Squires, "Depend on It; Learning to Trust Takes Time," *The Washington Post* (July 21, 1988): E1, E4.

4. F. Bartolome, "Nobody Trusts the Boss Completely–Now What?" *Harvard Business Review* (March-April 1989): 135–42.

5. J. R. Gibb, "Defensive Communication," *Journal of Communication* (September 1961): 141–48.

Chapter 19: Commitment

1. R. M. Steers, "Antecedents and Outcomes of Organizational Commitment," *Administrative Science Quarterly*, 22 (1), (1977): 46–56.

2. Ibid. (adapted).

3. R. Emery and E. Thorsrud, *New Designs for Work Organization* (Oslo: Tannum, 1969), n.p.

4. E. T. Hall and M. A. Morgan, "Career Development and Planning," in W. C. Hanner and F. L. Schmidt, *Contemporary Problems in Personnel* (Chicago: St. Clair, 1977), 206.

5. P. Hersey and K. H. Blanchard, *Management of Organizational Behavior,* 3rd ed. (Englewood Cliffs, N.J.: Prentice-Hall, 1977), n.p.

6. P. E. Conner, *Organizations: Theory and Design* (Chicago: Science Research Associates, 1980), 236.

7. E. E. Lawler III, "Individualizing Organizations; A Needed Emphasis in Organizational Psychology," in H. Meltzer and F. R. Wickert, *Humanizing Organization Behavior* (Springfield, Ill.: Thomas, 1976), 202.

Chapter 20: Affirmation

1. Adapted from A. J. DuBrin, *Leadership: Research, Findings, Practice, and Skills* (Boston: Houghton Mifflin, 1995), 69–70.

2. Adapted from B. M. Bass, *Leadership and Performance Beyond Expectations* (New York: The Free Press, 1985), 22.

SUGGESTED READINGS

Alderson, Wayne T., and Nancy Alderson McDonnell. *Theory R Management.* Nashville: Thomas Nelson, 1994.

Anderson, Leith. *A Church for the 21st Century.* Minneapolis: Bethany House, 1994.

————. *The Concept of Corporate Strategy.* Homewood, Ill.: Irwin, 1987.

————. *Dying for Change.* Minneapolis: Bethany House, 1990.

Ansoff, H. Igor. *The New Corporate Strategy.* New York: John Wiley, 1988.

Badaracco Jr., Joseph L., and Richard R. Ellsworth. *Leadership and the Quest for Integrity.* Boston: Harvard Business School Press, 1989.

Barker, Joel Arthur. *Future Edge: Discovering the New Paradigms of Success.* New York: William Morrow and Co., 1992.

Barna, George. *The Frog in the Kettle: What Christians Need to Know About Life in the Year 2000.* Ventura, Calif.: Regal Books, 1990.

————. *The Power of Vision.* Ventura, Calif.: Regal Books, 1992.

Bass, Bernard M. *Bass and Stogdill's Handbook of Leadership: Theory, Research, and Managerial Applications.* New York: The Free Press, 1990.

————. *Leadership and Performance Beyond Expectations.* New York: Free Press, 1985.

Beckhard, Richard, and Wendy Pritchard. *Changing the Essence.* San Francisco: Jossey-Bass, 1992.

Beer, Michael, Russell A. Eisenstat, and Bert Spector. *The Critical Path to Corporate Renewal.* Boston: Harvard Business School Press, 1990.

Bennis, Warren. *An Invented Life: Reflections on Leadership and Change.* Reading, Mass.: Addison-Wesley, 1993.

————. *Leaders on Leadership: Interviews with Top Executives.* Boston: Harvard Business School Press, 1992.

————. *On Becoming a Leader.* Reading, Mass.: Addison-Wesley, 1989.

————, and Burt Nanus. *Leaders: The Strategies for Taking Charge.* New York: Harper & Row, 1985.

————, Jagdish Parikh, and Ronnie Lessem. *Beyond Leadership: Balancing Economics, Ethics and Ecology.* Cambridge, Mass.: Blackwell, 1994 .

Block, Peter. *The Empowered Manager: Positive Political Skills at Work.* San Francisco: Jossey-Bass, 1991.

————. *Stewardship: Choosing Service over Self Interest.* San Francisco: Berrett-Koehler, 1993.

Bolman, Lee G., and Terrence E. Deal. *Leading with Soul.* San Francisco: Jossey-Bass, 1995.

————. *Transforming Organizations.* San Francisco: Jossey-Bass, 1992.

Bramson, Robert M. *Coping with Difficult People.* New York: Ballantine Books, 1981.

Buchholz, Rogene A. *Fundamental Concepts and Problems in Business Ethics.* Englewood Cliffs, N.J.: Prentice Hall, 1989.

Burke, W. Warner. *Organization Development: A Normative View.* Reading, Mass.: Addison-Wesley, 1987.

Burns, James McGregor. *Leadership.* New York: Harper & Row, 1978.

Byham, William, and Jeff Cox. *Zapp! The Lightning of Empowerment.* New York: Fawcett Columbine, 1988 .

Callahan, Kennon L. *Effective Church Leadership: Building on the Twelve Keys.* New York: Harper & Row, 1990.

————. *Twelve Keys to an Effective Church.* San Francisco: Harper, 1983.

Campolo, Tony. *Everything You've Heard Is Wrong.* Dallas: Word Publishing, 1992.

Cetron, Marvin, and Owen Davies. *American Renaissance: Our Life at the Turn of the 21st Century.* New York: St. Martin's Press, 1989.

Chapman, Elwood N. *Your Attitude Is Showing: A Primer on Human Relations.* Chicago: Science Research Associates, 1977.

Chewning, Richard C. ed. *Biblical Principles and Business: The Practice.* Colorado Springs, Colo.: NavPress, 1990.

————. *Business Ethics in a Changing Culture.* Reston, Va.: Reston, 1984.

Clifton, J. Robert. *The Making of a Leader: Recognizing the Lessons and Stages of Leadership Development.* Colorado Springs, Colo.: NavPress, 1989.

Conger, Jay A. *Learning to Lead: The Art of Transforming Managers into Leaders.* San Francisco: Jossey-Bass, 1992.

————. *Spirit at Work.* San Francisco: Jossey-Bass, 1994.

Connor, Daryl R. *Managing at the Speed of Change: How Resilient Managers Succeed and Prosper Where Others Fail.* New York: Villard Books, 1993.

Connor, Patrick E., and Linda K. Lake. *Managing Organizational Change.* New York: Praeger, 1988.

Covey, Stephen R. *Principle-Centered Leadership.* New York: Simon & Schuster/ Fireside, 1992.

————. *The Seven Habits of Highly Effective People: Restoring the Character Ethic.* New York: Simon & Schuster, 1992.

Cueni, R. R. *The Vital Church Leader.* Nashville: Abingdon, 1991.

Cummings, L. L., and Barry M. Staw, eds. *Leadership, Participation, and Group Behavior.* Greenwich, Conn.: JAI Press, 1990.

Dale, Robert D. *Good News from Great Leaders.* New York: Alban Institute, 1992.

———. *Keeping the Dream Alive: Understanding and Building Congregational Morale.* Nashville: Broadman Press, 1988.

———. *Pastoral Leadership.* Nashville: Abingdon Press, 1986.

———. *To Dream Again: How to Help Your Church Come Alive.* Nashville: Broadman Press, 1981.

Deal, Terrence E., and Allan A. Kennedy. *Corporate Cultures: The Rites and Rituals of Corporate Life.* Reading, Mass.: Addison-Wesley, 1982.

DePree, Max. *Leadership Is an Art.* New York: Dell, 1989.

———. *Leadership Jazz.* New York: Dell, 1992.

DeVries, Manfred F. R. *Leaders, Fools, and Impostors: Essays on the Psychology of Leadership.* San Francisco: Jossey-Bass, 1993.

_____, and Danny Miller. *The Neurotic Organization.* San Francisco: Jossey-Bass, 1984.

Dosick, Wayne D. *The Business Bible: Ten Commandments for Creating an Ethical Workplace.* New York: William Morrow and Co., 1993.

Douglass, Stephen B. *Managing Yourself.* San Bernardino, Calif.: Here's Life, 1978.

———, and Lee Roddy. *Making the Most of Your Mind.* San Bernardino, Calif.: Here's Life, 1983.

Driscoll, Dawn-Marie, and Carol R. Goldberg. *Members of the Club: The Coming of Age of Executive Women.* New York: The Free Press, 1993.

Drucker, Peter F. *The Effective Executive.* London: Pan Books, 1967.

———. *The Frontiers of Management.* New York: Harper & Row, 1986.

———. *Innovation and Entrepreneurship.* New York: Harper & Row, 1985.

———. *Management: Tasks, Responsibilities, Practices.* New York: Harper & Row, 1973.

———. *Managing for the Future: The 1990s and Beyond.* New York: The Penguin Group, 1992.

———. *Managing the Non-Profit Organization: Practices and Principles.* New York: HarperCollins, 1990.

———. *The New Realities.* New York: Harper & Row, 1989.

DuBrin, Andrew J. *Leaders: Research, Findings, Practice, and Skills.* Boston: Houghton Mifflin, 1995.

Eccles, Robert G., and Nitin Nohria. *Beyond the Hype: Rediscovering the Essence of Management.* Boston: Harvard Business School Press, 1992.

Eims, L. *Be the Leader You Were Meant to Be.* Wheaton, Ill.: Victor, 1975.

Engstrom, Ted W. *The Making of a Christian Leader.* Grand Rapids, Mich.: Zondervan, 1976.

———, and Robert C. Larson. *Seizing the Torch.* Ventura, Calif.: Regal Books, 1988.

———, and Norman B. Rohrer. *The Fine Art of Mentoring: Passing on to Others What God Has Given You.* Brentwood, Tenn.: Wolgemuth & Hyatt, 1989.

Fafenson, Ellen A. *Women in Management: Trends, Issues, and Challenges in Managerial Diversity.* Newbury Park, Calif.: Sage, 1993.

Fiedler, Fred W., and J. E. Garcia. *New Approaches to Effective Leadership: Cognitive Resources and Organizational Performance.* New York: Wiley, 1987.

Finzel, Hans. *The Top Ten Mistakes Leaders Make.* Wheaton, Ill.: Victor, 1994.

Ford, Leighton. *Transforming Leadership: Jesus' Way of Creating Vision, Shaping Values and Empowering Change.* Downers Grove, Ill.: InterVarsity Press, 1991.

Foster, Douglas. *Will the Cycle Be Unbroken?* Abilene, Tex.: Abilene Christian University Press, 1994.

Foth, Dick, and Ruth Foth. *When the Giant Lies Down.* Wheaton, Ill.: Victor Books, 1995.

Gabarro, John J. *The Dynamics of Taking Charge.* Boston: Harvard Business School Press, 1987.

Gangel, Kenneth O., and Samuel L. Canine. *Communication and Conflict Management in Churches and Christian Organizations.* Nashville: Broadman, 1992.

Gardner, John W. *On Leadership.* New York: The Free Press, 1990.

Garfield, Charles. *Peak Performers: The New Heroes of American Business.* New York: Avon Books, 1986.

Gentile, Mary C. *Differences That Work: Organizational Excellence Through Diversity.* Boston: Harvard Business School Press, 1994.

Gibson J. L., J. M. Ivancevich, and J. H. Donnelly Jr. *Organizations.* Plano, Tex.: Business Publications, 1988.

Gilbert, Jr., Daniel R., Edwin Hartman, John J. Mauriel, and R. Edward Freeman. *A Logic for Strategy.* Cambridge, Mass.: Ballinger, 1988.

Gouillart, Francis J., and James N. Kelly. *Transforming the Organization.* New York: McGraw-Hill, 1995.

Greenleaf, Robert K. *Servant Leadership: A Journey into the Nature of Legitimate Power and Greatness.* New York: Paulist Press, 1977.

Griffin, Ricky W. *Management.* Boston: Houghton Mifflin, 1993.

Habecker, E. B. *The Other Side of Leadership.* Wheaton, Ill.: Victor Books, 1987.

Hammer, Michael, and James Champy. *Reengineering the Corporation.* New York: HarperBusiness, 1993.

Handy, Charles. *The Age of Paradox.* Boston: Harvard Business School Press, 1994.

———. *The Age of Unreason.* Boston: Harvard Business School Press, 1990.

———. *Understanding Organizations.* New York: Oxford University Press, 1993.

Harrigan, K. R. *Strategic Flexibility.* Lexington, Mass.: Lexington Books, 1985.

Harrison, Allen, and Robert M. Bramson. *The Art of Thinking: Strategies for Asking Questions, Making Decisions, and Solving Problems.* New York: Berkley Books, 1982.

Heirs, B., and G. Pehrson. *The Mind of the Organization.* New York: Harper & Row, 1982.

Helgesen, Sally. *The Female Advantage: Women's Ways of Leadership.* New York: Business Ethics Network, 1990.

Hersey, Paul. *The Situational Leader.* Escondido, Calif.: The Center for Leadership Studies, 1984.

————, and Kenneth H. Blanchard. *Management of Organizational Behavior: Utilizing Human Resources.* Englewood Cliffs, N.J.: Prentice Hall, 1993.

Hickman, Craig R., and Michael A. Silva. *Creating Excellence: Managing Corporate Culture, Strategy and Change in the New Age.* New York: New American Library, 1984.

Hill, Linda. *Becoming a Manager: Mastery of a New Identity.* Boston: Harvard Business School Press, 1992.

Hill, Napoleon, and W. Clement Stone. *Success Through a Positive Mental Attitude.* New York: Pocket Books, 1977.

Howard, J. G. *The Trauma of Transparency.* Portland: Multnomah, 1979.

Howard, Robert, ed. *The Learning Imperative: Managing People for Continuous Innovation.* Boston: Harvard Business School Press, 1993.

Hunt, James G. *Leadership: A New Synthesis.* Newbury Park, Calif.: Sage, 1991.

Inrig, G. *A Call to Excellence.* Wheaton, Ill.: Victor Books, 1985.

Johnston, Jon. *Christian Excellence: Alternative to Success.* Grand Rapids: Baker Book House, 1985.

Joiner, Jr., Charles W., *Leadership for Change.* Cambridge, Mass.: Ballinger, 1987.

Jones, Laurie Beth. *Jesus, CEO: Using Ancient Wisdom for Visionary Leadership.* New York: Hyperion, 1995.

Kanter, Rosabeth Moss. *The Change Masters.* New York: Touchstone/Simon & Schuster, 1983.

Katzenbach, Jon R., and Douglas K. Smith. *The Wisdom of Teams: Creating the High-Performance Organization.* Boston: Harvard Business School Press, 1993.

Keirsey, David, and Marilyn Bates. *Please Understand Me: Character and Temperament Types.* Del Mar, Calif.: Prometheus Nemesis Book Co., 1984.

Koestenbaum, Peter. *Leadership: The Inner Side of Greatness.* San Francisco: Jossey-Bass, 1991.

Konek, Carol Wolfe, and Sally L. Kitch, eds. *Women and Careers: Issues and Challenges.* Newbury Park, Calif.: Sage, 1993.

Korda, Michael. *Power! How to Get It, How to Use It.* New York: Ballantine, 1976.

Kotter, John P. *A Force for Change: How Leadership Differs from Management.* New York: The Free Press, 1990.

————. *The Leadership Factor.* New York: The Free Press, 1988.

————. *The New Rules: How to Succeed in Today's Post-Corporate World.* New York: The Free Press, 1995.

Kouzes, James M., and Barry Z. Posner. *Credibility: How Leaders Gain and Lose It, Why People Demand It.* San Francisco: Jossey-Bass, 1993.

————. *The Leadership Challenge: How to Get Extraordinary Things Done in Organizations,* 2nd ed. San Francisco: Jossey-Bass, 1989.

Larson, Carl E., and Frank M. LaFasto. *Teamwork: What Must Go Right, What Can Go Wrong.* Newbury Park: Sage, 1995.

Leavitt, Harold J. *Corporate Pathfinders: Building Vision and Values into Organizations.* Homewood, Ill.: Dow-Jones-Irwin, 1986.

Levine, Stuart R., and Michael A. Crom. *The Leader in You: How to Win Friends, Influence People, and Succeed in a Changing World.* New York: Simon & Schuster, 1993.

Lewis, Phillip V. *Managing Human Relations.* Boston: Kent, 1983.

———. *Organizational Communication: The Essence of Effective Management.* New York: Wiley, 1987.

Likert, Rensis. *New Patterns of Management.* New York: McGraw-Hill, 1961.

Loden, M. *Feminine Leadership: Or How to Succeed in Business Without Being One of the Boys.* New York: Time Books, 1985.

McCaskey, Michael B. *The Executive Challenge.* Marshfield, Mass.: Pitman, 1982.

McConkey, Dale D. *MBO for Nonprofit Organizations.* New York: AMACOM, 1975.

MacDonald, Gordon. *Ordering Your Private World.* Nashville: Oliver Nelson, 1985.

McDonough, Reginald M. *Keys to Effective Motivation.* Nashville: Broadman Press, 1979.

McFarland, Lynne Joy, Larry E. Senn, and John R. Childress. *21st Century Leadership: Dialogues with 100 Top Leaders.* Los Angeles: The Leadership Press, 1993.

McGinnis, A. L. *Bringing Out the Best in People.* Minneapolis: Augsburg, 1985.

———. *The Friendship Factor.* Minneapolis: Augsburg, 1979.

McGregor, Douglas. *The Human Side of Enterprise.* New York: McGraw-Hill, 1960.

Mackenzie, R. Alec. *The Time Trap.* New York: McGraw-Hill, 1972.

Machiavelli, Niccolo. *The Prince.* New York: New American Library, 1952.

Manz, C. C., and H. P. Sims Jr. *Superleadership: Leading Others to Lead Themselves to Excellence.* Englewood Cliffs, N.J.: Prentice-Hall, 1988.

Maslow, Abraham H. *Motivation and Personality.* New York: Harper & Row, 1954.

———. *Toward a Psychology of Being.* New York: Van Nostrand Reinhold, 1962.

Mattson, Ralph T. *Visions of Grandeur: Leadership That Creates Positive Change.* Chicago: Moody Press, 1994.

Maxwell, John C. *Developing the Leader Within You.* Nashville: Thomas Nelson, 1993.

Means, James E. *Leadership in Christian Ministry.* New York: Doubleday, 1989.

Morrison, Ann M. *The New Leaders: Guidelines on Leadership Diversity in America.* San Francisco: Jossey-Bass, 1992.

Morrison, Matt. ed. *Sparks That Leap: Essays on Faith and Learning.* Abilene, Tex.: Abilene Christian University Press, 1991.

Murren, Doug. *Leadershift.* Ventura, Calif.: Regal Books, 1994.

Mylander, Charles. *Secrets for Growing Churches.* New York: Harper & Row, 1979.

Nair, Keshavan. *A Higher Standard of Leadership: Lessons from the Life of Gandhi.* New York: Berrett-Koehler, 1995.

Naisbitt, John, and Patricia Aburdene. *Megatrends 2000.* New York: William Morrow, 1990.

———. *Re-inventing the Corporation.* New York: Warner Books, 1985.

Nanus, Burt. *Visionary Leadership.* San Francisco: Jossey-Bass, 1992.

Nichols, Nancy A. *Reach for the Top: Women and the Changing Facts of Work Life.* Boston: Harvard Business School Press, 1994.

Nohria, Nitin, and Robert G. Eccles, eds. *Networks and Organizations: Structure, Form and Action.* Boston: Harvard Business School Press, 1993.

Ohmae, Kenichi. *The Mind of the Strategist: Business Planning for Competitive Advantage.* New York: Penguin Books, 1984.

Suggested Readings

O'Toole, James. *Leading Change: Overcoming the Ideology of Comfort and the Tyranny of Custom.* San Francisco: Jossey-Bass, 1995.

Owen, Harrison. *Spirit: Transformation and Development in Organizations.* Potomac, Md.: Abbott, 1987.

Pagonis, Lt. General William G. *Moving Mountains: Lessons in Leadership and Logistics from the Gulf War.* Boston: Harvard Business School Press, 1992.

Pascarella, Perry, and Mark A. Frohman. *The Purpose-Driven Organization: Unleashing the Power of Direction and Commitment.* San Francisco: Jossey-Bass, 1989.

Patton, Bobby R., Kim Giffin, and Eleanor Nyquist Patton. *Decision-Making Group Interaction.* New York: HarperCollins, 1989.

Peale, Norman Vincent. *Positive Imaging.* New York: Fawcett Crest, 1982.

Pegg, Mike. *Positive Leadership: How to Build a Winning Team.* San Diego: Pfeiffer & Co., 1994.

Peters, Thomas J., *Liberation Management.* New York: Random House, 1991.

———. *Thriving on Chaos: Handbook for a Management Revolution.* New York: Harper & Row, 1988.

———. *The Tom Peters Seminar: Crazy Times Call for Crazy Organizations.* New York: Vintage Books, 1994.

Peters, Thomas J., and Nancy Austin. *A Passion for Excellence.* New York: Random House, 1985.

Peters, Thomas J., and Robert H. Waterman Jr. *In Search of Excellence: Lessons from America's Best-Run Companies.* New York: Harper & Row, 1982.

Pfeffer, Jeffrey. *Competitive Advantage Through People: Unleashing the Power of the Work Force.* Boston: Harvard Business School Press, 1994.

———. *Managing with Power: Politics and Influence in Organizations.* Boston: Harvard Business School Press, 1992.

Porter, Michael E. *Competitive Advantage: Creating and Sustaining Superior Performance.* New York: The Free Press, 1985.

———. *Competitive Strategy: Techniques for Analyzing Industries and Competitors.* New York: The Free Press, 1980.

Powell, Gary N. *Women and Men in Management.* Newbury Park, Calif.: Sage, 1993.

Powers, Ray. *Christian Leadership.* Nashville: Broadman Press, 1979.

Quinn, J. B. *Strategies for Change: Logical Incrementalism.* Homewood, Ill.: Irwin, 1980.

Ray, Michael, and Rochelle Myers. *Creativity in Business.* New York: Doubleday, 1986.

Reddin, W. J. *Managerial Effectiveness.* New York: McGraw-Hill, 1970.

Reeck, Darrell. *Ethics for the Professions: A Christian Perspective.* Minneapolis: Augsburg, 1982.

Reynolds, Joe. *Out Front Leadership: Discovering, Developing, and Delivering Your Potential.* Austin, Tex.: Mott & Carlisle, 1994.

Ries, Al, and Jack Trouth. *Positioning: The Battle for Your Mind.* New York: Warner Books, 1981.

Richard, L. O., and C. Hoeldtke. *A Theology of Church Leadership.* Grand Rapids: Zondervan, 1981.

Rush, Myron. *Management: A Biblical Approach.* Wheaton, Ill.: Victor Books, 1983.

Sanders, J. O. *Spiritual Leadership,* 2nd rev. Chicago: Moody, 1994.

Schein, E. H. *Organizational Culture and Leadership,* 2nd ed. San Francisco: Jossey-Bass, 1992.

Senge, Peter M. *The Fifth Discipline: The Art and Practice of the Learning Organization.* New York: Doubleday Currency, 1990.

———, Charlotte Roberts, Richard B. Ross, Bryan K. Smith, and Art Kleiner. *The Fifth Discipline Fieldbook: Strategies and Tools for Building a Learning Organization.* New York: Doubleday Currency, 1994.

Shaller, Lyle E. *Getting Things Done: Concepts and Skills for Leaders.* Nashville: Abingdon, 1986.

Shawchuck, Norman, and Roger Heuser. *Leading the Congregation.* Nashville: Abingdon, 1993.

Shelly, Rubel. *The Lamb and His Enemies.* Nashville: 20th Century Christian Foundation, 1983.

Smith, Fred. *Learning to Lead: Bringing Out the Best in People.* Waco, Tex.: Word Books, 1986.

Stowell, Joseph M. *Shepherding the Church into the 21st Century.* Wheaton, Ill.: Victor, 1994.

Strebel, Paul. *Breakpoints: How Managers Exploit Radical Business Change.* Boston: Harvard Business School Press, 1992.

Sweeting, George. *How to Solve Conflicts.* Chicago: Moody Press, 1973.

Swindoll, Charles R. *The Quest for Character.* Portland: Multnomah Press, 1987.

Terry, Robert W. *Authentic Leadership: Courage in Action.* San Francisco: Jossey-Bass, 1993.

Tichy, N. M., and M. A. Devanna. *The Transformational Leader.* New York: Wiley, 1986.

Tjosvold, Dean, and Mary M. Tjosvold. *The Emerging Leader: Ways to a Stronger Team.* New York: The Free Press, 1994.

Tregoe, Benjamin B., and John W. Zimmerman. *Top Management Strategy: What It Is and How to Make It Work.* New York: Simon & Schuster, 1980.

———, ———, Ronald A. Smith, and Peter M. Tobia. *Vision in Action: Putting a Winning Strategy to Work.* New York: Simon & Schuster, 1989.

Tzu, Sun. *The Art of War.* London: Oxford University Press, 1963.

Von Oech, R. *A Whack on the Side of the Head.* New York: Warner Books, 1990.

———. *A Kick in the Seat of the Pants.* New York: Harper & Row, 1986.

Vroom, Victor H. *Manage People, Not Personnel: Motivation and Performance Appraisal.* Boston: Harvard Business School Press, 1990.

———, and Arthur G. Jago. *The New Leadership: Managing Participation in Organizations.* Englewood Cliffs, N.J.: Prentice-Hall, 1988.

Wagner, C. P. *Leading Your Church to Growth.* Ventura, Calif.: Regal, 1984.

Walton, Clarence C. *Corporate Encounters: Ethics, Law, and the Business Environment.* Fort Worth, Tex.: Dryden Press, 1992.

Wareham, John. *The Anatomy of a Great Executive.* New York: HarperBusiness, 1991.

Weisbord, Marvin R. *Organizational Diagnosis: A Workbook of Theory and Practice.* Reading, Mass.: Addison-Wesley, 1978.

Suggested Readings

Westin, Alan F., and John D. Aram. *Managerial Dilemmas: Cases in Social, Legal, and Technological Change.* Cambridge, Mass.: Ballinger, 1988.

Wheatley, Margaret J. *Leadership and the New Science: Learning About Organization from an Orderly Universe.* San Francisco: Berrett-Koehler, 1994.

White, Ernest O. *Becoming a Christian Leader.* Nashville: Convention Press, 1985.

White, John. *Excellence in Leadership: Reaching Goals with Prayer, Courage and Determination.* Downers Grove, Ill.: InterVarsity Press, 1986.

White, Morton. *The Age of Analysis: 20th Century Philosophers.* New York: New American Library, 1955.

Willner, A. R. *Leadership in Organizations.* Englewood Cliffs: Prentice-Hall, 1984.

Wren, J. Thomas. *The Leader's Companion: Insights on Leadership Through the Ages.* New York: The Free Press, 1995.

Youssef, Michael. *The Leadership Style of Jesus: How to Develop the Leadership Qualities of the Good Shepherd.* Wheaton, Ill.: Victor Books, 1986.

Yukl, Gary A. *Leadership in Organizations,* 2nd ed. Englewood Cliffs, N.J.: Prentice-Hall, 1989.

Zaleznik, Abraham. *The Managerial Mystique: Restoring Leadership in Business.* New York: Harper & Row, 1989.

For more information regarding the author, or leadership seminars and workshops for your church or organization, contact:

Leadership Resources
Drs. Phil and Marilyn Lewis
137 South Hacienda Avenue
Glendora, CA 91741–3806
(818) 963–3602